'This book for b
Government refu
like this is gold-dust. Clear, informative, straig
wonderful touches of respectful humour. Helping staff and their
overcome barriers and restart interrupted careers and lives.'

— Sheila Heard, Managing Director, Transitions London CIC,
Employment Services for Refugee Engineers and Business Services professionals

'Sarah Crowther has dedicated her life so far to making it easy for refugees in West London to get help, to access services, and to integrate into society. This wonderful book makes it easy for readers to understand why refugees come to Britain and the issues they face, and to know what to do to help a refugee in front of them.'

— Ezechias Ngendahayo, MInstF (Dip), Projects and
Training Coordinator, Development Team, Refugee Council

'This book will certainly help you to get a clearer, more realistic picture of the present-day challenges refugees face in the UK and worldwide, and it will also increase your understanding of the complexity of the lives of people in exile.

Reading this will inform you about all the relevant issues. More importantly, using this book will prepare you to become better at what you do whenever you help refugees and asylum seekers – regardless of your society, community, profession or ethnicity, as it provides a wealth of practical knowledge that you can use to develop a positive, proactive and progressive approach to your work and the work your organisation does.'

— Oleg Pasichnyi, Ex-Refugee, Member of REAP,
Professional Interpreter / Translator, Social Policy Researcher

'This book transformed my thinking by releasing refugees and asylum seeker from those static labels into becoming agents of their own lives; by creating a role for any of us to assist each refugee engage with the access points for public services. I liked the conversational style, supported with experience and resources.'

— John Murphy, London Churches Refugee Fund and Network

'The kind of book that can be read from any page and deserves a centre space of a home library.'

— Ayman Uweida, Member of REAP, Professional Interpreter and Refugee

'This book fully appreciates the struggles that refugees and asylum seekers face, such as: identity, health, language barriers, living conditions and education. It tackles these deep and complex issues with an honest and sensitive approach which is important if we aim to have an inclusive, supportive and productive society.'

– Khalida Obeid, Afghan Women's Support Group Coordinator

'With specialist support for refugees dwindling, this book argues we can all expand our roles and expertise to support refugees more effectively. The book offers helpful practical advice, but also successfully navigates complex policy and ethical terrain, providing a valuable snapshot of the state of refugee support in the UK.'

– Asif Afridi, Deputy CEO, brap (UK-based equality and human rights charity)

Working with Asylum
Seekers and Refugees

of related interest

A Practical Guide to Therapeutic Work with Asylum Seekers and Refugees
Angelina Jalonen and Paul Cilia La Corte
Foreword by Jerry Clore
ISBN 978 1 78592 073 8
eISBN 978 1 78450 334 5

Safeguarding Children from Abroad
Refugee, Asylum Seeking and Trafficked Children in the UK
Edited by Emma Kelly and Farhat Bokhari
Part of the Best Practice in Working with Children series
ISBN 978 1 84905 157 6
eISBN 978 0 85700 559 5

Art-Making with Refugees and Survivors
Creative and Transformative Responses to Trauma After
Natural Disasters, War and Other Crises
Sally Adnams Jones, PhD
ISBN 978 1 78592 238 1
eISBN 978 1 78450 518 9

Working with Asylum Seekers and Refugees

What to Do, What Not to Do, and How to Help

SARAH CROWTHER

Foreword by Debora Singer MBE

Jessica Kingsley *Publishers*
London and Philadelphia

All materials used or referenced from or via REAP have been
reproduced with kind permission from REAP

First published in 2019
by Jessica Kingsley Publishers
73 Collier Street
London N1 9BE, UK
and
400 Market Street, Suite 400
Philadelphia, PA 19106, USA

www.jkp.com

Library of Congress Cataloging in Publication Data
A CIP catalog record for this book is available from the Library of Congress

British Library Cataloguing in Publication Data
A CIP catalogue record for this book is available from the British Library

ISBN 978 1 78592 317 3
eISBN 978 1 78450 630 8

Printed and bound in Great Britain

Contents

List of Boxes

Foreword

Anyone could be a refugee.

Each of my parents spent their childhood within a comfortable middle-class family life, assimilated within their country. By their early teens, they had been uprooted by the war in Europe and were living across borders, learning a new language, a new culture, a new school curriculum. They were helped to adapt to their new lives by many British people, the kindness of strangers.

This book provides a brilliant pointer as to how best to provide such help to refugees arriving on these shores three-quarters of a century later.

Refugees are ordinary people fleeing extraordinary circumstances. Whether a man fleeing political oppression, a woman fleeing domestic violence, a gay man fleeing a forced marriage or a woman refusing to wear religious dress, refugees are fleeing some form of persecution. The definition of a refugee is complex, but the warmth radiating out of Sarah Crowther's book reflects a simple empathy that will benefit refugees however you define them.

Having worked with asylum seekers for 14 years, I am all too aware of the complexity of their situation. This can lead to a sense of helplessness. A sense of 'I don't know what I can offer' or, in many cases, 'there is nothing that I can offer'. This book provides a practical, no-nonsense response to this sense of helplessness. It will be welcomed by professionals and volunteers alike, whether in community work, health and social care, education, employment and many other disciplines.

I have known Sarah professionally for many years now and I have always had great respect for her work. I am honoured to write the foreword for this book. It reflects its author's long experience and sound expertise. Its wide-ranging and comprehensive nature will support those who are keen to engage with and support refugees in their midst but would like some advice as to how to go about this.

With this book in hand, the only thing a reader needs is willingness.

Debora Singer MBE
Senior Policy Adviser
Asylum Aid

Acknowledgements

This work exists because of the people I have met over the last 20 and more years; refugees, migrants, practitioners and activists, wise women and men, children.

I started a project management job with Refugees in Effective and Active Partnership (REAP) in 2002 on a two-year contract and have never left, despite other work here and there. I owe a huge debt of thanks to the members, staff and trustees of REAP. I especially want to thank Valey Arya, who started everything, and colleagues over the years: Anab Abdalla, Ayo Olaogun, Emina Cokic, Olesya Khromeychuk, Patrick Wright, Poornima Karunacadacharan, Rachaporn Slater, Renu Bhimbat, Stephanie Yorath. In particular, Ayo who taught me to pause and try to see the world as others see it, and Rachaporn for all her humour, tolerance and support since I started writing this book. Thank you to Stan, for patience.

Members – some now trustees – have opened windows and doors and given me innumerable insights: Oleg Pasichnyi and Ameem Bint Amir, Christopher Geake, Earl Phillip, Ezechias Ngendahayo, Fariha Bhatti, Janpal Basran, Khalida Obeid, Maria de Lourdes Pale, Peter Jones, Santiago Aristizabal. Thank you to the current trustees for permission to use REAP materials in this book. I can only mention a few of many wonderful earlier trustees: Anab Abdallah, Kiran Seth, Sala Salih, Samuel Nersisyan, Seble Ephrem, Yuusuf Guuled. Some individuals are thanked within the text, in relation to specific lessons and ideas for action.

It could also not have been written without the lessons I have learned and people I learned them from, through HEAR – London's Human Rights and Equality Network of voluntary and community organisations. Many years of thanks to Christine Goodall, Tim Brogden and Geraldine O'Halloran and to Mhairi McGhee, to Lisa and Andy, and the many hugely committed people involved in the network.

I have been lucky to meet many extraordinary professional peers and guides who have informed, encouraged and advised me over the years: some are acknowledged below. I would like to highlight Ceri Baldwin, Freda, Tina Wallace, Misak Ohanian, Judith Kramer – much missed. Special thanks to Sheila Heard who suggested I write the book and made it possible. Also to Debora Singer for her wonderful foreword. I am very grateful to Elen Griffiths and her team at Jessica Kingsley Publishers.

And to John Campbell for his expertise; to him and Alex, Eleanor and Nina, who, with Judith Foster and Nicky Crowther, have genuinely helped with their patience and belief in this project and hardly grumbled at all.

Individual chapters have been made possible by the knowledge and personal contributions over years from great numbers of people, including those above and to name just a few:

Accommodation: Ian Scott, Steve Hedley and Team.

English, education and employment: Marcin Lewandowski, Giles Strachan, Nafisa Rahman, Azar Sheibani.

Health, mental and emotional health: Diana Garanito, Helen Pool.

Refugee children: Sharon Long, Rabbi Aaron Goldstein.

Any mistakes, errors or omissions are all mine.

CHAPTER 1

Introduction

When You Find Yourself Working with
Asylum Seekers and Refugees

What do we expect?

Most of us expect to decide what kind of life we want to live. It might not be easy but we can choose what to study and where to live and whether to have a baby and how to work towards the kind of livelihood and lifestyle that suits us. We develop our own sense of identity and grow connections with friends and community networks. We make a home our own, and take care of our families, raise our children as we see best. We might detour on the way and we all make mistakes, but these are the choices we make.

Some people face day-to-day realities that remove all those choices: they face unreasonable and unjustifiable constraints, hostility and discrimination, humiliation, aggression and violence; they are impoverished and disempowered. Many ordinary people suffer abuse by powerful players in social or political systems where other people or the state or the legal system should be protecting everyone, but they fail to do so. Although many people stand up against such abuse, when abuse of a few becomes acceptable to the community, and those who have the power to protect society fail to do so, your only choice is to keep yourself and your loved ones safe. You change how you dress and act, change where you shop, change job. When that isn't enough, you have to look for a place where you and yours will be all right:

A wife leaves the house and moves ten miles away to a women's refuge.

A young man migrates south to London.

A father kisses his wife and children goodbye and gives the driver $500 to take them over the border.

To escape the harm done by inequality and unbridled discrimination, people like us leave behind their livelihoods and careers, and walk away from most of their family and all of their friends, and most of what they have owned and worked for. They leave the places where they learned everything they know, where they speak the language, understand 'the System', have contacts. These people end up in unfamiliar places, not knowing what their future will be, knowing their family is scattered across continents, and that they must start from scratch.

Why this book and who is it for?

Few of us escaped the heart-breaking image of a dead toddler, Alan Kurdi, washed up on a Mediterranean beach on 2 September 2015. For thousands of people across the UK, the immediate impact of meeting a refugee or refugee family for the first time has become a fairly regular, very personal experience. The family that has just walked through your office door is an ordinary family who couldn't carry on living where they lived. Now they are coping with the consequences of everything they have been through. They have to rebuild their lives in an unfamiliar society. Perhaps they will cope fine without your help, but they will probably cope better and rebuild a decent life faster with an extra hand.

In this chapter I am using 'refugees' to mean people who have the experience of coming to the UK to seek safety. In your work, and in later chapters in this book, different terms and definitions are sometimes needed, including those defined in immigration law and others, and I'll clarify those as we get to them.

You might specialise in health, mental health, education, English, youth work, social work, advice, housing, employment. Your field might be sports, arts, food, or engagement, campaigning and fundraising. You might already have extensive experience supporting vulnerable people, or focussing on women, or children with learning disabilities, or older people, for example. This book is for people who work in community, faith, voluntary or statutory organisations. It is also for activists, freelancers, trainers, trustees and volunteers. If you are part of any kind of group or organisation, or just have a new family move in next door and find yourself helping refugees, it is for you. Whatever your role, in most parts of urban Britain today, if you work 'hands on' and face to face in primary, community or local services of any kind, you will find yourself working with refugees.

> If you are a 'hands-on' practitioner or work closely with practitioners, and you find yourself working with refugees, then this book is for you.

Whether planned or not, you will find that with confidence and willingness to adapt, you already have most of the skills and experience you need. You will need a certain amount of new knowledge about refugee issues, entitlements and support, and ideas for adapting your existing activities to see your work through to your satisfaction. Your time and resources are no doubt already stretched, but hopefully you have team and management support and your other service users are sympathetic. But with or without team backup, the **first intention** behind this book is *to broaden awareness and provide information, sources of expertise and ideas to help you respond effectively to the person in front of you.*

Why this book now – has something changed?

Why this book now? Refugees have always come to Britain. Have the 'flood-gates' opened? Is this book necessary because our systems can no longer cope? In fact, no.

Visibility

With the coverage in the press, it appears that huge numbers of refugees are arriving in Britain, but this is simply not the case. Refugees have always come to the UK, and the asylum system is tightly controlled by the Home Office. Although there are short-term peaks and troughs in 'flow', the annual number of claims for asylum in the UK is little different now to the year 2000 as persecution and war persist around the globe. The number of people being given 'refugee status' has actually dropped (although the definition of 'refugee' needs proper attention and is discussed in Chapter 3).

What has changed is the *political visibility* of refugee flows. Our media revels in dramatic footage of desperate people (almost all of whom are still in other countries), and the news and electoral agenda in Britain swirl around attitudes to foreigners and migration of all sorts as migrant flows and net migration rise and fall. Since the global credit crash and before, 'austerity' policies and changing UK demographics have stretched services and housing in the UK. The public has become sharply aware of who gets what, and refugees are part of that discussion.

Visibility is a double-edged sword. Syrians have been in the news for several years and are met by both compassion and panic. People ring charities because they really want to do something; they offer Syrians a sincere welcome, food, clothing, a bed, money, kindness. But how many British residents are aware that similar numbers of desperate Sudanese are asking for asylum, and how many British people have even heard of Eritrea? As well as the swelling of sympathy, there is the reaction: a news commentator compared them to cockroaches; would-be politicians scream that we are at breaking point.

Apart from numbers arriving to seek asylum now, we don't really know how many refugees are in Britain. History shows that when a country becomes safe again, large numbers of people leave their place of refuge and return home to look for their lost sister, care for their mother, reclaim their land, rebuild their homes. The Home Office has no system for recording how many people who have sought refuge leave of their own will.

You might want to know how many refugees live in your area and where they are from. Such facts would help services prepare and plan. But those numbers don't exist either. We know the larger cities have substantial refugee populations, especially in more deprived areas where there is cheaper housing and there are larger migrant populations already. More asylum seekers are housed in the cheaper accommodation of the North West than anywhere else in Britain. Many young unaccompanied asylum seekers are in the care of the local authorities that cover the 'ports of entry' such as Heathrow (Hillingdon), Dover (Kent) and in Croydon, where the Home Office handles new claims. But in terms of readying yourself or your organisation, your awareness is what lets you see what isn't easily visible to others.

So this book is not written in reaction to a sudden increase in refugee numbers. Sadly, there will always be another Syria, or Sri Lanka, Srebrenica, Rwanda, Third Reich, Armenia, Tudor Reformation. Where will people flee from in the next ten years (North Korea? Iran?), and will we notice?

Organisations

Refugees have been among our service users for years. Practitioners have been supporting them as part of their daily work, addressing people's vulnerability, complex needs, inclusion and 'reaching the hard to reach'. But as individuals and British society have become more alert to refugees, refugees have appeared on the agenda of organisations that deliver services and support as a *distinctive category* of service user. 'Refugee support' has become a visible, legitimate and urgent concern for practitioners and finance directors alike. It is increasingly written into job descriptions, workplans and budgets.

There are two sides to any organisation. There is the textbook idea that organisations are structured and planned arrangements of people playing different roles, working together to achieve objectives that move towards an agreed goal. And there is the daily lived experience of individual staff and members with personal motivations and dynamic relationships with colleagues. They work within more or less helpful rules and targets, and have to justify their actions to others in the organisation, who in turn report to funders, commissioners and politicians outside the organisation who have different priorities. Senior staff, funders, commissioners and politicians have the power to cut off the resources staff need, in particular their salaries. Outsiders have the power to cut off the resources the organisation needs to exist. There never are enough resources, especially time.

Organisations that serve and support real people are always having to change and react to the complex, unpredictable and even chaotic lives of the people they serve. Unpredictable needs can disrupt organisational activities and processes in ways external judges might not understand. In this context, people within organisations often dread uncertainty and disruption because these create extra demands and could threaten their future.

Refugees' lives often introduce exactly that uncertainty and disruption to the organisations they approach. The people themselves may move through a series of crises, which are unpredictable and hard to manage resources around.

Refugees may be vulnerable on many fronts, and have interwoven needs all happening at the same time – some of which will probably be new to you and your colleagues. They often have few means to draw on as they work towards real-life goals: they don't have a car, or a bank account, or broadband. They aren't familiar with NHS and mental health service workings, nor the school system, local authority housing, tax, benefits, employment law, zebra crossings or other British institutions, systems, culture and manners. They don't have contacts and can be isolated (do *not* assume they have a supportive 'refugee community' to turn to). Some might have postgraduate degrees, but others might not be literate even in their own language. Like any migrant, they may not speak or understand or read and write English.

When you find yourself working with refugees, you will almost always find you are working beyond your job description: adapting plans, relationships, rules, priorities. You and your organisation find yourselves having to invest time and effort to learn new things, which is costly and might only help one person or family. There isn't even a guaranteed return on that investment, because the refugee may be rehoused, deported or may just move tomorrow. Later, when someone new arrives, she or he will be completely different and need different things. In the midst of these unfamiliar demands, you and your colleagues at all levels also have to look after yourselves and protect the organisation.

The **second intention** of this book is *to give practical assistance to your work with refugees, within the real-life world of the organisation.*

Nowhere else to turn

So refugees are more visible, and organisations are now paying them direct attention. The other thing that has changed is specialist support relating to refugees that you might have drawn on in the past. There never was enough, and shifting resources and ideologies in the past decade mean a lot of what was there has gone. Few local statutory or voluntary sectors have refugee services. There is less expertise available and a fraction of the communication links there were in the recent past.

As a consequence, refugees have fewer places they can turn to for help or that you can refer them to, and as a 'client-facing' practitioner there are not many places you can turn for advice/guidance or backup.

Take note, though: even when there were specialist services, there was a tendency across the social and community sector to refer a refugee away to 'a refugee organisation' or 'a refugee community group' because…

'We don't do refugees.'

This often appears to have been because practitioners assumed refugees are somehow different to 'us' – *other* people who needed *other* services, not the people *we* are responsible for helping. Or perhaps this tendency came from the sense that ordinary people like us cannot help them, we can't cope, we don't know enough, only 'refugee specialists' can help. This is not so. When a refugee has toothache, she or he needs to go to a dentist, not to a refugee organisation. When a woman refugee is isolated, she wants to meet other people, perhaps other women – it doesn't really matter if they are refugees or not, and it might be better if they aren't (see Box 1.1).

Box 1.1 **'We don't do refugees'**

A woman approached us who had a disabled child. She had financial and practical support in place but was lonely and finding it hard to stay positive. We found there was an organisation near where she lived that existed to bring together families and carers with disabled children to break down isolation and create opportunities to socialise and make friends. I was delighted; she was an isolated mother of a disabled child – exactly who they had set up to support.

We rang them and asked for details so she could join their activities. Their reply was: 'We don't do refugees.' All they heard was 'refugee' and they rejected her.

Ironically perhaps, the fact there are so few refugee specialist services left means this 'referring away' can't really happen any more, which might not always be a bad thing. The current situation is that organisations with a specialism in one field – be it children, emotional wellbeing or sport – are finding they must adapt and deepen that specialism to include refugees. This is not new, nor is it only refugees who are affected. Specialists in one field are always adding new expertise to existing expertise. Primary schools built expertise to integrate children with special needs. Disability organisations developed their services to support carers. Women's groups are debating responses to transgender equality.

In other words, there is a new role for hands-on staff who find themselves working with refugees now. Your role is no longer to find out who to refer to. But you don't need to learn a whole new specialism either. You just have to expand the specialist knowledge and experience you already have so you can relate it to refugees. The task will connect your expertise with a broad range of issues and other specialist fields. There is advice and guidance out there to back you up, but the services that produce and provide such resources can't take on the role of giving direct support to your participant, member or client.

So the **third intention** behind this book is *to help you deal directly with what you might previously have been able to refer onwards.* You need to expand your role and expertise, because there is no one else to do the job.

You and integration – What is 'refuge'?

Finally, when you find yourself working with refugees, you also find yourself a potential agent for integration and social change.

When you ring a women's centre and ask them to help you support a refugee ('No, thank you, I don't want you to Google a refugee women's group for me; the person I am supporting would like to come to *your* centre'), you change how they see their role towards refugees too.

When you challenge a doctor's receptionist ('Yes, they are entitled to register with a GP; no, they don't need to have proof of address; yes, I am sure about that. Would you like a copy of the NHS leaflet that explains it?'), you are improving access for other refugees (and other people) at the same time.

When you look someone in the eyes and treat them as an equal, normal human being, you create a slightly healthier, stronger society.

So my **final intention** through this book is *to do my bit so we all make this society a more meaningful place of refuge for people who have lost so much* (Box 1.2).

Box 1.2 Objectives

- To broaden awareness and to provide information, sources of expertise and ideas to help you respond effectively to the person in front of you.

- To give practical assistance to your work with refugees, within the real-life world of the organisation.

- To help you deal directly with what you might previously have been able to refer onwards.

- To make this society a more meaningful place of refuge for people who have lost so much.

Ordinary, unique, active

Throughout the book I am going to keep coming back to three central concepts about people who are refugees:

Refugees are ordinary.

Each refugee is unique.

Refugees are active agents of their own futures.

Refugees are ordinary

People are people. They worry about their mother, get cross with their kids, don't mind working but don't want to have to work all the time, like a nice meal, enjoy a good film, have happy and sad memories from childhood, have ideas for the future.

People who have had to escape persecution are still only people, only human, ordinary. They still worry about their mother. Through no fault of their own, they have been through extraordinary and often traumatic circumstances, and that might make them extraordinary to some extent. However, they are only extraordinary in the way any of us would become a bit extraordinary if we lived through extraordinary times and experiences. No miracles, no exceptional toughness or talent for survival. Not people who are 'better than us at handling death' or who are more used to oppression and loss and therefore don't feel it as much as we would.

> What does she do in those circumstances? What any of us would do, she depresses. It's an ordinary response, no one should be surprised about it. (Paraphrase from health visitor)

They are ordinary: persecution is not. To say refugees are ordinary is not to say it is ordinary to be a refugee. It is not ordinary to be subjected to discrimination, persecution, state-sponsored or state-tolerated aggression, abuse, injustice and violence. That is an entirely different matter. That is never ordinary. It must never become ordinary.

It is easy for you to feel a bit overwhelmed. You feel that if you faced what they have gone through, you would go under: I am just an ordinary person – how could any ordinary person cope with what he has been through? Mostly, like any ordinary person, this man you are talking to has just somehow managed to keep going despite everything. Maybe in similar circumstances I would just about manage to keep going, just about survive – maybe I would become a little extraordinary too? I hope I never find out.

If refugees are ordinary, what are they not?

Ordinary but not hopeless. People might have had experiences that crushed them. You will meet some people who are in the darkest places, but they do not stay there for ever. The seasons come and go, children learn to walk, new friends share delicious food. The past may have been appalling, the present may be tough, and there may be crises, flashbacks and delayed reactions for the rest of their days, but most of the time things are better than they were, and the future should be better than this.

Ordinary and not without standards. Refugees are trying to rebuild their lives and restore their dignity and a sense of pride and positive identity. They have standards and mostly they would like to raise those standards. Charities I have worked for have received 'donated' bin liners of old clothes that donors were probably sorting out to throw away, including stretched bikinis, worn-out and stained trousers, handbags with broken handles. Whether desperate or not, no one wants to be treated as if they are worthless. That is demeaning when really support should be enabling.

Ordinary and not in our debt. No person deserves to be a refugee, no person asks to be a refugee, so where a refugee is given help, it is a necessity, it is about decency – it isn't a loan. It does not mean they are in our debt.

There are lists of 'what refugees have done for us' that keenly proclaim how much more refugees put more into politics, society and the economy than they cost the country in the first few years. But this shouldn't be necessary. What is more, they don't have to earn the right to refuge – it is an essential element of a civilised country that it provides refuge to those who need it; as it is 'in our gift', so we give it. Refugees shouldn't even have to feel grateful. 'Grateful' implies supporters are doing something beyond the call of duty and deserve special recognition. It is fair that any person appreciates the effort another goes to for them, but 'grateful' implies that it would be acceptable not to help them.[1] However, as anyone who has worked with refugees will tell you, the gratitude and reciprocal generosity you sometimes receive can almost be embarrassing.

Ordinary and not angels. In the British population there are British people who are angelically kind and honest, people who are somewhere in the middle (most of us) and people who are genuinely hard to like. So it is with refugees. I am not talking about the crooks who cynically attempt to cheat the asylum system. I just mean average ordinary people, who have escaped danger to find safety, and happen to be truly lovely or actually not very nice. You might be bowled over by the warmth and sincerity of one refugee, only to find the next refugee grumpy, dismissive or a bit manipulative. You might be stunned by how frank and open one person is, while someone else is giving you highly selective information, dressing up the picture they present to you. You may be caught out by one person's liberalism in contrast to the lack of sympathy and sexism shown by another. Generally unpleasant behaviour might be a personal trait, but bear in mind that most of us ordinary people don't behave very well when we are miserable, short on resources, frustrated by endless bureaucracy and constantly anxious.

Ordinary and equal. Refugee does not mean more important or less important. It doesn't mean more entitled or less entitled. It doesn't mean better or worse. Ordinary means equal. People have a right to be treated as equals, with dignity and respect, neither better nor worse than anyone else, regardless of their sex, race and country of origin, religion, sexual identity, age, disability, marital status, whether pregnant or transgender. When we base our work and interactions on everyone being equal and with a right to equal treatment, we have a sound footing to go forwards on.

Ordinary and not 'other people'. The problem of people seeing refugees as 'other' people, 'them' and somehow different to 'us' will no doubt float up in your work, and it surfaces several times in this book.

---

1   Not always grateful. There is a wonderful article by Dina Nayeri called 'The Ungrateful Refugee' (*Guardian*, 4 April 2017), www.theguardian.com/world/2017/apr/04/dina-nayeri-ungrateful-refugee.

Each refugee is unique

> Each person who has come here for refuge is unique. (Just as every ordinary person is unique.)
>
> Each person's experiences are unique.
>
> Each person's response to their experiences is unique.

Therefore, their response to their current situation (and their relationship to you) is unique. One person might cry all day, another might stand for election.

There is a huge range of variables (and unique combinations) in each refugee's life: their sex, age, nationality, education, current family situation and so forth. What they went through individually (and with their family) will be completely different to the person from the same town who stands next to them. Their journey though Britain's asylum system will be different to their sister's (Chapter 2).

You will find patterns, though – probabilities and likelihoods. Their entitlements and access to support are fixed by a combination of their asylum or refugee status and other cross-cutting legislation around health and social care, equality, human rights, children's rights and more (Chapter 3). Refugee populations face multiple disadvantages linked with equality characteristics, such as mental health disabilities that make individuals vulnerable to discrimination and compound poverty and disempowerment over time (Chapter 4). Many people will struggle with access processes and have limited means and language to engage with you (Chapter 5). They often need your help to negotiate with other organisations (Chapter 7). But these general patterns don't tell the whole picture, and, above all, do not tell you about the person you are talking to today.

To summarise, start from the knowledge that nothing is certain; there is no typical experience or normal refugee. You might see similarities, but look for differences. You can't simply learn a set of facts and reactions to a standard set of 'refugee problems', so your preparation has to be about your readiness to learn, to listen and build trust from the first contact, and your ability to find and make new contacts and resources to help you in your work.

Refugees are active agents

Refugees are active agents of their escape and adaptation. They are survivors, not victims. They are coping, recovering and working to rebuild their lives, which includes not only practical necessities for themselves and their dependants, but less visible priorities such as caring about distant family members or a sense of who they will be in the future.

As they build, they will pursue their own priorities and that means preserving and using their assets in the way they think best. They will shop around, might test the boundaries now and then and perhaps accept a little more than they should at times. You might not always approve of their choices, but be careful before you judge. What they choose to do now is a tactic in a longer-term strategy, not their end goal, and most people want to get on with it.

You are a witness to their efforts; your actions facilitate theirs. You bring an essential toolkit of knowledge and skills. But they are not waiting for you to solve their problems. You, of course, are one of the assets they are juggling, so don't be surprised if things don't always go the way you thought they should. No matter what your skills or what you can offer, you are not in control of this relationship.

Learning from refugees and this book

This book exists because of refugees' own voices; it has grown from what I have learned when meeting and listening to individual refugees and families over more than 15 years. The testimonies, quotations and sometimes anecdotes are meant to give insight and ground what you are reading in the humanity and complex daily realities of a hugely diverse range of real people. Where I include direct quotations, they are anonymised, although I give what background I can where relevant, and please note the Acknowledgements which mention key individuals to whom I owe a lot. I also include real-life examples from my observations; some of the boxes are composites of several stories I have heard directly from people and gathered from primary sources over the years.

The book also combines expertise from many practitioners I have met or worked with over 25 years, many of them refugees. Their valuable knowledge, advice and expertise run through all chapters. Several have given their wisdom and knowledge freely and generously for this book, including input on accuracy and completeness, but any errors are mine alone.

The content and approach of this book have been shaped and tested by more than 15 years of giving direct support to primary and community practitioners who are *not* specialists in refugee issues but have found themselves working with refugees. I have learned from people on site, in meetings, in training and interactive workshops and by responding daily to practitioners' questions.

In this book I aim to answer practitioners' key questions:

What matters most?

What do I need to know?

What can I do?

I offer pragmatic ideas, working definitions and plain English rather than legal, clinical or pedagogical terms, although I make it clear where it is important to use specific terms in a more precise way. The way it is structured and presented, including the Table of Contents, Index and Appendices, is designed to help the reader make good progress through the book, or to pick and mix over a cup of tea, but still be able to flick through the book while you are on the phone and quickly find what you need. You are welcome to quote in letters, reporting and bids if you think it will help: please do acknowledge the source.

The book falls broadly into two sections, Chapters 1–7 discuss experience and knowledge, definitions and information, diversity and approach, with, from Chapter 5, a growing focus on action. Chapters 8–10 are practical chapters by theme, addressing what you can do about the issues that refugees are likely to face, starting from most basic needs around surviving destitution and homelessness (Chapter 8), then health, mental health and disability (Chapter 9), and learning English, training and employment (Chapter 10). Chapter 11 is an overview of issues faced by refugee children and young people and options for supporting them. Chapter 12 draws some final conclusions about deeper meanings of 'refuge' and 'refugee'.

In some chapters there are 'Long Boxes' with more detail on specific topics. There are a great many organisations and resources you can find online, but be careful that the site is not out of date as things change fast. Appendix A lists all organisations mentioned in the book, including the considerable number mentioned in practical chapters from Chapter 8 to Chapter 11. If you ring organisations for advice, please respect their time.

Box 1.3 **Monitoring your own learning**

Put a mark on the lines below to record where you think your knowledge is, and add a date. Revisit now and then.

I have a good overview of refugees' experiences and issues they might face.

0% ——————————————————————— 100%

I have an adequate working knowledge of refugees' entitlements for my job.

0% ——————————————————————— 100%

I am confident my current activities and practices give effective support to refugees.

0% ——————————————————————— 100%

I know where to find expertise or how to go about finding it when I need it.

0% ——————————————————————— 100%

I have clear priorities for what I want to know next, to help me support refugees.

0% ——————————————————————— 100%

CHAPTER 2

Why It Matters

Introduction

I have spent many rather cross hours arguing the big ethical, policy questions about the UK giving refuge to people who need it, and about why and how it matters to the UK and society as a whole. There are ethical *and* rational arguments in favour of welcoming and supporting refugees. This is a practical book, however, and even though the big national and international policy questions are gripping and often emotive, they probably aren't why you are reading it. Even so, for practical work you have to start by asking yourself: 'Why does it matter?' You need to be clear in your own reasoning because your views will affect what you do when you meet a refugee.

Our individual views and histories affect how most of us feel about helping refugees: maybe you have personal experience of violence or loss and rebuilding a new life; or your grandmother came to Britain as a refugee; or you feel the person whom you helped last year might have been taking advantage of you. You might be undecided or somewhat sceptical. It might not surprise you to learn that I think it matters a great deal whether or not we support refugees, and that we do so properly. Compassion and justice matter. Mutual respect and recognition matter. Preparedness and sensible resource allocation matter.

This book is for readers who are involved in supporting people who are recovering and rebuilding lives in the UK having escaped persecution and danger in other countries. Even if this is not your primary role at work, it is important to get this support right. To do that, you need to be clear what *your* answer is to the following two questions:

Question 1: Does it matter whether or not hands-on workers support refugees?

Question 2: Does it matter whether the people I am supporting are refugees or not refugees?

Question 1: Does it matter whether or not hands-on staff support refugees?

Polarised yelling matches aren't usually helpful, and the amount of yelling in Britain in the past few years has made people nervous about expressing their views and asking questions. There are several arguments for why hands-on staff need to support refugee individuals or families, and several points where people have genuine doubts and concerns. You, the reader, might be uncertain how to explain your position in the face of opposition. It is good to look at the range of reasoning.

Many people make the ideological case that support for refugees is a matter of compassion and respect for human life, about common humanity and the collective and individual duty of a decent, civilised society. Then there is the argument that if you are in a line of work that supports people who are struggling, you cannot legitimately ignore the vulnerability and struggles that are a daily reality for so many ordinary people who have sought refuge here. You will have your own views on these arguments already.

One of the more abstract points of view can be expressed as 'There, but for the grace of God, go I' (Box 2.1). Are you someone who could be (or has been) discriminated against? A woman? A man? A religious believer? An atheist? Could it get worse rather than better?

Discrimination and persecution do happen in the UK, whether one looks at contemporary hate-crime and wage discrimination, the treatment of Irish people in the 1950s, the Reformation (c. 1520–1550) or the massacre of the Jews in York (1190). Discrimination is an underlying reality in any society – it's really only a matter of scale. So it could be you; it could happen here.

Box 2.1 **There, but for the grace of God, goes John Bradford**

John Bradford was an English religious reformer – a Protestant Christian. The phrase 'There, but for the grace of God, go I' comes from him. He was imprisoned in London for his religious beliefs and campaigning. From his prison window he would watch people being led out to execution. He was burned at the stake in 1555.

   Many other Protestants like him became refugees, fleeing to other countries in Europe to escape persecution, indefinite imprisonment, torture and execution by the royal family and the state in Britain.

Where would you go if the situation turned nasty here? Without an EU passport, you can't just hop over the North Sea or the Channel. Perhaps you can cross into the Republic of Ireland, but can you stay? Will America let you in? Will Iraq welcome you? Will a family in Eritrea give you a room in their house? One conclusion from such reasoning is that we had better support other people seeking refuge, because we never know if one day we might need them to return the favour.

The simplest argument to make within formal organisations is that we must support refugees effectively because the law says we must and there are consequences if we don't. Under equality law we must ensure that all the people we support receive the same standards of support, working towards the same good outcomes, and this includes asylum seekers and refugees (see Chapter 4).

There are other obligations under other laws. You might not think the law is reasonable, and you have probably met several people who believe various laws and rights should be done away with. Nonetheless, this is how the law stands at present, and we must comply or face the consequences.

Finally, pragmatically, getting it right first time saves resources and builds trust that makes future working relationships more productive.

Doubts and concerns about whether to support refugees

Many people have genuine concerns about whether supporting refugees is a risk to Britain in the long run. *Hostile reporting* that plays to people's fears also scares people who dread the rise of intolerance. *Sympathetic reporting* tends to dwell on moral imperatives and the scale of need, which scares people who are concerned about consequences and who are upset about being labelled inhumane and racist.

Ideally, different views about our roles – and possible consequences of giving refuge – would be a source of creative debate and critical reflection, not least about practice. But at present different views are a source of damaging conflict, simplistic contradiction and rejection. It is important to think through doubts and concerns for ourselves and ensure that our own views are well informed from many sources. Then we can act with confidence, knowing our actions are justified, and we can keep learning and engaging with others – including those who have different views.

Doubts and concerns can be loosely grouped into three: Why us? Is it fair? Can we afford to care?

Why us? There are many who recognise that refugees have a legitimate need but have questions such as: Why us? Why do they all come to us? Aren't there other countries, other towns, or other organisations who should support them? Are we soft? Shouldn't they help themselves?

Higher visibility has given a distorted view of how many refugees there are in the UK. Very many countries are, of course, supporting refugees, many of them in far higher numbers and with fewer resources than Europe. The United Nations High Commission for Refugees (UNHCR), for example, estimates that Ethiopia hosts nearly six times as many refugees as the UK, and Pakistan 13 times as many (Refugee Council 2016).

Asylum seekers and refugees are not evenly distributed across the UK. Those asylum seekers who are housed by government are housed in economically depressed urban areas, where there is cheaper housing and multiple occupancy. Refugees settle where they can, which tends to be cities, starting in the poorer wards. These two factors have concentrated asylum seekers visibly in areas where there is usually already serious deprivation. It is interesting to note that the more ethnically diverse areas seem to be the least worried about this. This doesn't appear to be because earlier migrants and refugees are more sympathetic

– in fact, the opposite might even be true, but perhaps with more familiarity there is less concern about impact.

In some fields your organisation might be *wrong* to try to help – for example, immigration case work or counselling for post-traumatic stress that you aren't qualified to do. In terms of other organisations, there may be bodies who *should* be supporting the refugees who are coming to you. (Perhaps their response is 'We don't do refugees'.) It is important to ask around. In this case your organisation should not step in to fill the gap another organisation should fill, but you will probably find your role becomes helping your refugee client or member get past misinformation and climb through the necessary hoops to access the services they are entitled to.

But when you ask around, you could be surprised how little is there. Since cuts already noted in Chapter 1, there is often no 'other organisation' or 'other service' to help. Social Services are only obliged to support asylum seekers or refugees if they are assessed to be 'children in need' or disabled or on a few other grounds. Many local authorities have set up Syrian Resettlement services for selected Syrians, but don't support other refugees – even Iraqis or Syrians who came here overland all fleeing the same conflict. Refugees' own organisations and refugee specialist services in the voluntary sector have largely gone or are cut so thin you can see through them. Where they remain, they can connect expertise and perhaps run some restricted projects, but they rarely have capacity for the kind of holistic work they once did. Chapter 1 introduced the view that refugees have few places to turn, meaning specialists in all fields now need to work inclusively, broadening their expertise to include refugees, as they can no longer refer refugees elsewhere.

Regarding helping themselves, refugees are active agents of their own regrowth, and are constantly striving to improve their own situation. Sometimes that's enough and they don't need you. Sometimes their best efforts aren't enough, and they need an extra hand to move on and up. If people don't present to you as refugees in need of help, you may not notice they exist – you only meet those who come to you for help.

Is it fair? A second area of doubt revolves around whether it is fair that we pay for refugees from our taxes. Are they coming over here just to get our benefits, NHS and education for free? Our jobs? We paid tax – they haven't! Are they cheats? Are they crooks? Are they terrorists?

Within any system there are people who rip it off, but that doesn't mean the system isn't needed or is necessarily failing. Think of politicians' expenses: some Members of Parliament work flat out for 25 years for their constituents and claim exactly what they need or less; one person buys a duck house.

To some extent these 'Is it fair?' questions rotate around whether our asylum decision-making system works. Yes, there are people who try to exploit the asylum system, but it is not easy to get away with it. The British system is tough.

Some would say too tough, to the point of risking injustice. Broadly speaking, the British government is looking for ways to keep people out or refuse their claims. So if the Home Office or the Courts decide the person in front of you is a legitimate refugee, you can be pretty sure they are. There are plenty of other people who have suffered and asked for refuge, and are refused.

About benefits: people need to eat. Our 'benefits' system stops refugees (and other British subjects and eligible women and men) living under flyovers and suffering long-term (expensive) health problems related to malnutrition. Homelessness is not an option. Sofa-surfing is unsafe and unsustainable. Night shelters are an expensive emergency patch. The average lifespan of someone sleeping on the streets in the UK is apparently three years. Flight from war and persecution is often a matter of life and death; benefits and services can be about life and death too.

People want to earn a decent living instead of relying on sub-poverty-line benefits, and as soon as they have the permission and opportunity to work and pay for themselves, they will. Our staff time spent on education and health is not wasted on refugees. It is as much an investment in them as in any member of society – it enables them to contribute to society, as ordinary members of society, in the future. Not paying back a 'debt' – just enabling them to contribute skills and productivity, look after themselves and their family, and pay normal taxes.

Do criminals and terrorists try to get into the UK through the asylum process? Yes, they probably do try this route, and many others. That is, if they aren't born here and living here already with British family. If people are determined to do British people harm, they will use what means they can. The asylum system makes us neither more nor less vulnerable to attack. Other factors are at play.

Can we afford to care? or **What about my mum?** Concern is often connected with the feeling that supporting refugees means British people will lose out. We know we are a rich country. Everyone knows we can afford to support some refugees, but how many is too many and have we reached the tipping point? Will our living standards change? Will our culture change? Will change be for the worse? What about my mum's hip replacement?

Britain changes all the time and always has. So no doubt the refugees and migrants arriving now will change the country as so many other things in the past have changed this country. Eritrean culture might be new to Britain, but refugees aren't, and nor is social change. Land enclosures, the slave trade, industrial revolution, colonialism, women's suffrage, world wars, cars, the pill, privatisation, broadband have all had a huge effect on Britain's economy, society and politics. Changes arising from the arrival of refugees are part of that picture. Taking the long view, most people would say the arrivals of Dutch Protestants under Elizabeth I or Jewish children escaping Nazi Germany changed many aspects of British society for the better, despite initial hostility and even violent conflict in some quarters. But it is slightly risky to argue that we can 'afford' refugees because we gain from refugees, as it is a return to the view that refugees have to earn the right to be here.

Whether we can afford refugees is an area where issues about migration and about refuge get mixed up. We need to keep these issues separate. Even though refugees are one kind of immigrant, this book isn't addressing migration or immigration as a broader issue. Some of the points in later chapters about working with refugees will apply to any work you do with any migrant person (including students, tourists, workers and business people, EU nationals, family members joining spouses, undocumented migrants, etc.), but the experiences of refugees coming to the UK are completely different to those of other migrants and many of their needs are different too. The number of refugees compared with overall migration figures is small: about 30,000 people ask for asylum per year, although it varies year to year and 2016–2017 was higher. Roughly a quarter – about 8000 – are allowed to stay. Many go home when home becomes safe. By comparison, after the Brexit vote, overall net migration figures *dropped* to 230,000 in 2017 (www.ons.gov.uk).[1] Thirty thousand asylum seekers is a substantial number, but it isn't a flood. Looking only at the larger number of asylum seekers (rather than people given status and Leave to Remain), it works out to 46 people per Parliamentary constituency (650 constituencies) if spread evenly, although refugees tend to end up in deprived urban constituencies. An average constituency has 70,000 voters. The source of these figures, and the best quick reference source for anyone needing statistics, is the Refugee Council Quarterly Asylum Statistics; this data is from May 2018.

Successive decisions by Her Majesty's Governments about how to spend our tax money also get confused with issues about refuge. Political ideologies about the role and value of the welfare state, public services and public workers, and social housing shape decisions about how money is spent and what resources are available to the people of Britain – including my mum – now and in the future. Those are the decisions that fix who has to wait how long for what. But when someone's hip replacement operation is delayed, people tend to look for an immediate solution. We can't ignore the fact that some interests in the UK manipulate perceptions to promote certain agendas. Pictures of a thousand people at a border point stir fear of a future in which Britain will cease to exist as we know it, as poverty-stricken and desperate strangers pour in. If frustrated members of the public are pointed towards a visible group of 'other' people (who are not likely to stand up for themselves), they appear to have a simple solution for the problem: 'I'm worried public services will let me down: stop refugees and migrants and the problem will be solved.'

---

1   Net migration is calculated by the total number of people coming in per year minus the total number leaving per year – therefore, the overall increase or reduction in numbers of migrants in the UK.

Question 2: Does it matter whether the people I am supporting are refugees or not refugees?

Refugees' needs are different to other service users', participants', members' needs. But also the same. This second question comes down to how we treat refugees. Should we treat them differently to other people or not? Having picked up this book, this question is probably already in your mind. It is a great question to start off a training session or team discussion.

There are plenty of hands-on workers who will say with pride, 'We don't single people out', 'We don't agree with labelling people', 'We treat everyone the same', 'Everyone has equal opportunities here', 'We accept people as they are'. Some reply cautiously, 'We don't like to ask in case they feel stigmatised', or 'in case they think we won't help them'.

But I am less ambivalent about my bugbear, 'We don't do refugees' (see Box 1.1). Perhaps these organisations 'do' everyone? Or they really mean 'our' services aren't for 'them': refugees aren't like us. Perhaps like a respondent to a survey REAP did, who said, 'We do housing for gay men; we don't do refugees' as it hadn't occurred to him that gay men might be refugees, or that refugees might be gay men. Maybe 'don't do' comes from confusion about refugees, like the man who replied to the same survey, 'We do not encourage refugees to access our services as our funders would not be happy about us providing services to people who are not supposed to be here...' (see Box 4.8; REAP 2009). Refugees can appear as 'other' people – exotic, threatening, scary, extraordinary. In these cases it matters very much if the people who need support are refugees or not, because if they are, in that organisation's view, they can shove off.

I fully agree it is all wrong to label people, pick them out as 'different' and judge them for something that is outside their control. However, refugees have had extraordinary experiences and therefore some of their needs are likely to be out of the ordinary too. There are also legal constraints. If we don't recognise differences, including where there are extraordinary needs, we cannot support people in the ways they need supporting. 'Equal opps' is not treating everyone the same; it is treating everyone differently. You don't have to know for sure that someone is a refugee, or what their immigration status is or any detail about what they have been through, but you should be aware they might be a refugee, because you need to take that possibility into account as you work out the best way to support them. If treating everyone the same means responding to all individuals with respect, listening and learning, and taking responsibility for our decisions, then, absolutely, we should treat everyone the same.

> If treating everyone the same means responding to all individuals with respect, listening and learning, and taking responsibility for our decisions, then, absolutely, we should treat everyone the same.

Experiences

You need to be aware of what people *might* have been through (see Box 2.3). In current narratives about refugee experiences, we are very aware of war and violence and horrendous journeys across continents. But most people's experiences of persecution go back further and start with less dramatic experiences, with more subtle impact.

People may have experienced direct and indirect discrimination, social and economic losses, intimidation and invasions into their lives for years, even generations before they eventually leave their country. 'The community' and even their own family might have been the perpetrators or just did nothing to stop the attacks. The police and government turn a blind eye, 'fail to protect' and perpetrate or even promote persecution. People are disempowered and impoverished. Abusive social and political structures cut back their options and opportunities.

Perhaps they stand up and fight back, or perhaps they don't. They adapt to cope and survive, trying to look after themselves and their loved ones. There will be a series of losses and departures. If you were in this situation, you might change how you act, your livelihood and what you aspire to, how you dress, how you raise your children. People make little moves. Your daughter moves desks in her maths lesson so the kid next to her can't kick her any more. You move flat because the neighbour was aggressive, then say goodbye to your father and move the family to a bigger city where you can get on with life but be less visible. Your son goes to university over the border.

You start to run out of options. Hostility develops into theft, violence, imprisonment and torture (Box 2.2). You decide it would be best to leave the country. There may be triggers to departure: a new prime minister makes a speech, a bomb in the market place, your uncle is taken away. You and your children and your parents fly or drive or walk over the border, perhaps to stay with a cousin, perhaps to a camp, where you will stay for now; perhaps you will head for another country where you have contacts or you think you might be able to find peace and rebuild a home for your family to join you.

Box 2.2 **Aware of current dangers**

It is good to be informed about other countries so you realise what this person might have gone through or witnessed at first hand. Congo has a long history of torture. Iran hangs gay men. Bosnians witnessed neighbour turning on neighbour.

But make sure you have the historical context too: Syrians who came to the UK before the current war travelled from a liberal and prosperous country.

The journey is hard and you have to pay lots of people who take most of your money off you and tell you what you must do. You stay in crowded places, suffer assaults, lose weight and get ill. You feel anxious all the time, you don't know what will happen next, you can't reach your family by phone, you live off rumours, you keep going.

You arrive in a country and ask to be allowed to stay – a claim for asylum. You have to explain your traumas and why you left over and over again to strangers via an interpreter who is also from your country. You don't quite trust him. You don't want to talk about the rape but you have to. You don't know who is on your side. You get a letter that says no, go home, you were not in danger, you will be safe enough there. Your solicitor writes more reports and fills in more forms for an appeal. Then you wait. You are in a hostel. It is with a lot of other asylum seekers; the people living in the area don't like you. People come and try to sell you drugs, documents and opportunities for cash-in-hand work. Everyone tells you what to do but they all tell you different things. There is a nice woman in a nearby community centre who gives out food and soap. She looks at you as if you matter.

You go into a court. You've never been in a court before. There is an interpreter and they ask you questions and the legal people talk. Then you go back to the hostel and wait.

A letter comes; it says you can stay. You have 28 days to find a place to live and apply for benefits before you have to leave your accommodation and they cut off your money. There are no interpreters at the benefits office. The nice woman helps you fill some forms and gives you food and a paracetamol. In the end you promise someone £20 per week to let you sleep on the floor, and after three weeks you manage to find a room and your first benefit money arrives. Your relief is overwhelming.

Box 2.3 **A discussion tool: I am a refugee 'by experience'**

I feel I am a refugee. I came here for safety.

I survived and adapted, coped with bullying and discrimination in my home country.

I had to leave because it was too dangerous. I left one place after another: moved college, moved town; finally, I left the country. A lot of people like me face crises, danger, violence, fear; some can leave with their families, some have to leave alone.

I travelled through other countries where I could not stay. I lost most or all the people I know and all my things, and I had to pay a lot of money to get people to help.

I arrived in one country where I think I can stay, and have asked to stay, or I might only be able to stay for a while. I don't know what will happen next.

They said yes, I can stay. I have refuge! I have asylum, safety, a chance to recover and rebuild. But I need to learn the language, new systems, new people; I don't know anyone and no one knows me.

They said 'no', I have to go. Now what?

Questions to ask the group

What impact might these experiences have on a person's ability, sense of identity and mental health? What impact might these experiences have on parents' ability to nurture their children? On their ability to engage with you and your organisation? On someone's ability to plan their future? On their financial situation?

Refugees are different to other migrants but also the same

Refugees are migrants, but not all migrants are refugees.

Refugees face the full range of issues that all migrants face, but not all migrants face the issues refugees face.

Chapter 3 looks in depth at definitions of 'refugee' and entitlements, and Chapter 5 at the issues refugees and other migrants face when trying to engage effectively with staff and structures in formal organisations. But there are points that need noting here in relation to whether we treat refugees differently to other people, which includes whether we treat them differently to other migrants.

Box 2.4 | **Similarities between refugees and migrants**

Migrants with work, student, spouse or several other visas may be here a long time and put down roots here. They have made friends, made a home and started a business; they have a life here. Love affairs and divorces happen; children are born and start school; life gets complicated. The prospect of leaving can be traumatic.

On the surface, this person and a person seeking refuge are both suffering, facing the same dire anxieties about being forced to leave. They need letters of support, they are still struggling with English, they are extremely anxious about deportation. There is a human sitting in front of you who has done nothing wrong and is desperate to stay.

They present with such similar needs that they get mixed up. But they aren't really the same. The non-refugee person has not been through the same experiences of powerlessness, fear, loss, transit, insecurity and the asylum process. They can go back safely even if they really don't want to. They have the prospect of applying to return.

In my work I have repeatedly been asked how to help 'a refugee' but then found that the person is some other kind of migrant entirely – a Commonwealth national on a student visa perhaps, the spouse of a person here on a work permit, or even an EU national (see Boxes 2.4 and 2.5). We all do what we can. But the majority of migrants have different visa arrangements and entitlements to refugees, especially those still in the asylum process (see Chapter 3). More important than that, other migrants have different reasons for being here and different experiences of leaving their original home, in transit and since arriving in the UK. Which is not to say that other migrants don't have genuine needs, or that life is necessarily easy for them. But their situation is different. They were safe, they chose to come, they can go back any time they want, and may be able to return to the UK after that (Box 2.4). These days there is often no right place for any migrant to go for advice, so any migrant might come to you. But the support refugees need starts from a completely different base to other migrants.

Box 2.5 **Differentiating between refugees and migrants**

Sometimes the fact someone is from a 'refugee exit' country such as Lebanon, Somalia or Syria leads supportive workers to assume they are refugees. Sometimes just being from abroad or having brown skin or being Muslim is the sole basis on which people make this assumption. One time a young British black man was referred to us – a refugee charity – for housing advice. We didn't offer housing advice. He wasn't a refugee. He wasn't a migrant. I assume this ridiculous decision was well intentioned, but we had to conclude that it was founded purely on his skin colour and it was actually racist.

All migrants face a big challenge with communication in English, especially with bureaucrats and professionals such as medics or solicitors. Any newcomer to any country will find the accents, manners and local terminology new at first. Those with little or no English may have to invest years in learning the language to be able to communicate effectively in the UK. Some never do, remaining poorly informed or dependent on others all their lives.[2] Even fluent arrivals lack the cultural familiarity and competence that helps smooth out interaction – for example, use of body language or how to interact with the opposite sex.

With or without good English, it takes all migrants time to cope with unfamiliar institutions in a new country, and to learn how to negotiate access and prove eligibility to organisations that control useful resources. Although some people will gain the essential knowledge, skills and contacts (and documents!) to function effectively in months, others might still struggle with basics years later. Refugees have to do more of this than other migrants. Most migrants will have their documents and necessary evidence. Refugees often don't.

At risk of repeating myself, the biggest difference between refugees and other migrants is that most migrants chose to leave their country and come to the UK – mostly for economic reasons or to develop their lives in other ways. People in most categories of migration can work from the minute they arrive, but not asylum seekers, who are still waiting for a decision on their application for refuge and will be heavily penalised if caught working (see Chapter 3). Refugees who are allowed to work often aren't ready to work, as they lack relevant skills, recognised qualifications, job contacts.

Add to this the fact that other migrants who are in the UK were given permission to enter usually before they travelled. They will have made

---

2 Children can be extraordinary at learning languages, but don't succumb to the temptation of using them as interpreters (see Chapter 5).

arrangements for the family they leave at home and will have prepared for life in Britain before leaving, reading about it, choosing what to pack – probably with a degree of excitement. They have a good sense of what will happen after they arrive. Family members may be allowed to visit or join them while they are here. Such 'voluntary' migrants are more stable, less vulnerable. They are likely to have higher levels of physical and mental health than refugees.

All migrants are likely to experience a degree of homesickness, changes in family and personal relationships, and especially pressures and concerns about distant family. Being in a new social context often includes isolation in some form and challenges to a person's sense of identity and direction. Refugees will feel all these things, but for refugees the homesickness might be for places and experiences that no longer exist. Their family may have changed for ever and they might not even know where some family members are or what has happened to them.

Certain migrants may not have originally fled persecution but nonetheless have similarly traumatic experiences to refugees and end up in similarly vulnerable situations. For example, people who were trafficked into the UK, male and female migrants being forced into marriage, escaping domestic abuse or at risk of abuse linked to culture. They may end up in the asylum process as they ask the UK for protection. They are also coping with what they have experienced as they wait to find out if they will be allowed to stay.

Consequences for them and for you

What refugees have experienced has consequences for them, and therefore for your work. Each person deals with what life has handed them in their own unique way, but there are patterns and probabilities to be aware of with refugees that are additional to those you might find in your work with other people – plus, of course, the practical issues of entitlements and eligibility.

Refugees are often wary when dealing with **authority** – for example, being visited at home by a health visitor, deciding whether to report a crime to the police, or just filling in a form. You are an authority figure. Their perception and ability to build a relationship of trust with you will be shaped by earlier experiences before and after leaving their original home, and having come through the British asylum system.

They are also sensitive about **stigma and hostility** from the public, whether that is a neighbour or fellow student or a stranger insulting them as they walk home. This extends to caution about letting staff and volunteers in organisations know they are refugees, particularly where they fear discrimination could prevent them accessing the help they want or need.

Refugees are often dealing with short-term horizons, instability, vague but critical deadlines, insecure housing, health and financial situations that can easily tip into crisis. It takes time and stability to build up resources and resilience, and a 'shock' such as a car accident or losing a job, which you or I might overcome relatively quickly, can do long-term damage. Their impoverishment over time leaves them short of assets and forced to make difficult choices with their limited cash, time and energy. Their physical, mental and emotional health is often compromised, further challenging their confidence and scope for action, including what they aspire to in the future.

It all affects whether and how they engage with you and how easy it is to build an effective working relationship.

Summary and conclusion

So my answer to Question 1 is yes. I believe it matters that we support refugees. It matters that we support refugees because they have suffered and lost. They are struggling with British bureaucracy. They are recovering and actively rebuilding their lives, and if aware and informed people help them along the way, they will be able to build decent lives more quickly. The more effectively we do this, the better value we get from our scarce resources.

Likewise for Question 2, yes. It also matters that we know whether the people we are supporting are refugees or not because it has consequences for what we do.

1. You need to reflect on your own practice in light of who refugees are.

   They are ordinary and equal. Be professional, but connect as a real person too. Be aware that there may be serious issues at play. But don't poke. Find out what you need to know. But don't dig.

   Each refugee is unique. This means nothing is certain. Act with sensitivity. Don't assume the worst happened to the person in front of you, but don't assume it didn't either.

   Refugees are active, strategic agents of their own futures. Allow time and space. Let trust grow. Facilitate. Be flexible and prepared to respond to what emerges.

2. Refugees may have experienced powerlessness, fear, loss, transit, insecurity and struggles with the UK asylum system and bureaucratic processes. You need to be aware of what refugees might have been through and the possible consequences:

   • mistrust of authority, a series of crises, difficulty negotiating access to British organisations and institutions, reluctance to engage (Chapters 6 and 7)

   • poverty, homelessness, insecurity bordering on destitution (Chapter 8)

   • impaired physical, mental and emotional health (Chapter 9)

- struggles with language, skills and accessing opportunities and work (Chapter 10 – see also Chapter 6)

- all the normal trials and tribulations of life – for example, growing up and growing older.

3. Practically, you have to be aware of different ways 'refugees' are defined in different contexts that relate to asylum seekers' and refugees' entitlements and constraints, which are introduced in the next chapter, with details on practical topics in Chapters 8–11.

To conclude: as I see it, whether or not we support refugees depends on what kind of society we want to live in. What do we want 'British Values' to be? Clearly we have the potential to make a difference. The alternative is to walk away and leave refugees struggling, or just leave them swimming in the Mediterranean. What impact does that have on us? What do we gain by walking away? What do we have to lose by helping?

What I don't think Britain can afford is people who could be self-sufficient, and who could even contribute to society, being made poor and incapable, their lives wasted and their children disadvantaged. It doesn't make sense to save £100 on English lessons now, and spend £1000 on unemployment benefits later.

When asked whether we should give special treatment to refugees (What about people escaping domestic abuse? What about kids with HIV? What about my mum?), my answer is no. Being a refugee doesn't make a person more important. Being ordinary makes them important, as important as anyone who has suffered, lost, struggled, has the chance to rebuild and who needs meaningful support at this moment in time. If we focus on the experiences these people have faced, their current vulnerability and the possible long-term consequences for their lives and families, then the fact they are refugees becomes less significant, and so does the way immigration law defines them. It becomes instead about responding to the actual needs of real people whom we are in a position to help. If your services are set up so you can respond effectively to people with real and diverse needs and constraints, then you can respond better to everyone, including my mum.

CHAPTER 3

Defining 'Refugee' and Practical Entitlements – on a 'Need to Know' Basis

Introduction

This chapter makes the transition between *why* we help refugees in the opening chapters and *how*, which is the rest of the book.

You have to be able to define who *you* mean by 'a refugee'. Your definition will shape what you do.

You have many choices, ranging from legal definitions in international law right through to people's own descriptions of how they see themselves. Different bodies use different definitions for different reasons.

This book is meant to help you in the day-to-day world of working with real people. So this chapter looks at the practical implications of different bodies' definitions. It considers subjective definitions, a pragmatic summary of immigration, legal and governmental definitions, and some attention to popular uses of 'refugee'. Whoever *you* decide to consider a refugee, you still need a sound working knowledge of language from immigration law because government uses legal categories to set people's entitlements and to constrain certain people's actions and agency. Popular uses of 'refugee' are likely to come up in conversation with colleagues or volunteers and can have an impact on your freedom to support people as you think best. The right definition at the right time matters.

When you understand the language to use in different contexts, you can explain yourself clearly and confidently when you advise, reassure or even argue with your colleagues. This applies to trustees and even funders. Having the right words for the right moment means you get the correct information to and from other professionals, so you give accurate support to the individual, especially in matters of access, entitlements and benefits. Knowing the language means you can communicate and collaborate with other practitioners to improve processes and systems, especially when you need to prioritise scarce time and resources.

The Glossary lists the terms and various definitions given in this and other chapters. Appendix A lists all organisations mentioned. Appendix B is a collection of documentation and evidence referred to in the book.

WARNING! This chapter is not giving legal definitions or advice. The definitions discussed in this chapter are *not* for immigration-related case work or advice. If you aren't licensed to do immigration work, don't do it!

Box 3.1 'A workshop on "How to stop refugees duping us"?'

I was asked to run a workshop on how to stop support organisations being duped by refugees. I asked for further explanation. It emerged the enquirer didn't know the people's actual immigration status, but as they were males from Asia who had not been in the country long, it had been assumed they were refugees. One had been aggressive and manipulative towards staff and was probably involved in criminal activity and exploiting other migrants. Another had tried to defraud members of money and goods.

They assumed the problem was about refugees. I saw it as more about their own supervision and safeguarding procedures. They were not looking at what mattered, and by labelling them 'refugees' they merged criminal behaviour and refugees as if they were the same thing.

A subjective definition of 'refugee' – based on people's experiences

The previous chapter was about *why*. It concluded that the reason we should support 'refugees' is that they have suffered and lost and must rebuild their lives. On top of this they are often struggling with British systems and culture. It all centred on people's experiences.

It also set the scene for *how*. Chapter 2 concluded that practitioners need to be able to distinguish between refugees and other people, such as other migrants. This is necessary because refugees' experiences shape their situation at present, and what they are able to do about it. Therefore, people who have faced traumatic losses may now be struggling with mental health problems. People impoverished and disempowered by persecution and flight are probably facing an ongoing series of practical crises. People asking the UK government for refuge have their movements and activities limited and have fixed rights and entitlements. It all impacts on people's effectiveness and their willingness to engage with you. Chapter 2 noted that you need to be aware of these additional factors as you work out how to help.

This adds up to a strong argument for hands-on workers to have a core working definition of 'refugee' that starts from people's subjective realities.

A subjective definition of 'refugee'

So if we take 'a person who has fled persecution' and make it subjective, we can start from:

'a person who feels she or he has fled persecution'.

But often refugees flee from what has not yet happened, but that they fear will happen next. (A 'fear of persecution' is also embedded in international law – see Box 3.4). So adding this we get:

'a person who feels she or he has fled actual or potential persecution'.

So far this locates people's experiences in something that happened to them before arriving in the UK and is now done and over. But a meaningful definition needs to reflect the new reality too, so perhaps:

'a person who has found refuge in the UK, feeling she or he has fled actual or potential persecution'.

However, many people don't feel they have *found* refuge here – people who are scared of their neighbour, or are still in the asylum system and dread the post each morning. Which gives us:

'a person who feels she or he has sought refuge in the UK, from actual or potential persecution'.

A subjective definition like this is inclusive – it includes people who other observers might say are not refugees. For example, it could include someone still in the asylum process. It could even include someone that the government has refused to accept as a refugee, and I will return to this conflict of definitions later.

But this subjective definition can include other people too, unrelated to government categories. Some time ago I helped organise an event where I met two impressive women: Prossy and 'Lily', both lesbians. Prossy was gang-raped, tortured and abused by national police in her country of origin because of her sexuality. She struggled with negative decisions, deportations and appeals through the British asylum system for years, before she finally won the right to remain in the UK. Lily is from the United States of America. She and her British partner felt they would never be able to live freely in Lily's home town. So they moved to the UK where they could live openly as a couple.

You need to decide for yourself if this definition includes people fleeing war. Some say yes, war is appalling, there is great suffering and loss, and they are seeking safety so it is essentially the same as people fleeing persecution. Certainly, war usually involves persecution. Even if root causes are economic and political, violent conflict worsens or is worsened by national and ethnic and/or religious and political alignments. Aggression is often played out along lines of identity. The extreme 'macro' persecution of war is often brutally manifested at the micro level through abuse of selected individuals, families or whole villages.

People who have been trafficked, women being forced into marriage or people relying on spousal visas who have been abused by partners while in the UK have suffered and lost – and are allowed to ask for permission to stay in the UK in their own right, via the asylum system – and so fulfil part of the criteria of this definition.

Some who are concerned about suffering and loss might include people escaping natural disasters as 'refugees'. The most inclusively minded may include 'economic refugees'. They argue that history, powerful economies and leaders have caused such misery through exploitation and inescapable poverty and hopelessness that people have no choice but to flee.

Few would deny the suffering of these groups, or deny them sympathy. But some consider the aspect of persecution makes refugees' experiences fundamentally different. Not necessarily worse or more important, but still different.

A subjective and therefore inclusive definition leaves the practitioner having to make choices. We can't do everything, we can't help everyone.

We might decide to help anyone (any refugee) who comes to us, to the best of our ability, for as long as we can. It is a kind of 'non-decision' option. But it raises the question whether the people who need support most are the ones who get it – a question revisited in Chapter 5. I would argue that 'If you don't ask, you don't get' is not a good method for rationing services.

So with this subjective and inclusive definition, we are left still having to judge between Prossy and Lily. *Whom* do we prioritise and *how* will we help them?

So how do we judge? We haven't the information to judge objectively. We know barely anything about the person in front of us and it is unacceptable to dig. We can't start setting tests and making people compete for who has the worst trauma – although I have filled in a few funding applications that feel that way.

It ends up being a somewhat risky judgement call. We combine what people tell us, papers they show us, what we have learned about refugee issues over the years. We make good use of peer advice. Most of us also draw on a degree of instinct and trust and/or cynicism that goes a bit beyond accepting what we are told at face value. We start with a cautious approach. Over time, we shrink or expand the space within which they can engage us. We hope that we build mutual trust and respect and that the working relationship grows.

This book uses this subjective, inclusive definition as its 'default'. When the text simply says 'refugee', this is what it means:

> A person who feels she or he has sought refuge in the UK, from actual or potential persecution.

Home Office definitions of 'refugee' – based on future likelihood

This section goes through what 'refugee' and other important terms such as 'asylum seeker' mean in immigration law. It touches on processes the applicant goes through. (Entitlements are outlined later, towards the end of the chapter.)

The precise governmental department handling refuge (and other immigration) moves around every few years, but it remains the responsibility of the Home Office overall.

Several Immigration Acts have been passed by Parliament in the past 20 years and new Bills will almost certainly continue to arrive in Parliament. Although details and entitlements change a lot, essential definitions change little. This section aims to gives a pragmatic understanding of key terms and processes.

This section is *not* provided so you can give immigration advice or comment on whether someone is likely to succeed in their asylum claim. Even if you stay up to midnight searching the internet several nights in a row, you *will* get it wrong. You could jeopardise someone's whole claim. Leave it to the lawyers.

It is provided for practical reasons. You need working knowledge of Home Office definitions or you won't appreciate the impact they have on people seeking refuge. You need to understand something of what the refugee is experiencing as she or he goes through asylum and immigration processes. You will need to be familiar with essential legal and Home Office language to know how to help with practical needs, especially accommodation, money and work. Confusion on your part could mean a lot of wasted time and effort for you and, more importantly, for the refugee.

Home Office decisions about who does or doesn't fit the definition of 'refugee' are meant to be objective and based on evidence. But each case is unique. Situations change fast. There are a great many staff and other professionals involved in the decision-making system, with different knowledge and different interpretations of evidence, process and law. Home Office decisions are based on predicting the likelihood of certain things happening in the present and future, discussed below. With many uncertainties, and people's lives at stake, campaigners constantly scrutinise and challenge the system. Many thousand Home Office decisions on individual cases are challenged by those individuals and their solicitors each year.

'Asylum seeker' in immigration law

The law distinguishes between 'asylum seekers' and 'refugees' and gives them different rights and entitlements. The meaning of asylum seeker can be pragmatically summarised as:

> someone who has asked to stay in Britain on the grounds that if s/he goes 'home', s/he will be in danger; and is still waiting for a final answer.

They might still be waiting for an 'initial decision'. Or they have had their case refused and have appealed for the decision to be changed and are waiting for the result, in which case they are still considered an asylum seeker.

Initial claim for asylum. Starting the process of claiming asylum can be as simple as saying 'Asylum' to the right official. Most of the people you meet will have applied for asylum when they arrived in Britain. A large proportion make their *initial claim* at the airport or docks, although some go to a Home Office building such as Lunar House in Croydon after arriving overland, possibly helped by smugglers. People who are already here on student or other visas can claim asylum if trouble has broken out in their country.

Initial screening. Having made the claim, the asylum seeker might be detained until initial screening (conducted without a lawyer), which should happen within a matter of days, usually in Croydon or Belfast. Home Office officials process the paperwork and 'screening' interviews. Most people are released after the screening interview.

Where previously they had 'temporary admission' while they waited for a decision, now they are technically on 'immigration bail'. They will receive an Application Registration Card (often called an 'ARC card' by users) with a photograph and Home Office number. You can see images of these and other documents mentioned on the internet (Appendix B has more details). They may need to comply with reporting and other requirements, including being prohibited from work.

Detention. They could be detained again during their time in the asylum process. Men who are considered likely to abscond might be detained in centres near Heathrow (Harmondsworth, Colnbrook) and throughout the UK; women are mostly detained in Yarl's Wood in the Midlands and Lanarkshire. Detention centres are officially not prisons, so people wear their own clothes and can move around within the buildings. They can have visitors and make phone calls.

Unless you are involved in visitors groups such as Yarl's Wood Befrienders, AVID (Association of Visitors to Immigration Detainees) or BID (Bail for Immigration Detainees), for example, you are only likely to meet people after they have come out of detention. You may find yourself dealing with some of the after effects of their detention. People who were imprisoned or tortured before fleeing their original country, or who are vulnerable for other reasons, can become seriously distressed by detention, with longer-term impacts. Freedom from Torture has a number of personal testimonies on its website (www.freedomfromtorture.org).

Reporting. People might be required to 'report' or 'sign on' weekly, monthly or six-monthly to a reporting centre which might be a Home Office base or a police station. These can be some distance from where the person is staying and travel can be a problem although people on National Asylum Support Service (NASS) get travel costs refunded. At any one of these reporting appointments they might be detained pending deportation. People often find reporting distressing. It is important they don't miss a date, as that increases the likelihood they'll be detained.

There is meant to be some flexibility for people with disabilities or women with babies, for example. You can help with phone calls and letters even if you aren't licensed for immigration advice, although it can be frustrating.

Building a case. After screening, they need to build and make a case. Roughly speaking, they must prove they will be in actual danger if they return to their original country now. They must argue the state there cannot or will not protect them, either as someone who is a member of a particular group of people or as an individual.

They also have to show they are 'credible' – that is, honest and telling the truth (Box 3.2).

Box 3.2 Credibility – showing you are honest and telling the truth

As well as building a case, the asylum seeker will need to show they are credible – in other words, honest and telling the truth. They need to prove their ethnicity, nationality, identity and age, and how long they were in the UK before making a claim. The Home Office may 'dispute' the person's age if they claim to be under 18 (see Box 11.7). A late claim or being caught working for cash, for example, can undermine someone's credibility.

Credibility is also judged by gaps and inconsistencies in people's cases, or evidence and details that are added later. Even the testimony of highly respected organisations such as Freedom from Torture and the Helen Bamber Foundation may be ignored if it is submitted later in the process. This is particularly controversial when asylum seekers have been traumatised by torture, deaths, rape or other experiences and are only able to articulate their experiences after or over a length of time.

They should document their case with help from a licensed and specialist solicitor. Not all solicitors are licensed and not all licensed solicitors are equally good (Long Box 3.3). You cannot advise them on their asylum case, but you can help in other ways such as reading and writing letters in English or ringing their solicitor to check progress.

Next is a face-to-face substantive interview with a Home Office 'case-owner' who will follow this person's case through to decision.

To check their credibility, the individual's story and evidence will be checked against what is known to have happened in the country they have left. For example:

- If someone claims to have been persecuted when living in a certain town, or imprisoned in a certain jail, they or their solicitor will need to provide evidence that this kind of event happened at that time and place.

- They may be asked for details such as the name of certain streets where they lived, as this can be checked to prove they really are familiar with the place.

- The solicitor may call on an expert witness – someone like an academic who knows the country and its politics in depth.

Long Box 3.3 Solicitors, Legal Aid, OISC and what you can do

Getting the right solicitor. If you are assisting someone who wants to claim asylum and does not have a solicitor, don't look in Yellow Pages. The asylum seeker might have been given a list of licensed solicitors by the Home Office, but it is best if you contact your nearest community law centre, the Office of the Immigration Services Commissioner (OISC), or the Law Society of England and Wales, Scotland or Northern Ireland, and ask for a recommendation. You can also ask the Refugee Council or Coram Children's Legal Centre. Asylum applicants sometimes instruct solicitors who are not approved immigration solicitors, perhaps because of a recommendation or because they speak the same language. Changing solicitor is complex and costly – try to get someone good first time.

Legal Aid and fees. It changes fast and often. At the time of writing, solicitors can take up someone's case on Legal Aid for the initial claim, preparing and submitting appeals, and a stay of deportation. They cannot get Legal Aid for representation at Appeals Tribunals, or submitting human rights cases against removal. Legal Aid can be used to pay for expert witness reports.

Free or 'pro bono' advice and even representation can sometimes be gained via law centres, and also law schools at universities might take up cases. If a young migrant's case might be useful to make case law or for practice, the Refugee Legal Fund might fund it. Local Citizens Advice bureaux and other formal advice agencies often have someone with OISC1 (see below) who can give free advice.

OISC/Getting licensed yourself. Anyone can study and apply for an OISC licence at Level 1. It is a one-day intensive course (costing around £500) plus study, but you will need to register with OISC and may have to pay a registration fee of up to £500, although some non-profit organisations are exempt, and be supervised after that by an approved body, such as a law centre. The supervising body might be registered already, saving you the registration fee. If you find a free course, grab it – you will be better informed and could collaborate with a local registered body to be able to give basic advice. In addition, Right to Remain (righttoremain.org.uk) has tutorials for general knowledge. They also have self-help tutorials in other languages.

Decision. The applicant will get a 'positive decision' or a 'negative decision'. Positive is yes, you can stay (though see variations under 'Refugee with Leave' below). Negative decisions might be appealed, in which case the person continues as an 'asylum seeker'.

At this point, one of the big differences between a subjective definition of refugee based on (past and present) experience and the Home Office objective process (present and future likelihoods) becomes very clear. The Home Office might agree the person is credible and there was genuine persecution. They might agree the person is genuinely fearful. But if the Home Office considers the danger to be over, or that the person could live safely in another part of the country ('relocate') and live 'discreetly', it will probably refuse the application for asylum. So if you meet someone who says they are a refugee because of what has happened to them, but the Home Office says they are not a refugee and has refused them permission to stay, it doesn't mean the person is lying. It just means the Home Office is reasonably sure it won't happen again. In this situation, if your definition is similar to the subjective definition above, you would continue to work with them. If you are working in line with Home Office definitions, you might turn them away.

Appeal. When people are refused, they get a detailed letter explaining the reasons for their refusal. They have 14 days to put in an appeal, from the date of the written reasons for refusal, so if someone comes to you for help in this situation, you need to get them to contact their solicitor immediately. Immigration issues can crop up overnight, so keep your contacts up to date.

Asylum appeals will be considered on grounds that there was a failure in Home Office decision-making processes or reasons for refusal did not have enough evidence. The next step is First-tier Tribunal.

Of between 10,000 and 15,000 who appeal per year, about 36 per cent overall are successful (Refugee Council 2018). However, it is worth noting that a higher proportion of women's appeals are successful than men's. Asylum Aid (2017) argues this is an indication that those making the first decision may not fully understand issues about gendered forms of persecution.

Waiting. An initial decision should take three to six months, but can take years. An appeal might take months or years. There are backlogs and delays at all stages. During the wait, asylum seekers and their families are in limbo. If the decision is taking too long, you can help the person to make contact with their Member of Parliament. They can get an appointment at a constituency surgery session (ask your local library for dates). Or they can write (with your help) via the House of Commons, SW1A 0AA.

Refused asylum seekers

'Refused asylum seekers' are people who have asked for asylum and received a 'negative decision'. Their claim and any appeals have failed and they have been told the UK will not give them refuge. They might have been refused any further appeals ('Appeal Rights Exhausted'). You sometimes hear them called 'failed' asylum seekers.[1]

Fresh claims. If the situation in someone's original country significantly worsens, a refused applicant's lawyer might prepare a 'fresh' asylum claim delivered by the applicant in person to the 'Further Submissions Unit'

---

1   Although the government has said, based on future likelihoods, they are not refugees, you might consider a share of them to be refugees in the subjective sense, based on their past experiences. For that reason, the situation and entitlements of 'refused asylum seekers' are included in this book.

in Liverpool. If it meets certain standards, the asylum process starts over again, although a decision might be made faster.

Notice to depart. In their refusal letter, refused asylum seekers may get notice to depart, saying that they must take steps to leave the UK and return to their country of origin, that they may be 'subject to deportation'.

- Some will apply/appeal for a Stay of Deportation if their solicitor thinks they have grounds, for example, for a further appeal.

- They might make a case under the Human Rights Act 1998 – for example, if they are getting treatment for HIV or severe mental health problems which they will lose if they are deported (Article 3 'Freedom from cruel and inhuman treatment'), or because they have a family life here (Article 8 'Right to family life').

- Some leave.

- Some 'take steps to leave' – buying a ticket, for example. For a few people this might involve taking the option of Voluntary Assisted Return and Reintegration, when they receive a small amount of assistance to resettle on strict conditions.

- Some refused asylum seekers are detained pending deportation and might be put on a flight within a day of being detained.

- Not everyone can be deported, though. For example:

  - People under 18 can only be deported if there are suitable 'reception facilities' for children in their country of origin.

  - People can only be returned to their country of origin, but there are some countries that simply refuse to allow them back in, which would make them 'stateless'. It is prohibited under international law to make someone 'stateless', so the UK cannot deport them.

Some refused applicants will 'drop out of sight' and live 'off the radar' of the authorities. This might only be a short-term strategy. They might survive by trading and working cash in hand. They avoid coming into the vision of authorities. They may not even access the limited health care they are still entitled to (e.g. treatment for TB) because they are nervous about being reported to the Home Office. Other people who are 'off the radar' might include 'undocumented migrants' (which certain newspapers call 'illegal immigrants') or 'overstayers' (tourists or students whose visas have run out). Someone in this situation might contact you now and then. You do not need to report them. If you intend to help them in your professional role, check your organisation's funding restrictions (especially if using 'public funds') and policies (eligibility/ safeguarding/confidentiality and data sharing?). At times it will be better to consider what you are comfortable doing as an individual. You could get advice from a relevant outside body such as a community law centre, food bank or homelessness charity (see Appendix A).

Refugee with Leave – in international and UK immigration law

Although there is only one legal definition of 'refugee', several other legal categories have been defined which the hands-on worker can include under the name 'refugee'. The differences are usually quite minor for social, health, community and other local workers.

Most people assume 'refugee' means someone who has been given the right to stay under the International Refugee Convention 1951, making them an 'International Refugee'. The shorthand you'll hear most often, and which is used in this book, is a **'Convention refugee'**. For practitioners who support people in health, education and so forth, the most useful notion of refugee from the angle of immigration law is a bit wider than that. But let us start with Convention refugees (Box 3.4).

Box 3.4	**Refugee defined in the International Refugee Convention 1951 and Protocols 1956**

'…owing to a well-founded fear of being persecuted for reasons of race, religion, nationality, membership of a particular social group or political opinion, is outside the country of his nationality and is unable or, owing to such fear, is unwilling to avail himself of the protection of that country; or who, not having a nationality and being outside the country of his former habitual residence as a result of such events, is unable or, owing to such fear, is unwilling to return to it.' (www.unhcr.org)

When you meet Convention refugees in the UK, they either got their status within the international system, before arriving in the UK, or they got a 'positive decision' after applying 'in-country', within the UK. People who already have Convention status when they arrive have often been in refugee camps or in the care of the UNHCR.

This has been the case with people fleeing the war in Syria via camps in Lebanon and other neighbouring countries that are providing a home and some level of support to millions – that is, *millions* – of Syrians and Iraqis. David Cameron agreed Britain would take 20,000 Syrians with greater needs from those camps. But this is spread over five years. So, on average, that means 4000 per year, which works out to roughly seven Syrians per MP's constituency per year – perhaps two families. Some local authorities have refused to take any.

Going back to look at people who asked for asylum in the UK system, many who get positive decisions do not get Convention status but receive some other form of 'Leave to Remain'. Having Leave to Remain is like having a visa or permission to stay here. Their experiences are very similar to Convention refugees who claimed in the UK:

- They went through the asylum process.

- The Home Office decided their case to stay was strong enough.

- They have very similar rights and entitlements to Convention refugees.

Very often you will need to know if someone has leave, or 'status'. It is the first question most other professionals will ask you when you are discussing someone's situation: 'Has s/he got status?' But if you don't work in immigration law, there will be only a very few instances when you need to know if they have Convention status or some other kind of leave. Because of this, when the discussion needs to distinguish people by their immigration status (rather than subjective experiences). I will use **'refugees with Leave'** to mean those who have come through the asylum system and got some form of 'Leave to Remain'. (I am including Convention refugees who received their status abroad.)

Box 3.5	A sample of countries and numbers claiming asylum, and outcome of decisions		

At the end of 2017 the largest number of new applications for asylum came from:	Number of applications	In the same quarter, refusal rates for applicants from those countries were:
Iraq	786	80%
Iran	674	56%
Pakistan	607	88%
Sudan	446	62%
Eritrea	412	21%
Bangladesh	383	95%
Afghanistan	362	65%

(Refugee Council 2018)

After a positive decision, the next most significant thing is whether people get **temporary** or **permanent** forms of Leave to Remain. Convention status used to mean protection for life, wherever you went in the world. But it may surprise some readers that the UK now gives Convention refugees protection for just five years at a time, although this is usually renewed for a further five years. Other temporary or 'fixed-term' forms of leave include 'Discretionary', 'Humanitarian Protection Status' (HPS – often for people fleeing war), 'Unaccompanied Asylum-Seeking Child Leave' (UASC-Leave), 'Leave outside Immigration Rules' and others. (There are some older forms of leave such as 'Exceptional' or 'ELR' that no longer exist.) The refugee with temporary leave gets permission to stay for one, two, three or five years. For UASC-Leave, it is until they are 17.5 years old (Chapter 10).

The problem with **temporary leave** is that the refugee is still insecure. They have to apply for an extension before their leave runs out, but can't submit the application more than three months or, in some cases, one month in advance. Then they wait, again, not knowing what will happen or when. If their new decision is a refusal, the whole appeal/reporting/risk of deportation process starts again.

On a day-to-day basis, temporary leave shrinks refugees' options. You can't get credit. Universities won't let you start a three-year course – you'll probably do better to get a low-skilled job than go to college and get qualifications anyway. A pregnant woman might choose between having the baby and having an abortion. Mortgages and pensions are out of the question.

Permanent leave is much better. People who got Convention status before 2005, or who have 'Indefinite Leave to Remain' (almost always called just 'ILR') are secure. Convention refugees with five years initially seemed to get their five years extended to ten years without too much trouble, but the Home Office steadily tightens the rules, so most refugee specialists expect this to get tougher. With permanent leave, you can work towards applying for British nationality and a British passport. You can get on with building the rest of your life. After five, six or ten years, depending on status and 'legal residence', comes the possibility of applying for British citizenship or naturalisation.

Migrants of all sorts will take this step, but where refugees have little hope of ever being able to return to their country of origin, it sometimes has an extra resonance. No longer an exile? Perhaps no longer a refugee. No longer here for refuge, but belonging here, and your children and grandchildren belonging, and their children too.

Box 3.6	Becoming British – what they need to do and ways you could help

To apply for citizenship or 'naturalise', they need to:

- Pass the 'Life in the UK' test. You could use questions in the test as themes for discussion in support groups, host a study group, do a quiz night fundraiser based on official 'Life in the UK' questions (available from HMSO.gov.uk).

- Pass an intermediate-level English test (about ESOL Level 2; see Box 10.6). You could help with English, find where they can do the exam, help people get on to proper ESOL courses (see Chapter 10).

- Have two referees.

- Give evidence of where they have been throughout the whole ten years, explaining any gaps or travels. You could (should) keep old attendance records in good order for at least 15 years! Make sure you keep up good data protection services.

- Add evidence that they are helpful members of society. You could write a letter, create or broker opportunities for people to volunteer (e.g. help them apply to volunteer at a food bank).

- Download a form, fill it all in and send it off to the Home Office with the better part of £1000. Reassure them they *don't* need to pay someone extra money to do this for them. You don't need an OISC licence to help with this.

- Attend an interview. You could rehearse with them.

- Take part in a Citizenship Ceremony. You could be part of the audience!

When is a refugee not a refugee?

There are times when there is something (in law) about a refugee that defines their legal rights and entitlements more powerfully than their immigration status.

Any person who is present in the UK:

- …is protected by the Equality Act 2010 from direct and indirect discrimination and through the Public Sector Equality Duty, although some exceptions are allowed under immigration law.

- …has all the human rights laid down in the Human Rights Act 1998 which protects them from a wide range of abuses, although there are qualifications and some articles are 'relative' – for example, around detention (Chapter 4).

- …who needs primary or emergency health care will receive it and other care too (Chapter 9).

Any disabled person has the same entitlements to additional care and support under the Care Act 2014 as any person who is 'ordinarily resident' in the UK, regardless of their immigration status, although many statutory and voluntary sector bodies are not aware of this (Chapter 9).

Any child, from birth to the day before their 18th birthday ('0–17') is first and foremost a child in British law. So any child in a family claiming asylum or with Leave, any 'unaccompanied' child, any children of a refused asylum seeker, any child born in the UK to refugee parents – they are *all children* in British law and their rights as children laid out in the Children's Act 1989 and other related legislation, including care and education, all of which override their immigration status (Chapter 10).

Popular and political definitions and confusion

You can't leave daily conversation out of the picture. Most people muddle through using 'migrant', 'asylum seeker' and 'refugee' interchangeably. But where people are uncertain about what the terms mean, there is a risk of wariness or tipping into being overcautious. That's when people start to say things like 'We don't do refugees' or 'You should go to a refugee organisation'. It results in turning people away whom they could and you might think should have helped.

Language has suffered in the polarised debates of our times. Meanings have been blurred and words are politicised (Box 3.7). Many commentators in the British Press and on both sides of debate in the local pub use 'refugee' to mean a whole mix of people. People with different views select different words to strengthen arguments for and against refuge. But value-laden usage adds to uncertainty, and feeds into the doubts and concerns acknowledged in Chapter 2 (see also Box 3.1). The clearer you are on meanings, the easier it will be for you to increase the level of reasoning in the discussion.

Box 3.7 **The politics of language**

Because the debates on asylum and refuge are so polarised, language has also become polarised. Language has real power to change the tone and direction of debate and perception. The problem comes when value judgements are then applied to the whole massed body. It is used as a tool (or weapon) by one party against others to change the nature of the debate and strengthen or deny the legitimacy of refugees to our support. For example:

Migrant **v** refugee

UASC (unaccompanied asylum-seeking child) **v** UCSA (unaccompanied child, seeking asylum)

illegal asylum seeker, illegal immigrant **v** overstayer, undocumented migrant

failed asylum seeker **v** refused asylum seeker

removal centre **v** detention centre, prison

So let me mention a couple of groups who are not refugees, but get called 'refugees' in ways that are unhelpful and bring very negative undertones to the debate.

There are a few people who are cynically abusing the asylum system by claiming asylum as a way to stay in the UK even though they know they have no legitimate claim (Box 3.8). They are not 'refugees' by any meaningful definition of the word, no matter which immigration channels they use and what documentation they obtain. What they are doing is unethical and dishonest, although they are not breaking the law and there is no crime of which they can be convicted. They may be a minority, but cynical, false asylum claims undermine political and social support for refuge. When observers and politicians don't trust the system, the system gets redesigned to focus on cheats rather than on people who have suffered already. Cynical claimants waste our scarce time and resources. People who work with refugees day to day get angry about this.

Box 3.8 **A fishing trip**

One woman who had overstayed a student visa was referred to the refugee charity where I worked, for advice. She had just found a job and wanted to stay. She quite seriously asked me whether she should claim asylum. I was more cross with the organisation that referred her to us than with her. They had decided not to help her, so they sent her to a refugee charity! Did they think we would knowingly help someone abuse the asylum system?

People smugglers are not refugees. Many decent Germans risked (and lost) their lives smuggling Jews out of Germany in the 1940s. Refugees often need someone to get them out of a country and across borders in secret. They have to pay people with boats to get them over a stretch of sea. They need documents, so they buy what they can off people who have made it into a profitable business. They ask smugglers what they should say and do.

It is not illegal for the refugee to do any of these things, as it is recognised that refugees may have no other way to get away from danger to a place of safety. The fact that someone has paid a smuggler for help does not mean that person is a crook, coming here to abuse the system. It does mean they are desperate.

Many other migrants also turn to people smugglers, but that does not make them refugees.

The international community has not tackled the problem of providing safe passage to places of refuge. So 'commercial' smugglers continue to operate and make a lot of money. Some are dangerous. Smugglers are all mixed up in debates about refuge.

People traffickers are not refugees. Traffickers are the lowest of the low. Trafficking is a specific crime in international law and different to smuggling. Traffickers buy and sell people, they own people and move people around and across borders with or without their consent in order to exploit them for labour, sex, benefits fraud, body parts or 'modern slavery'. Some refugees are so desperate that they have little choice but to enter into such slavery, or they are tricked into thinking this person will smuggle them out of or into a country without knowing what is really going to happen to them.

People being deported after criminal sentences are not refugees. People who have been convicted of a crime and completed prison sentences of over a year can be deported if they are migrants or dual nationals (foreign national offenders). This can include people who are naturalised, even refugees. Post-prison deportees are often kept in the same removal centres as refused asylum seekers while appealing against or waiting for deportation. Please do not confuse deporting people at the end of a prison sentence with deporting refused asylum seekers (also see Box 3.9). Refused asylum seekers are at the end of a legitimate process. They have not broken the law.

Box 3.9 **Persecution should not be confused with prosecution!**

People cannot get refuge to avoid legitimate prosecution in other countries for crimes they have committed. However, they might make the case that their 'prosecution' is actually 'persecution' – that is, they are being unjustly accused of wrongdoing by a government that wants to silence them. This latter case is what Julian Assange of WikiLeaks claimed when he sought asylum in the Embassy of Ecuador to avoid being extradited from the UK.

Entitlements to publicly funded support and services

If you can define categories of who is and who isn't and who can and who can't, you are very powerful. It is a great responsibility.

Whoever defines the category decides:

- who belongs to it – eligibility
- what they have to do to prove they belong in that category
- what evidence they must provide (see Appendix B).

They decide who decides.

Whoever defines the category also defines what rights and entitlements the people they put in that category have:

- how people are treated once it is decided they belong to that category
- what they can do and what they can't do
- what they have to do
- what services, money, opportunities and so forth they can get
- what they have to do to access their entitlements
- when and where the entitlements will be delivered and by whom.

Again, they decide who decides.

Formally or informally, all our organisations define people into categories and have rules on who is entitled to what. The 'rules' aren't always clear or written down, especially when the organisation finds itself facing something new, like refugees. Different people within an organisation might work to their own 'rules'.

This rest of this section looks at what the Home Office has decided asylum seekers, refused asylum seekers or refugees (i.e. refugees with Leave) can do and the services and support they can receive from public funds – in other words, paid for with taxpayers' money. Other areas of law noted above – for example, concerning disability – override Home Office definitions.

Just because someone is entitled to support or a service does not mean they always get it when they need it. The problem with access is drawn out in Chapter 5 and is a theme running through all the practical chapters.

This is just an introduction. Box 3.10 gives a 'quick reference' outline of entitlements and refers you to Chapters 8–11 for fuller practical details.

Even this introductory outline comes with a warning: things change fast! You will need to research details to get the right information for each unique individual. Advice from specialists is always valuable where you can obtain it.

Asylum seekers

Accommodation and living costs. In outline, asylum seekers can apply to the National Asylum Support Service (NASS) for accommodation and subsistence/ living costs. At its simplest, they fill in a form and send in evidence that they are destitute. The process is described in Long Box 8.15. If successful, they will be offered one option for 'dispersed' accommodation in a sub-contractor-run hostel, shared accommodation or flat/house somewhere around the UK, away from the ports of entry (Dover, Heathrow, etc.).

For living costs, the successful applicant will get about £38 per week. A family will get that amount per head with a few pounds extra for pregnant women and babies. The money is provided via an 'Aspen' card which can be used broadly as a debit or cash card (Box 8.9). Pregnant asylum seekers get a one-off maternity grant of £300. Costs are refunded for travel that is required by the Home Office – for example, for reporting.

Health, disability and social care. In summary, regarding health, mental health and disability, asylum seekers are fully entitled to most NHS services, although access can be a problem as GP practices are often unsure about entitlements. The local authority must assess the support and care needs of all disabled people, which includes disabled asylum seekers. It must provide necessary additional support as identified. This might mean free local transport, hearing aids and so on, although there are no fixed rules on this. It could even mean adapted accommodation if the assessor finds this is needed, but they do not go ahead of other people in the queue.

English-language training. The introduction of immigration bail conditions in 2018 potentially prohibits almost all adult asylum seekers, as well as undocumented migrants, from studying. Until then adult asylum seekers could study if they could afford fees or find places on free English-language or other training courses, although free places were in short supply. Asylum seekers can challenge immigration bail conditions set by the Home Office through their legal advisers, including prohibitions on study.

Employment. Asylum seekers *may not take paid work* (there are some very rare exceptions). They can volunteer with some restrictions.

Asylum-seeking children and young people. Asylum-seeking children, with or without families, have full access to education up to 18. Families with NASS support will get free school meals and might get other state help if the child is considered to have special educational needs, for example, depending on the individual school and local authority. Unaccompanied children seeking asylum will receive care as children in need and/or looked after children regardless of immigration status, with variations as they approach 17.5 years. There are also variations if the government or local authority disputes the age the child claims to be.

Refused asylum seekers

For refused asylum seekers, the situation is harder and more complicated. They start from having 'No Recourse to Public Funds' – usually called NRPF or 'No Recourse'. It means they get no financial support and cannot use any of the facilities, resources or services that are provided with public tax money. This group of people has minimal legal means of support beyond any savings or gifts of help from contacts or charities/religious bodies. The online NRPF Network is very useful, especially for local authority workers.

Accommodation and living costs. However, if refused asylum seekers agree to deportation, they can apply for continued support from NASS. They may be allowed to stay on in any previous NASS accommodation if their claim for Section 4 is handled quickly.

Health. People with NRPF are allowed GPs, public health, emergency and other NHS care and treatment for free, including crisis mental health care. In Scotland and Wales they can also have free urgent care and medicines. In England they will be given urgent treatment if needed, but will be invoiced for the full cost. Disability assessment and care as above.

Employment. Refused asylum seekers may not take paid work.

Children. Even if a family is NRPF, children must still go to school free because of children's law. If the family does not have NASS support, the children might not get free school lunches.

Refugees with Leave to Remain

Refugees with any form of Leave (except UASC-Leave – see Chapter 11) have much the same entitlements as each other. They have nearly the same entitlements as UK nationals.

Accommodation and living costs. There is a cliff-edge moment when asylum seekers get the letter informing them they have Leave. From the date of the letter with their positive decision, they have just 28 days before their asylum support is cut off. If they are in NASS accommodation, in some cases they may be able to stay where they are, or they have to find new accommodation. The process is explained in Chapter 8. They have 28 days to access and start receiving mainstream benefits such as Universal Credit, Child Benefit, Housing Benefit – there is often a gap.

Health, training, employment. They have full access to NHS services and assessment/care relating to disabilities, as other resident UK nationals. They can access English-language and other courses, training, apprenticeships and other opportunities, and these are often free for refugees with Leave if they are also receiving benefits related to employment.

Refugees with Leave can take paid work.

Travel rights for refugees. People with Leave, other than Convention status, can travel on non-British national passports if they have them as long as they don't leave the UK too often for too long. Convention refugees have a 'travel document' which they can in theory use for travel anywhere in the world except to their country of origin, although actual processes, visa arrangements and inaccurate advice cause problems. All will face additional scrutiny on return.

They are likely to need evidence of their movements at some point – for example, if they apply for British nationality. So remind your refugee contacts to keep records of dates, flight numbers, itinerary reference numbers and details.

Family reunion for refugees. Adult refugees with Convention status and Humanitarian Protection status can apply for family reunion immediately, which would allow them to bring dependants, spouse and older parents to join them in the UK. If successful, the family members who join them automatically receive Convention status. It can get complicated in cases of divorce or domestic abuse and they/you will need to turn to licensed legal advice.

	Outline of entitlements for asylum
Box 3.10	**seekers and refugees with Leave**

Accommodation
Asylum seekers can get NASS housing 'dispersed' across the country, and refugees with Leave can apply for Housing Benefit/Universal Credit and social housing on the same criteria as any UK person (Chapter 8).

Money
Asylum seekers can get some money to live from NASS; refused asylum seekers might get a little money (and housing) if they agree to leave the country. Refugees with Leave can apply for mainstream benefits including Universal Credit and Child Benefit (Chapter 8).

Health
Everyone is entitled to a GP free, even including 'off the radar' individuals. Everyone can get family planning, HIV, TB and other public health care, and emergency care including care for life-threatening mental health crises free. Everyone will be given urgent care, but in

England some refused asylum seekers and other migrants will then be charged. Some pay for prescriptions (Chapter 9).

Disability

Everyone can have their support needs assessed by the local authority where they are 'ordinarily resident'. The local authority provides for any specialist needs identified (Chapter 9).

Work

Asylum seekers and refused asylum seekers can't work; refugees with Leave can (Chapter 10).

Children

Every child gets the same state support, education and care as UK national children until they are 18, regardless of immigration status, with minor exceptions (Chapter 11).

School

All under-16s must go to school; under-18s can access education (Chapter 11).

Further reading/training

For organisations that provide detail and training on status and entitlements, see the relevant practical chapter and Appendix A for organisations.

Summary and conclusion

Box 3.11 **Summary of definitions used in this book**

To make best use of this book, check you can distinguish between the following:

- Refugee – a subjective definition, used throughout this book: 'Any person who feels she or he has sought refuge from persecution, in the UK.'

- Asylum seeker – legal term, summarised as: someone who has asked to stay in Britain on the grounds that if she or he goes 'home', she or he will be in danger, and who is still waiting for a final answer.

- Refused asylum seeker – legal term, summarised as: people who have asked for asylum and received a 'negative decision' – the UK will not give them refuge.

- Refugee with Leave – shorthand, used in this book especially in relation to entitlements: a person who has claimed asylum in the UK and been given some form of 'Leave to Remain'.

- Convention refugee – shorthand for people who have been given International Refugee Convention status (Box 3.4).

You might like to revisit Box 1.3 Monitoring your own learning. See also the Glossary.

Whom you support and *how* go together when you work with refugees. You have to have a proper way of deciding whom you help because you can't help everyone. Having clear but pragmatic definitions for your working relationships with refugees isn't about dumbing down, but about doing the job (Box 3.11).

You need to know where your definition might *clash* with others' definitions, both within the organisation and where there are obligations to funders and regulators such as Ofsted and the Care Quality Commission (CQC) who have their own categories and requirements. Members of the public may have their own views about who should get what. Be especially aware of potential clashes with Home Office definitions and rules. They can't be ignored.

Look out for immediate limits and constraints so you don't waste your time, energy and resources, or the refugee's. Be certain you are not encouraging someone to do something that could get them into trouble, such as taking paid work when they are still in the asylum system.

Other definitions and rules shape the *space* within which the refugee lives. Equally important, they shape their choices and potential to get on with rebuilding. At the same time, definitions you might not like but cannot ignore are framing the space you have for action in your role, although you have more flexibility than refugees.

You have *discretion*. Or you could call it wriggle room. Discretion is your ability to choose to do more or to do less to help someone.

You can *negotiate* the rules – not necessarily formally. You can stretch, interpret and argue, and at times choose to ignore rules.

You have *agency* – you can change things by engaging with others from a position of confidence and knowledge: change views, change definitions, change the rules.

But be careful. Without a good enough understanding of the whole picture, you can get it wrong.

With a subjective, inclusive definition of 'refugee', your *responsibility* is to make decisions; decide whom to support and decide on the best plan of action, even when you know you don't know enough. There are things you won't know – experiences that people are not ready to reveal, the things that desperate people are hiding. There are some people trying to get things they aren't entitled to. It is quite likely that at some point you will look back on a decision and wish you had or wish you hadn't.

There are four implications for you and your organisation:

1. Decisions over categories and entitlements are forms of power that restrict opportunities for whole groups of people. Hands-on workers need to look at each contact with a refugee with fresh eyes. You need to *keep on learning and sharing* your reflections on best practice.

2. As you and your team are making the best decisions you can on partial information and somewhat on principle, the organisation as a whole has to be willing to *share the responsibility* if it turns out you made a mistake. Talk to colleagues; keep them informed.

3. There are always risks when people interact, whether 'provider and client' or a mix of participants, members and service users. You still need *effective supervision and safeguarding procedures* in place.

4. Collaboration and good-quality referral to other services is important for the people you decide you can't help. Your *knowledge of other services* is an important part of your expertise.

CHAPTER 4

Refugees in All Their Diversity – Equality, Discrimination and Positive Action

Introduction

Can anything demonstrate the importance of protection from discrimination and inequality more clearly than the arrival of people asking for asylum?

People from around the world are escaping from people who abuse their power and discriminate aggressively against those whom they see as different. The persecuted often face humiliation and abject impoverishment, as their intolerant societies strip away their goods, their identities and their futures. Their own governments fail to protect them (see Box 4.2)

The utter injustice is that the people who have been abused are the ones who give up everything. They may live in limbo for years, disempowered and their potential wasted.

They lose. Discrimination and abuse win.

According to British equality laws, everyone is equal, and people who come for refuge should be equal with everyone else and equally protected. Though, to quote an old friend of mine, 'Should?… Schmould!'

Discrimination exists in many ways in British society. Refugees are often on the receiving end of asylum-hate, but also more subtle forms of discrimination, when professionals create policies and processes that unintentionally leave people disadvantaged, and the decision-makers don't see the impact of what they have done.

Inequality is a real and current issue for refugees in the UK. They usually start with almost nothing in a society where people already have so much, but it is more than that.

First of all, take 1000 refugees and compare them with 1000 people drawn randomly from the UK population. More of the refugee group or 'population' will be struggling with disabilities, more will be religious believers, all are of ethnic minorities. These and other 'characteristics' are known to be linked to patterns of inequality and poverty in Britain.

Second, refugees often have poor English, few resources and little familiarity with British structures and culture. But such things don't need to disadvantage people if the necessary services can be adapted and provided in an equitable way that responds to the needs of diverse individuals. It is often a matter of awareness and willingness.

Do you have to read this chapter? It is perfectly OK to skip over it – at first. Especially if you are looking for something to help someone who needs something done for them today.

But you should read it as part of your organisation's longer-term planning. Learning about equality law and relating it to your work is a bit like flossing your teeth. We all tend to put it off, but you'll feel better once you've done it and in the long run you'll be really glad you did.

Making use of the Equality Act 2010

This chapter makes use of the Equality Act 2010 ('the Act'). The legislation has been put in place to protect people from discrimination: the very protection refugees were lacking in their original countries. But this is not a briefing about the law (see the suggestions for finding out more in Box 4.13). It is about how you can use the ideas and principles spelled out in the Act to help make sure refugees – and other disadvantaged people in the UK – get a fair crack at things.

The Act is designed to make sure people and organisations – private, voluntary and statutory – avoid discrimination and try to improve equality. Of course, it is a tool for enforcement so there is an element of 'stick' to it. You can be challenged by users or outsiders if you don't comply (Box 4.1). It isn't optional.

Box 4.1 **Does the Equality Act 2010 apply to my organisation?**

Almost certainly. The Act applies to any organisation that provides services, regarding how it treats its service users, employees and volunteers. Your organisation is responsible for the actions of any staff member and, to some people's alarm, for the actions of any person or other body who is 'your agent' or 'carrying out your instructions'. This means your organisation is responsible for the behaviour and actions of your trainees and volunteers, and if you have other organisations working for you, you are also responsible for them as they are also your 'agent'.

As well as 'stick', however, there are potential 'carrots' in terms of relations with funders and statutory bodies, whether proving work is worth funding or your ability to lever changes in local statutory services. Changes in council or local NHS policy and services could benefit refugees well beyond the scope of anything most organisations could provide alone. This latter point is covered in Chapter 7.

The Act can be used in other practical ways.

- It spells out many useful concepts that can raise awareness about diversity among refugees – and any of your members or service users for that matter.

- It helps you scrutinise your organisational practices for any risk that what you are doing and the way you are doing it might accidentally make life harder for some of the people you aim to help (see Chapter 5).

- You can check you aren't doing certain things you mustn't do ('direct discrimination', 'indirect discrimination', 'positive discrimination').

- You can use the Act to justify taking 'positive action' if you think some special actions are needed specifically to help refugees, so they can catch up more quickly, although you still need to have evidence of the need.

The final reason equality law is valuable for practitioners who work with refugees goes back to the immigration definitions in Chapter 3. It is hard to use immigration law to help your work. It is imposed on you and is probably outside your original field of expertise. But equality law is already part of your working world and relates directly to everyone you support, not only refugees. Equality law is consistent with work responding to lived experience, unique individuals and subjective identities – where immigration law often clashes. Where immigration law controls and limits refugees, this chapter will show how equality law gives you tools to facilitate them.

Box 4.2	Protection from persecution – what happens when you don't have equality laws

Refugees are living evidence of what happens when you don't have equality laws and protection.

Different social, economic and political structures play out in different ways in different countries, but the protection in the UK's Equality Act 2010 is not provided in many countries across the world. In some countries, people of certain ethnic populations can only work in prescribed tasks. Disabled children are often secluded, refused education, even denied food. Girls are forced into marriage and sexual service; women are burned when they are disobedient. People in minority religions are moved into ghettos. Children work as unpaid labour. Gay men and lesbian women are beaten to death.

Protecting refugees from discrimination after they arrive in the UK

International refugee law specifies protection for 'race, religion, nationality, membership of a particular social group or political opinion' (see Box 3.4). Certain characteristics, such as sex, disability or sexuality, were not recognised initially, but have had to argue for protection as 'particular social groups' (Box 4.3).

Box 4.3 Women and other 'particular social groups'

Certain populations, such as women, were not initially recognised as being subject to persecution. Women refugees have had to argue for refugee protection for women as a 'particular social group' and this is now established in international practice. It also took a long time to get British decision-makers to see gendered and sexual acts inflicted on women as acts of persecution and not just general aggression to be expected in war. The battle is still not securely won.

Activism by equality campaigners in recent years seem to have created space in UK asylum debates for more thorough consideration of certain social groups, in particular around sexuality and disability. The work of the UK Lesbian and Gay Immigration Group (UKLGIG) and Micro Rainbow are good examples.

British equality law names 'protected characteristics', including race, religion, sex, disability, sexuality, transgender and others (Box 4.4). Anyone with any of these characteristics should be protected from discrimination and persecution while they are in the UK.

Box 4.4 Nine protected characteristics in the Equality Act 2010

- **Age.** A person who has a particular age in number of calendar years (e.g. 32-year-olds) or range of ages (e.g. 18–30-year-olds).

- **Disability.** A person has a disability if she or he has a physical or mental impairment which has a substantial and long-term adverse effect on that person's ability to carry out normal day-to-day activities.

- **Gender reassignment.** A person in the process of transitioning from one gender to another. (This also includes people who are intersex, transsexual or transgender.)

- **Race.** A group of people defined by their race, colour, nationality (including citizenship), ethnic or national origins.

- **Religion and belief.** Religion has the meaning usually given to it, but belief includes religious and philosophical beliefs including lack of belief (e.g. atheism). Sincerely held, observant, a belief that affects your life choices or the way you live.

- **Sex.** A male or female (man/woman girl/boy = gender/age).

- **Sexual orientation.** Whether a person's sexual attraction is towards their own sex, the opposite sex or to both sexes.

- **Marriage and civil partnership.** Civil partners must be treated the same as married couples on a wide range of legal matters.

- **Pregnancy and maternity.** Maternity, considered the first six months after birth.

So let's be clear what 'protected characteristic' means.
We all have 'characteristics'.

- I am right-handed. I am wearing jeans, etc.

Some of our characteristics are lifestyle choices which we can or could change:

- I can't become left-handed. I could change into a skirt.

Some we can't change, although they might change:

- I need stronger glasses each year.

We share many of our characteristics with other people.

- I am one of a couple of dozen people in my street who drives a car.

- The last census showed about 65 per cent of the people who live in my town are white English; about 95 per cent are British.

Some characteristics that we can't change and we share with a number of other people have been and are used by other people to disadvantage us:

- I am female. In some professions, employers tend to choose to employ men so I am at a disadvantage, through no fault of my own, if I want to go into that profession. The same applies to men being disadvantaged in other professions.

The Act protects everyone in the UK from discrimination on the grounds of any of the 'protected characteristics'. Therefore, any woman refugee has the same rights to equal treatment as any woman in the UK, and is also entitled to treatment that is as good as that shown to any man. Or any male refugee the same rights as any man; any child, young or older person; believer or non-believer, or any person residing in the UK has the same rights as anyone else in the UK with whom they share any of the nine 'protected characteristics', and also with those who don't share those characteristics. And your organisation has to treat them all equally, giving equal opportunities and perhaps equitable support – with an extra hand up here and there where people are behind.

Campaigners are challenging the Home Office and NASS to ensure they are fulfilling their duty to give equal opportunities and equitable treatment to people with diverse characteristics who are in the asylum process. The Women's Asylum Charter, for example, has challenged the Home Office regarding interview processes that disadvantage women and has had some real success (Asylum Aid 2018).

Refugees and race. Refugees are not specifically named as a protected group in the Act, but they are directly protected under the characteristic of 'race'. It is illegal to discriminate against people because of their colour, their nationality including citizenship, and their ethnicity or national origins.

Under 'race/nationality' the Act does not just ban discrimination against someone because she or he comes from a certain country, such as Afghanistan, but makes it illegal to discriminate against any person on the basis that she or he is not a British national. In other words, non-British people in the UK must be treated as well as people with UK nationality.

Exceptions affecting refugees. There can only be exceptions to the ban on discrimination if a law is passed by Parliament that makes it legal to discriminate in certain situations. Immigration laws passed in the past 15 years have made it legal to treat asylum seekers, refused asylum seekers and refugees with Leave differently, and less well than British nationals. But it isn't a general licence to discriminate. The different treatment allowed is only what is specified in the legislation. Against that, as noted in Chapter 3, are other areas of law such as children's, health and social care laws and mental health law that override immigration law. Ultimately, nothing can override the Human Rights Act 1998.

Box 4.5	How laws override each other, but nothing overrides human rights

So it could go like this. A refused asylum seeker is in labour. The Equality Act 2010 says all people in the UK should receive equal health services. Immigration laws (in England) says refused asylum seekers are an exception, and can be charged or refused some care and treatments. The Human Rights Act 1998 Article 2 says public bodies such as hospitals cannot violate the right to life, and Article 3 enshrines freedom from inhumane and degrading treatment, so the hospital will take care of her during childbirth and give any further urgent treatment needed. But they send an invoice later.

For the hands-on worker, it is important not to look at a refugee and see only a refugee. People are complex and unique: queer or questioning, young and growing older. People persecuted them because they didn't like who they saw them to be. Now in the UK, they still have all their previous, complex characteristics, plus now that of being a refugee. Refugees are often categorised under race or 'BME' labels (Black and Minority Ethnic), or maybe 'BAMER' (Black, Asian, Minority Ethnic and Refugee). But if you want to avoid discrimination, you need to look at the whole person, with a whole mix of characteristics, all of which are significant in their lives and the support we offer them. (For an example, see Box 1.1.)

What you mustn't do

Now to you and your organisation. What mustn't you do?

Discrimination really does happen in the daily activities and life of many organisations. Staff may feel secure that colleagues or volunteers would not express direct hostility towards refugees. But there must always be concern about people misusing wriggle room – their discretion to do more or to do less. There is also the risk that a policy that was meant to help everyone accidentally makes it worse for a certain population with a shared characteristic.

Direct discrimination

Direct discrimination is when a person is knowingly treated less favourably than another in the same or a similar situation. It might seem reasonable to segregate people by a certain characteristic, but unless there is an objective reason to do this, it is direct discrimination. Therefore, although the Home Office is allowed to treat non-nationals differently to British nationals, you aren't – except in the ways the Home Office tells you to, such as letting asylum seekers apply for a job vacancy.

Hostile and insulting behaviour on grounds of people's characteristics is direct discrimination. This includes voiced expressions of 'asylum-hate' such as telling a refugee to 'go home' or 'go back to where you came from' (Box 4.6). It also includes some actions that would probably never see you in court, but which get noticed by people who are on the receiving end.

One little cut that a lot of migrants feel is when people make no effort to pronounce their name correctly, or make it sound ridiculous, or anglicise it without permission, as if it is unreasonable that a person has a name from their original culture. These little 'micro-aggressions' belittle and downgrade the receiving person's humanity, and express implicit hostility and a sense that the person is not equal in the perpetrator's eyes.

Box 4.6 | **Direct discrimination from local life – Case Studies A and B**

Case Studies are referred to in the text as 'CS/A', 'CS/B', and so on.

A   A refugee member's young daughter was verbally insulted by an adult volunteer at her school, who told her she had no right to be here and made her cry. The situation was dealt with swiftly and emphatically by the school to the parent's satisfaction.

B   A Tamil woman on her way to a workshop we were organising about equality and refugees was waiting to cross the road with her baby in a front-facing pushchair, when the passenger of a passing van yelled abuse at her and squirted water at the baby.

In most services, professional and hands-on staff have a great deal of discretion in whether and how they serve someone. If someone gives refugees lower-quality support than they give non-refugees, because of personal hostility or cynicism, that is direct discrimination. It might be as simple as deciding not to book an interpreter, even though they could. It can also be direct discrimination when people repeat the way they acted for one refugee for different refugee, because they assume 'they are the same' (see also Box 4.7).

Box 4.7 Forms and examples of illegal direct discrimination, including 'positive discrimination'

- Discrimination 'by association' – for example, not sending someone who cares for a disabled person on a course that other staff go on, because you assume they will take time off.

- Discrimination 'by perception' – for example, someone who insults a woman because they think she is going out with an asylum seeker, even if she isn't.

- Deliberately causing disadvantage (by comparison) – for example, not letting a refugee volunteer with an older person's lunch group because the participants and other volunteers might not like it.

- Harassment, unwanted conduct – for example, deliberately telling jokes about gas chambers in front of a Jewish person (association and perception apply).

- Victimisation – picking on someone because they complained or protested about discrimination affecting them or anyone else.

- 'Positive' discrimination: favouring one person or group over another for no objective reason – for example, giving one of three equally good candidates a job because she is a refugee and you want to help refugees. Please note: this is illegal discrimination (but see 'positive action' below).

Indirect discrimination and 'We don't do refugees'

Indirect discrimination is when a practice, policy, set of eligibility criteria, and so on is set up and applied generally, but in a way that means a whole body of people with a shared characteristic is accidentally ruled out or unable to access the resources for no good reason. It might be a long time before people within the organisation notice a whole group of people are not using their services, so it is very useful to take a fresh look at patterns in take-up or get an outside view now and then.

For example, if a hospital gets all its interpreters through agencies that require interpreters to be self-employed, it makes it likely that a substantial block of migrants will be stranded in insecure employment with limited rights, career prospects, insurance and pensions. If there is a more mixed group of people within the hospital, with equivalent levels of skill and responsibility, have regular job contracts and full rights, the policy of sourcing interpreters through agencies may be indirectly discriminating against migrants, or, in other words, indirectly racist.

> ## Box 4.8 When not understanding leads to discrimination – Case Studies C–E
>
> **C** During a survey of support organisations of and for lesbian and gay people in 2009, looking at awareness of lesbian and gay refugees, one organisation told us, 'We…are fighting AIDS; we don't have a service for refugees' (indirect discrimination).
>
> **D** A second said, 'We do housing for gay men; we don't do refugees' (indirect discrimination).
>
> **E** A third said, 'We do not encourage refugees to access our services as our funders would not be happy about us providing services to people who are not supposed to be here…' (direct discrimination).
>
> A participant in the survey review workshop commented: 'Sometimes individuals, groups and organisations start to impose their own "migration law", by making it a condition which the law does not actually state.'

It can be difficult to avoid discriminating if you are unclear about immigration status and want to avoid getting your employer into trouble. Immigration law, exceptions, case law, judicial rulings, entitlements and documentation have been changing constantly for 20 years. The result is widespread confusion and misinformation about refugees' rights and entitlements. Few people outside refugee specialist bodies are confident about the definitions and differences between asylum seekers, Convention refugees and others.

With pressure from government not to employ, treat, serve, house or educate people who are not entitled, there is a risk that hands-on staff will err on the side of caution and refuse to serve a refugee, perhaps saying 'We don't do refugees' because they don't want to make a mistake. But this is how mistakes are made: refugees are disadvantaged without justification; refugees who *are* entitled and in need are wrongly turned away. This is discrimination (Boxes 4.8 and 4.9).

When social services incorrectly refuse to assess a disabled asylum seeker's needs because they think non-nationals are not entitled to local authority support, that is discrimination.

> ## Box 4.9 When confusion leads to discrimination – Case Study F
>
> **F** When one of our members was refused accommodation by a landlord because he was an asylum seeker, the landlord apologised but explained he didn't want a fine for housing an illegal immigrant. A letter enclosing the government guidance with relevant passages highlighted reassured him and he happily let our member move in.

There are also times, especially under pressure to cut costs, that structures designed to improve efficiency disproportionately disadvantage refugees and other migrants. For example, cuts to child care at colleges particularly affect migrant women who cannot access English classes if they have children under school age, preventing them from even starting on the ladder to employment and integration. Even attempts to avoid discrimination might unintentionally discriminate – for example, a recruitment panel that wants to avoid personal assumptions might anonymise application forms in an effort to be fair to all, but set criteria such as minimum qualifications that candidates need to have to be considered. In doing so, they could accidentally exclude migrants and refugees who are qualified but whose qualifications are non-UK, without ever knowing, because their qualifications aren't on the approved list.

If you see something that seems discriminatory, or have it reported to you, there are some straightforward things you can do, starting with a gentle nudge. See Chapter 7 for details and what you can do next if a nudge doesn't work.

What you can do to improve equality

You can't treat people less favourably, or disadvantage them because of their protected characteristics, but you can treat them differently and do things especially for them.

You can differentiate. In fact, you must. There is no point giving a deaf person braille to read or a blind person sign language interpreters. It is not about splitting resources 50/50 for men and women. You can't avoid discrimination by calling everyone 'person' or 'friend' or 'community members'. You don't help refugees gain an equal footing and an equal stake in society by ignoring the fact they are refugees and 'treating everyone the same' (Chapter 2).

It is fully legitimate to differentiate refugees and argue that refugees are so disadvantaged that they must be treated as a high-priority equality group. Refugees have many difficult characteristics, often linked to disadvantages they have faced and unfair new challenges now. They need to be at high risk of discrimination and disadvantage alongside other high-priority groups. This is *not* a hierarchy, or competition for who is most disadvantaged; many people in British society are seriously disadvantaged and struggling with multiple disadvantages – refugee populations are one of those groups.

When you differentiate between people, you can then get proper information about their needs and provide the right support for them. Different treatment is fine as long as it is based on the person's actual situation at that point, and is *appropriate* and *proportionate*. You also need to differentiate within a population – for example, Iranians with mobility difficulties, Iranian teenagers, Iranian lesbians (Box 4.10). The key is the quality and detail in your organisation's data, your working relationship with the refugee/s and your own awareness and knowledge.

Box 4.10 Hostility and discrimination within 'communities'

'Community' as in 'refugee community' is not a helpful concept for hands-on workers.

The feel-good implications of 'community' gloss over 'refugee' problems such as the long-term impact of civil war, inter-family, inter-tribal, inter-regional, inter-ethnic or inter-faith conflict between people from the same country, ethnic group or religion.

So bear in mind that people within the same ethnic or national population, who 'share a characteristic', do not necessarily like each other or approve of each other. Discrimination and intolerance are not ruled out by having one or two things in common. A relatively small number of people with the shared characteristic may develop a shared, positive identity and build forms of social organisation on that, but that can raise issues about the loyalty and conformity required for people to 'belong', often denying diversity and cultural change.

It is especially important to be aware of this if you work to support 'a community', such as 'the Iranian community' or 'the gay community'. Some 'members of the community' might actively discriminate and exclude and even persecute others whom they see as different even if you see them as similar.

'Community' inverts the real absence of any kind of meaningful connection between people who happen to share a certain characteristic, and implies they all know and care for each other. Its ideological undertones assume a degree of solidarity, self-help and shared identity that are not usually realistic and tend to give a sense that if public authorities let people down, some kind of mutual self-help system will function in their absence.

'Community' overemphasises place, locality and proximity. It ignores stigma and fear of being made visible as 'a refugee'. Often outsiders treat the few who make themselves visible as 'community leaders' if they typify and/or represent and can communicate with the many.

You can make reasonable adjustments. All service providers and employers have a duty to make reasonable adjustments for someone with impairments, to ensure she or he is not disadvantaged by things that could be avoided. Where feasible, they should change practical activities and facilities or put in extra support, so an individual with an impairment can participate or benefit to the same level as someone without that impairment. Ideally, employers and service providers should also be looking ahead to what might be a barrier.

With refugees, this might include a policy of always using plain English or having a contact list of interpreters to hand if needed. Mental ill health is considered a disability and is a frequent challenge for refugees, so making waiting, treatment or working environments for service users less stressful is a very reasonable adjustment.

'Reasonable adjustment' is a good principle, one most people are familiar with, and difficult to argue against. It is a good tool to use in your organisation to improve opportunities and make your services more responsive and accessible. What is good for one disadvantaged person is sometimes good for others: plain English and a less stressful working environment are usually a good thing all round.

Where budgets are tight, people might feel they have little room for adjustments, but thinking ahead might include arguing you need a budget line for reasonable adjustments in next year's budget or bid – funders are often supportive of a realistic budget for reasonable adjustments. It is after all about complying with a legal duty.

You can take positive action. Positive action is one of the great assets created by the Act. It gives service providers permission to do extra things for some people only, if those actions will help them catch up and avoid future disadvantages. It lets you put extra effort and resources into helping certain people; you can treat them *more* favourably than others, as long as you have evidence that there is a need. You can take positive action to:

- Overcome disadvantage (about the past): Your extra, targeted project, service or resources will help people get over the harm done by inequality and discrimination that held them back in the past, or if, as in the case of newly arrived refugees, their circumstances mean they are far behind people who are like them in other ways (age, ability, etc.). For example, free English lessons would be a positive action to help people who have arrived in Britain without English to learn more quickly. Another example could be a 'migrant immunisation catch-up' project.

- Facilitate participation (about the present): This is the extra things you can do to make sure particularly disadvantaged groups don't miss out on current opportunities, when they might have trouble accessing them without extra help. Your local research might show Tamil-speaking refugees are unaware of a certain course that would be particularly useful to them, or they can't afford your normal course fees, or can't get child care and so can't attend. You might do a Tamil-language publicity leaflet, offer some 'refugee bursaries', ask a Tamil-speaking crèche worker to provide play activities in the next room, even though non-Tamil speakers might also want help with child care.

- Meet their different needs (about the future): Where there is an aspect of people's lives that will probably continue to be a source of challenges, you can set up ongoing specialist services that are only of use to them and no one else, to stop these being disadvantages in future. This positive action relates only to those ongoing needs. An example could be a Pashtu-language counselling service for young Afghan refugees with post-traumatic stress disorder.

You have to have evidence that refugees need positive action before you can provide it. You need to gather data and evidence which you can present to non-refugees who might challenge what you are doing as they might accuse you of discriminating against *them*. This can be direct from your organisation's monitoring and research with users, or from local and/or national sources (see Box 4.13 and Appendix A).

Your positive action has to be for people who are disadvantaged in comparison with the general population. You don't have to put on positive action for all the disadvantaged groups you identify, or even the most disadvantaged. And positive action has to be related to the particular disadvantages showing up in your evidence.

So if your evidence shows that recent Sudanese refugees arriving in your area are suffering from dental problems, you can put on something to help with their teeth. You can't take them all out for a day trip to the seaside and call it 'positive action', no matter how much everyone would enjoy it.

Remember to be careful that your 'positive action' is not 'positive discrimination' (see Box 4.7).

You can monitor equality characteristics. It is not only all right, but very important to monitor the diversity of who uses which of your services, who is and isn't satisfied with services, your applicants for volunteer or paid positions, diversity of staff, trustees and more. Characteristic monitoring will show you whether the people involved in and using your organisation are coming from all protected populations or just some. Then you can decide if that is a problem. It can even show you whether there are different patterns in use or different levels of satisfaction for people with certain combinations of characteristics too, such as African women or older Muslims.

Saying you can and should monitor for equality characteristics is not to say it is easy or popular. There are no one-size-fits-all equality characteristic monitoring forms or processes that will work for everyone. You need to design a process that will make refugees visible. Funders often have their own set forms, which usually renders the process meaningless for the organisation that has to get people to fill them in. See Box 4.11.

Box 4.11	Equality characteristic monitoring (ECM) and looking for refugees

- You want your ECM to make refugees visible, so that you can see if they are using your service. You will usually need to adapt your form and process.

- Don't use other people's categories. Start with the nine protected characteristics but decide what will make refugees visible within your respondents.

- Does 'Asian' give you meaningfully differentiated data? With refugees? No! Asian = Chinese, Russian, Afghan, Tamil, Turkish, Palestinian, Indonesian, Korean, Vietnamese, Myanmar, Bangladeshi, Pakistani, Iraqi, Iranian, Syrian, Yemeni, Indian, Nepalese, Japanese and more.

- You can invite people to describe their ethnicity, religion, and so on in their own words, which is more meaningful for them, although it will cause difficulty collating. You need to do your research to find out which of the ethnicities are likely to be refugees.

- Collect it, collate it, analyse it, discuss it, report on it, act on it. If you aren't going to use the data, don't ask people for it.

The Public Sector Equality Duty (PSED)
– what they (and you) must do

It is worthwhile investing time in understanding the Public Sector Equality Duty (often just called 'the Equality Duty' or PSED). You can use it to help refugees when you are dealing with other organisations, and practical suggestions for advocacy and lobbying public sector bodies are given in Chapter 7. It has potential to help people with all characteristics, of course, but this section gives a simple overview, and highlights points that have particular relevance to refugees.

In Chapter 3, I noted how having the authority to define people gives a body great power over their lives and over the actions of those who support them. The body that can define categories decides what someone is and isn't, what they can do, what support and services they will get and how.

Many public or statutory bodies – councils, the NHS, colleges – also have scale. Where the decisions a small charity makes about its priorities might affect 30 people, or 300, a governmental body might make changes that affect 3000 or 3,000,000. A change of plan could help a great many people but, without any ill intention at all, mess things up for some smaller groups. Refugees are one of those groups.

The Act places the Equality Duty on all 'public authorities' – roughly, bodies using taxpayers' money – and their 'agents', which might include your organisation (Box 4.12). If they fund you, you should comply with the Equality Duty and the public authority might check you do.

> ### Box 4.12 — What are public authorities? Does this affect my organisation?
>
> A public authority is, broadly, any state body that has powers given to it by law and/or which operates with taxpayers' money – so councils, police, the NHS, most schools, and so on are public authorities.
>
> Other organisations doing work for these bodies also count as public authorities because they are directly or effectively operating on behalf of the state body. This can include your organisation, if it is using funds from a contract or grant from a public authority. The public authority must make sure you comply. Public authorities and their agents must comply with the whole Equality Act 2010, including the Public Sector Equality Duty (PSED).

The Equality Duty is meant to push public authorities to take far more care about indirect or what used to be called institutional discrimination. There is no doubt it has potential to bring about change for the better, both for refugees and my mum.

'Due regard...' Under the Act, public authorities must have 'due regard' to the equality needs of staff and services users. Due regard means the public authority has to be proactive in checking for inequality and always look for ways to improve the situation. It is not just about avoiding discrimination. It is about equality in a broader sense. If a group of people have substantially lower living conditions, education, health, etc., the public body has to address this. Refugees are very much in this category.

For example, many Afghan women have had no schooling and are illiterate and innumerate in any language. They often live in family structures with strict gender roles. They tend to have poor health, partly because they rarely take up preventative screening or treatment and often present to health professionals when illnesses are advanced. If a public authority is paying due regard to inequalities across its area, and has an Afghan population living within its boundaries, it should be aware of this. It must make sure the way it runs local services does not reinforce or worsen this inequality. Staff can take positive action – for example, health workers can target activities to improve Afghan women's take-up of preventative and primary health.

A service provider can't tackle all inequality in their area at once. So it is all right to support a health group for Afghan mothers, even if it means a public authority does not have enough resources to run an exercise group for men with diabetes – as long as the decision is based in sound evidence. However, the Equality Duty is an ongoing duty. Although organisations can prioritise, they cannot ignore other existing inequalities: the needs of the diabetic men must not be forgotten.

The Equality Duty says public authorities must work to:

- *'Eliminate discrimination, harassment, victimisation and other conduct that is prohibited by or under the Act.'* This means they must make sure no staff behave badly, that decisions are always properly made and their implications for people who might be disadvantaged are thought through, and that administration and organisational management, such as eligibility criteria, access routes and evidence noted in Chapter 3, have no bias.

- *'Advance equality of opportunity between people who share a protected characteristic and those who do not share that characteristic.'* This means reviewing and making changes and creating strategies, including positive action, so that both staff and volunteers in the organisation and diverse members of the public all have a fair chance of gaining equally good outcomes from what the organisation offers.

- *'Foster good relations between people who share a relevant protected characteristic and those who do not share that characteristic.'* Public authorities must encourage mutual knowledge and positive relationships between populations and among the mass of diverse individuals in its area. This includes tackling intolerance or hostility and preventing or dealing with hate-crime.

Equality Duty procedures. The PSED lays out certain documents and procedures that public authorities have to have in place, although they often go under different names. These procedures are designed to improve local data, ensure long- and better short-term planning, and stop people relying on guesswork. Where these processes are weak, refugees and many small disadvantaged populations will always be at risk of being passed over.

The various documents and procedures are an asset for practitioners and any member of the public who wants to feed into decision-making. You can use Equality Duty processes to get refugees on authorities' agendas, encourage better refugee-related data and heighten attention to refugees in design, planning and commissioning/funding, and reviews of how effective something has been. You can trigger positive actions that will benefit refugees – perhaps with you as a partner in the delivery.

Equality Evidence Review. The Equality Evidence Review should include local primary data from local statistics from the Census and Joint Strategic Needs Assessment and any reliable local source. There are few local statistics about refugees, and the Census doesn't record immigration status. Refugee populations change too fast for the Census to keep up. But detailed ethnic and language data in the Census can be useful, and schools and NHS also collect language and even interpreter data if you can access it.

The Evidence Review should also have qualitative data from consultations, case studies and local voices, which is where you can get refugees' voices heard. It should use evidence from respected sources and can include national bodies, including specialist bodies in the voluntary sector such as the King's Fund and the Refugee Council. The amount of good-quality national work on refugee needs and good practice can make up somewhat for the lack of local statistics (see Appendix A).

Equality Objectives. Every public authority must agree Equality Objectives for the organisation at the highest level and publish them so the public can see them. The choice of Objectives should come from the Evidence Review. Equality Objectives state what the public authority's priority populations will be for the next few years, and what changes it aims to bring about for those populations. Equality Objectives should then, in theory, be included in plans (including plans for positive action) and monitoring across all activities. It doesn't usually work quite that well.

Equality Objectives create space for action. If you can get refugees, or Afghan women, for example, named in the Equality Objectives, it gives the authority's staff more freedom to do something about the disadvantages they face. You could well see some big local improvements for them in the years ahead.

Annual Equality Duty Review. Every January the public authority should publish a review of updated evidence, and the progress they have made towards their Equality Objectives.

Equality Impact Assessment (EIA) and mitigating actions. Every time there is a substantial change in policy, new, changing or decommissioning (ending) of services, the public authority must assess what impact the change will have on the 'equality' populations in their area. The purpose is to spot any damage to certain groups 'in the community' before it happens, so staff can put in mitigating actions to avoid the harm. Any shock-prone group with high needs and low means, such as refugees, is vulnerable in times of change where information and rules change, especially as new teams set up new access structures which usually start off as one-size-fits-all.

EIAs use the data in the Evidence Review and should also gather fresh local participatory data and relevant national research in relation to the proposed change. The EIA can be used to trigger 'mitigating actions'. Where positive action is about making things better, mitigating actions try to stop things getting any worse than they have to.

Equality characteristic monitoring. This has been mentioned already. If done correctly, especially if integrated throughout feedback and evaluation, equality monitoring provides stronger data for the Evidence Review and future Objectives and EIAs. Get your refugee participants to fill in the forms – they will probably need reassurance and your help to understand.

Summary and conclusion

Box 4.13 Further sources on anti-discrimination and equality

There is a great deal of high-quality training and writing to draw on, face to face and online. Look for Equality and Human Rights Commission, Equality and Diversity Forum, National Equality Partnership reports (NEP has ended), Open University, British Institute of Human Rights, HEAR and brap and other regional networks that have managed to keep going. Also, Race on the Agenda (RoTA), Women's Resource Centre, Age Concern, Disability Law Service, Stonewall.

Regarding refugees with protected characteristics, see Asylum Aid (women), Forward (women and girls/female genital mutilation – FGM), UKLGIG and Micro Rainbow (sexual orientation), JCORE, Children's organisations in Chapter 11.

The Equality Act 2010 gives you a structure that you must comply with but also a range of concepts, opportunities and tools of real use. You might use it to advance the interests of refugees and protect them from harm. But any step towards better access and equality is good for all your vulnerable clients. Equality law is there for all of us.

Already wary of authorities, refugees are unlikely to stand up against discrimination and for equal treatment. They often rely on the bodies they should sometimes be challenging. Stretched thin as they are, they are more likely to suffer a long-term impact from discrimination – or from poor policy and planning. 'They are particularly vulnerable to discrimination as [unlike other migrants] they do not have the choice to leave the UK and go back to their countries of origin' (EDF and REAP 2011, p.2). Refugees, like everyone, care about having a reasonable chance to get on with life. No country can afford to ignore discrimination if it wants a healthy society in which people can fulfil their potential. Inequality makes it harder to design your own future, and more likely that a person's or a group's potential will be wasted. They don't usually articulate their frustration in terms of inequality. 'As long as we are human beings we face challenges,' one workshop participant said.

If people who have left behind discrimination and persecution find themselves limited to an underclass existence here, we can hardly claim to have given them refuge. Sadly, refugees often accept discrimination as normal.

But you don't have to.

CHAPTER 5

Engaging with Refugees

Introduction

I could have called this chapter 'Working with Refugees', or 'Dialogue and Interaction with Refugees' or 'Participation, Agency, Empowerment and Integration', 'Responding to…' or 'Creating spaces for…'. But 'Engaging' gets across a sense of urgency, of *negotiating a creative relationship*. As a friend of mine said about his daughter who had been struggling with mental health and drug issues, 'She's engaging with us, and that's good enough for me.'

'*With* Refugees' emphasises that this is not about getting *them* to do something, but about *mutual influence and communication*. This is communication in its full sense, as dialogue between diverse parties that builds new knowledge and helps all parties grow and develop. Fluent English language is helpful, but there is more to it than that.

It is crucial to see what you and your organisation do *as refugees might see it*. As any detective film says, you have to figure out their motives, means and opportunities. Then reflect that in your practice. What motivates someone who has to rebuild a life? Given the hoops refugees have to jump through, do they have the skills and assets they need to make that leap? Are there timely, local openings they can take advantage of and use in their strategies?

> You have to figure out their motives, means and opportunities.

Refugees are just ordinary people, all different and doing the best they can. They will shop around – engage where and when they believe they can get the best out of their scarce resources. Don't see this as cynicism. Nor is it some kind of failure in the relationship. They are making their own decisions, taking responsibility for their own lives. What comes out of it might not be quite what you expected. Can you adjust?

Chapter 2 highlighted how refugees' experiences and current pressures might affect their willingness and ability to form good working relationships with people like you, especially if they see you as an authority figure. Then there are the broader issues all migrants face, such as working in an unfamiliar language and culture. Some stability lets the relationship grow. You will need to be clear, adaptable, build mutual knowledge and trust to gain a degree of collaboration.

This chapter is about practical action. About *how*. It starts with understanding issues about access that everyone needs to recognise, and then seeing the view from where refugees stand. The ideas come from many lessons and voices over the past 15 years: from refugees, practitioners and my own experiences and observations. But it isn't a 'How to...' manual. It isn't a ready-to-eat cake or even a 'results guaranteed' packet mix. Please think of it as a cupboard of ingredients to pick from as you mix and flavour for your needs.

Access

The first step in any work to engage people is understanding 'access'. Whether or not the resources refugees need exist is certainly a big issue. Whether they are entitled is another. But when something out there could be useful for them, the most significant issue is: can they access it? Have they got the knowledge, documents, skills to negotiate access, and is it worth the effort? Britain may have some of the best justice, education, medicine and arts in the world, but what good is that to refugees if they can't access them?

You can start with the well-established idea of three 'access stages' that people have to work their way through to use formal services. Think of a job application. First, you submit an application form and they look at two or three key points to check you meet the minimum requirements – a work permit, an appropriate qualification, etc. If you don't, your form goes in the recycle bin. If you do, you are through 'the gate' and they will consider your application. They read the whole form carefully and compare it with all the other applicants' forms, while you wait to hear if you are shortlisted for interview. That is 'the queue'. The interview is a face-to-face 'encounter', where people see you, hear you and judge you on the spot.

In other cases, encounters are the moments of direct interaction when the staff or the organisation negotiate exactly what they will offer you, which might include them making some reasonable adjustments and the decision-maker using a degree of discretion. Some services may also be provided directly through encounters – you get your injection, you sit and learn English, or you talk with a therapist.

One refugee I discussed access with said that for him what he called the 'pre-gate' was even more important. He needs a wheelchair to get around, but for his first two years in Britain he didn't know he could get help to get a wheelchair, he didn't know buses had ramps and he had never heard of independent living centres. 'I just sat in the four walls of my room.' He says many refugees (and people in all walks of life) don't even know there is something useful out there. Or even when someone knows something is possible in the UK – for example, you can get a wheelchair – they don't know how to find the service, or how to tell if it is the right one for them or good quality, or even whether the provider might rip them off. They never get as far as the gate. (See Box 5.1.)

In asylum, assuming people know what to do (pre-gate), the initial asylum claim and screening interview (gate) usually includes face-to-face interaction with officials (encounter). Then knowing how to find a decent solicitor (pre-gate) and get to an appointment (gate) to brief them on your case (encounter). Then gathering evidence and documents to build that case while you wait (queue) for your substantive interview (encounter). Then you wait and chase people for news (queue). Asylum seekers can write to or contact their MP at constituency surgeries (gate/encounter) to ask for help to speed thing up (queue), but few asylum seekers know this (pre-gate). During this waiting period you find the number (pre-gate) to ring the subcontractor (encounter) who screens your eligibility for NASS support (gate); then you submit your application for support (gate) and wait (queue), possibly with no money, nowhere to stay and no food (pre-gate-foodbank). If you get Leave to Remain (gate) you go to a Jobcentre Plus…and so it goes on. There is a kind of sequence but it is more loops. You are judged by anonymous strangers on paperwork and in face-to-face encounters throughout.

Box 5.1 Challenges to access with examples

Challenges to access		Examples
'Pre-gate'	When people are not even aware that a service exists or that they might be entitled to it, or how to find it or how to choose between different options.	Never having heard of an independent living centre. Not knowing you need to register with a GP (or how) to get free health care. Not knowing that as you have impairments you can ask your council for a community care assessment. Having a list of solicitors (or child care, or college courses) but having no idea how to choose.
Gate	The point a person first comes into contact with an agency and has to persuade 'gatekeepers' that she or he is eligible for the resources and services that the organisation provides or controls.	Asking a GP receptionist to register you with the GP. Asking your GP to refer you for specialist counselling. Filling and posting an application for NASS support (subsistence funds/accommodation; see Chapter 3). Going into a bank with ID papers to try to open a bank account. Open the door of a café and walk in.

| Queue | Submit and wait for your request or claim to be dealt with, as it is assessed for completeness, credibility, entitlements and priority compared with need and with others; waiting for an appointment, a decision. Might request special treatment, a quick decision, priority over others. | Waiting in the Accident and Emergency department of a hospital before and after triage. Sending extra letters and documents to strengthen your claim for NASS support, answering further questions, ringing for news, getting an advocate to ring for you. Waiting to hear about your asylum appeal. Asking your solicitor or MP to support you. In a café, you catch the waitress's eye. |
| Encounter | Face-to-face or other direct interaction with a decision-maker and/or person providing the service, who tells you what they will provide for you, with some discussion/negotiation. Depending on the service, it might be provided in this or another encounter. 'Encounters' are often also 'gates'. | Triage nurse examines you. A duty nurse treats you. A family support worker spends an hour with you helping you fill a form. You meet the bank manager to discuss a loan for a college course. The waitress brings your food. |

'Access stages' is rather a neutral term. Each stage is an anxiety-provoking hurdle, another mini-crisis that refugees have to get through as they try to sort out their lives. Whether you run a little local play group or a 980-bed hospital, to engage effectively with refugees your organisation needs to make sure that what happens day to day in all four different access settings is equitable and easy for a refugee to deal with. Long Box 5.2 has several examples of ways – good and bad – that organisations arrange access to their services.

Even if an own-language leaflet improves things pre-gate, and empathetic staff are wonderful at making encounters productive, neither means anything if a reception volunteer (gate) turns the asylum seeker away, saying you can't help. I have an alert word when looking at access: 'just'. As in 'they just need to…' I instantly know there is going to be a problem.

> I have an alert word: 'just': As in 'they just need to…' I instantly know there is going to be a problem.

	Different ways organisations handle access,
Long Box 5.2	**good and bad – Case Studies A–I**

Pre-gate

A This organisation established its professionalism with local social services and staff are permitted to work directly in a hostel for young refugees. They spend quite a lot of time there each week, and because they go to where refugees are, they make contact and support people who have just arrived, even though they could be moved to other regions soon.

B Several organisations created a shared list of groups to be distributed. But the list only reaches refugees who are already connected with services such as primary school or other groups. The majority of new group participants still come because of word of mouth.

C This organisation runs services in an area with a substantial refugee population. It serves hundreds of people. When asked how many refugees use their services, a staff member answered, 'We don't want to stigmatise by asking, but at a guess, one or two.' Because they do not monitor, they can't find out if they have refugee users or not. They have no way of knowing whether they should be putting special effort to avoid indirectly discriminating against refugees by leaving them outside the gate.

Gate

D A local advice service gave out appointments by a first come, first served queuing system where people waited from 8am to get an appointment. Ironically, when cuts bit hard it improved the access, as the service linked up with two others to set up a single freephone number which people ring and most now get initial advice by phone. Face-to-face appointments are only given if absolutely necessary.

E An adult learning team offered a four-session 'Boost Your English' course funded by a Government source which needed ten people to go ahead. About 18 people arrived the first week, several of whom spoke almost no English and struggled to understand instructions. As well as proof of identity and address, they were unexpectedly asked to prove they were refugees and prove how long they had been in the UK. Women who had refugee status through their husbands were told to come back with evidence of their husbands' refugee status plus their marriage certificates. The 'Boost Your English' team didn't have a photocopier so they told people to bring their own photocopies the next week. There was no time for any English. The course was cancelled before the second week.

F Freedom from Torture's reception area in Birmingham has warm soft colours, open windows, sofas and chairs with cushions, attractive art works done by clients, tissues, fresh fruit; a low-level desk which the calm and experienced volunteer receptionist sits behind, with a vase of flowers, a photograph board showing good-sized photos of staff, their names and roles; a clean toilet with tampons and condoms available for anyone to take; one neat short list in large print of key advice services and no other notices or signs, except a couple on the back of the toilet door about confidential domestic violence or sexual health services.

Queue

G   A social housing bidding system sends emails to people when a property comes up. Registered individuals bid online, and viewings are allocated on a first come, first served basis. One of our members had to go to the library just to read her emails, causing such delays that she had no realistic chance of a successful bid and gave up. The IT system that worked very well for some people meant she had no chance of getting off the bottom of the queue.

Encounter

H   A session with free food was held at a local church hall. Volunteers say a blessing before distributing the food to their diverse applicants. 'Mostly people don't mind,' one said.

I   Regular participants at an English group had very little English but were familiar with signing in, a regular circle exercise for greeting everyone, role plays and how to work the tea urn. They made sure new people know what to do and took part in what was going on.

So far this view on access does not do justice to the critical *relationship* between a hands-on worker and a service user. That relationship is not a fifth 'stage'. It is fundamental to all the challenges that access presents to refugees and, ultimately, to whether they get what they need.

A relationship can exist without trust, but it is more productive with, and there is a mutual need for honesty and appreciation to get the best outcomes. Much of what refugees have been through makes trust all the more precious. They might hold back while they observe you and decide if they can trust you. Make sure they know what you are doing and why, and what is being written on forms and on computers. Trust is about your credibility and earning their respect, not about getting them to like you. Friendly? Yes. But not friends.

> Trust is about your credibility and earning their respect... Friendly? Yes. But not friends.

Don't ever risk your credibility by being vague. Be honest about what you don't know. Be upfront and clear about your role and limits. And only ever promise what you are certain you can deliver.

The end reality is that you – the staff member – hold all the control cards. Power here is very one-sided whether you like that fact or not. In many cases the only way a refugee can take control is to walk away.

However, in any interaction, and especially in face-to-face encounters, there is an element of influence in both directions as you ask them questions and their answers change your awareness and knowledge. They appeal to your discretion and you consider your potential to change wider systems. Make space for refugees' influence and the relationship can become more creative and productive.

Motives, means and opportunities – reflect and boost

The chapter opened with the need to look at your own work as refugees might see it, figuring out the motives, means and opportunities refugees have when they engage with you. Then you have to adapt your work so it reflects their motives and means and creates opportunities that work for them, rather than necessarily for you.

At times you don't know enough; so try things out and do it better next time. At times adapting everything around their perceptions and priorities just isn't possible. But think through the issues, and do what you can. And make sure you talk to people who *don't* come as well as those who do.

Motive to engage with you

Refugees are active agents of their own development. They are motivated to act. But to what end? What would you or I care about if we had been through what they have been through? Are we offering refugees what they feel they need?

> Question from workshop trainer: 'Any methods you have tried that did not work?'

> Answer from participating professional: 'Anything, when they don't wish to communicate.'

People are motivated to pursue their subjective interests. These are by no means selfish interests but a drive to improve the things and usually benefit the people we care about. Personal standards and principles also matter.

Many of us are familiar with Maslow's hierarchy of the needs which motivate people to act. It is a good place to start. We go from rudimentary human needs for 'survival' – safety and welfare, food, shelter, warmth, physical safety. Then the needs around 'security' – personal and family stability and independence, current and future livelihoods. Then the need for 'self-actualisation' – dignity, status among peers, an ability to express oneself. In reality, they co-exist.

I recently heard Journalist Yasmin Alibhai-Brown tell an anecdote about a refugee she had known for years who got her first job. She rushed up to Alibhai-Brown shortly after starting and waved a handbag at her. 'Look! I bought it myself! I bought my own handbag.'

As people pursue their interests, they may be interested in getting *resources* such as money or food, but usually their actions are about *access* – getting a job, or obtaining a voucher for the food bank. Some may be motivated by the wish to be *more in control* of their lives, more independent, less at the mercy of other people or the vagaries of institutions. For example, they might take a job that pays only the same as Universal Credit but frees them from the Benefits Agency.

People may have an element of calculation in what they do, of balancing different priorities and weighing up a choice of actions with different costs and possible benefits. But they rarely act only for rational reasons. Nothing is certain; refugees' lives change fast, and priorities shift: 'Sorry, teacher, my solicitor needs to see me.' Unpredictability is a feature of refugee life.

As a support worker, you may have a sense of a refugee's motives, but you can't say what individual priorities are. Plus each refugee is unique. So your engagement work and your activities need to relate to several possible interests at once, which might motivate people to engage with you for more than one reason. You absolutely cannot work on a one-size-fits-all, 'typical' refugee (Box 5.3).

Box 5.3 Understanding refugees' motives and improving engagement – some ideas

- Find out more about people's motives. For example, do a 'school gate' survey and find time to talk to parents picking up primary-age children over several days.

- Address common motivations. What do most of us care about? Our parents, our children, money, a home, a decent job, enjoying some sociable time? For example, offer training in employable skills such as interpreting or food hygiene. Build from there.

- Address multiple motivations at once. For example, English groups relate to future employment, the ability to interact and look after your own interests in Britain, making social contacts within the group, a sense of personal progress and better self-esteem, access to other activities and services provided by group leaders/host organisations.

- Include 'self-actualisation' and social interests – socialising but also status such as recognition ceremonies, framed certificates for people who have completed a course or 50 hours' volunteering, a written acknowledgement that can be used as a reference.

- Work in a little rational cost–benefit calculation. For example, 'This workshop will help you save money because...'

Means to engage with you

The *means* to engage are skills and assets such as financial or practical resources, a sense of energy and agency, and contacts. They are the tools we need to get things done, including jumping through hoops that other people set us (see Box 5.8).

Migrants generally have fewer practical assets and less knowledge to draw on than life-long UK residents. Refugees have even less. Do our practices ask too much of their current resources? Can we adapt our practices so they demand less of refugees' means?

Money and time. Refugees are usually low on money, whether that means no cash, irregular income or no access to banks and reasonable credit (see Chapter 7). They make careful choices (Box 5.4). Financial poverty results in people having to use a lot of their time on daily practicalities, shopping around, waiting for off-peak buses or walking home. It leaves them short of time for other activities and limits their mobility and freedom of choice.

Box 5.4 **The debate about charging for services**

I was involved in offering a full Level 3 interpreting qualification course for free. People on the course didn't value it and completely wasted the opportunity. When we charged, attendance was 100% and all participants submitted all assignments.

The English groups where I worked were free for years, then we started to ask for £1, although we waived it if people had no money. Attendance stabilised and people came on time and participated better. But two people certainly stopped coming because of this, and we never were sure about the decision.

Means to keep in touch – phones, post and IT. Keeping in touch nowadays requires phones and IT. The post can work but be aware of misspelled addresses and the lack of security in blocks of flats, shared houses or bed-and-breakfast accommodation. For convenience and security, most refugees see a mobile phone as a top priority, mostly using top-up cards so they can keep in touch cheaply by text and various free apps, even internationally. They may have no other access to IT or printing and copying. The 'digital divide', where parts of the population zoom along online and other parts are completely sidelined, is very significant for refugees who frequently lack both access and skills (see Long Box 5.2, CS/G).

Documents. For refugees, documents and evidence are critical (Long Box 5.2, CS/E). Documents have already been mentioned in Chapter 3 and Appendix B includes details. Refugees and especially asylum seekers often don't have all the evidence they need, because they are at the Home Office or solicitors, or people didn't have them in the first place (e.g. birth certificates) or can't get them (e.g. National Insurance number).

English language, literacy and confidence to speak. One of the most immediate and obvious means for successful engagement – or challenges to it – is how well refugees can communicate in English. It isn't usually about how good their vocabulary and grammar is – although, of course, that is a factor. It is a great deal to do with confidence. People often understand better than they speak, but with confidence they will look you in the eyes and have a go (Box 5.5). They'll use smart phones and dictionaries and get by. Those who don't have the confidence to try or to say they don't understand are more likely to miss out (see Chapter 6).

Box 5.5 Communication in English

I recommended a man for a Level 3 interpreting course once. I thought he was fluent in English, but he failed the language assessment by a mile. He was so good at communicating that I simply never realised his level of English was far too low for interpreting.

A few years before that I had turned down a fully qualified interpreter for a job because, despite his accurate grammar and technical vocabulary, he spoke so fast with such a strong accent that I couldn't understand half of what he said.

Knowledge, skills. Knowledge of rights and services is an important 'pregate' asset. Skills with IT, language and office practices are valuable, particularly for handling the gate and the queue.

Cultural competence. Social skills and understanding of social context and interaction and culture in Britain are probably more important in a successful encounter than they really should be. Body language, for example, is highly cultural. One person will use space, their eyes, face, hands, touch, and their whole body position to encourage (or discourage) someone else, but the other person can't interpret these physical displays. Choice of words (even when both are fluent in English), turn taking and knowing how to interrupt, and understanding whether/how people ask/answer questions and agree/disagree are all cultural.

Many refugees and migrants with limited experience of British culture act or behave in the way they would expect to act or behave if still in their home country, which might be out of place or misinterpreted here. People have assumptions about hierarchies by gender, age, race, disability, faith, education, profession and combinations of these. They read different messages and have different responses to how we express ourselves, whether I am wearing a Mulberry scarf or tongue and eyebrow piercings. Behaviour is shaped by different experiences of the client/professional, supplicant/patron, customer/salesman, master/servant relationship. If they act on earlier rules that don't fit their new cultural context, they might waste good advice and ignore instructions, or cause offence and lose support (see Box 5.6).

Box 5.6 Tolerating intolerance?

When you live within an established culture, and you find yourself working with people who are facing new social concepts and beliefs, you will inevitably get clashes of idea and opinion about gender, sexuality, race, values, power and much more. It takes time for new arrivals to recognise the differences, learn what it all means and work out their own position. They have to learn new skills for agreeing and disagreeing to avoid causing offence.

Nobody has to tolerate hostility or discrimination; whoever you are working with, there are still boundaries. But we need flexibility (and support) to learn and engage with people whose views and behaviour might sometimes be challenging to us personally and ideologically.

On the other hand, if you are a teacher or medical clinician reading this book, you might have been taken aback by the degree of respect and deference you have been shown. (It can be a pleasant relief, but also alarming as you feel the weight of someone's dependency falling on your shoulders.) It is particularly disconcerting when gifts of some value appear on your desk, and it is useful to cite an 'organisational policy' of not accepting gifts, so you can politely refuse, with grace and gratitude (see Box 5.7).

Box 5.7 Food as a gift of love

I love it when people bring in food they have cooked. It tastes great. It is an expression of pride and skill and positive identity. There is no monetary value to cause embarrassment. It means I have really done something right. As one of our earliest members said, 'Food is love'.

Although some people learn and absorb and adapt quickly, others – especially older people – may never gain the bi-cultural fluency that would make their lives so much easier. It is probably hardest for those who don't get into work – asylum seekers, parents, carers, older people and people without necessary skills.

Contacts and networks. In juggling their scarce resources, refugees probably depend more on peers than on workers within formal organisations. Reciprocity and collaboration among peers, including sharing knowledge, helps people cope with life. The down side is that people will often accept friendly but inaccurate advice (and pressure) from peers rather than listen to you. People compare and choose, and your credibility is critical in whether they follow your advice or their friend's.

Very many asylum seekers and refugees don't have local peer networks because of multiple moves, social or mental health issues, lack of opportunity to meet and consolidate acquaintances, all leaving them increasingly isolated. Or they might have a limited view because language leaves them relying on peers from similar ethnic and cultural backgrounds. Do *not* believe the romantic notions about a 'refugee community' where people are just waiting to look after each other (see Box 4.10 for a critical view on 'community').

A sense of agency. Over the years I have come to the conclusion that a sense of agency – a firm belief in one's own ability to bring about changes – is the most important means for refugees to engage effectively with formal organisations. It requires self-belief and energy to keep going through the hassle of dealing with multiple institutions. A sense of agency makes people strategic and helps them get over knockbacks. It might not get a person everything she or he wants, but it helps a lot.

Box 5.8	Understanding refugees' means and improving engagement – some ideas

- Money: Pay travel expenses, give top-up cards as thank-you gifts instead of flowers.

- Time and mobility: Bus routes matter, free parking less so. Piggy-back activities – for example, book the benefits adviser to come directly after an English group session, not the next day.

- Means to keep in touch: Set up group texting from your computer. Have group apps on an organisational mobile. Hint: Don't leave voicemail messages on mobiles – recipients have to pay to listen to them.

- Making the post work: When people hand-write addresses, check you can read it before they leave. Look out for 1 and 7, 2 and 3, 0 and 6.

- Documents: Provide proof of address. Post a formal letter to them showing charity/company number and an original signature to their current address. Include their full name, date of birth and immigration/NASS reference numbers (see Appendix B).

- Communication in English/confidence to speak – see Chapter 6.

- Knowledge and skills: Training, volunteering, experience, of course, but consider peer-building approaches – for example, 'Connectors'.

- Cultural competence: Don't be shy to tell people 'You should shake hands now', 'You must be on time'. We all want to get it right. Be assertive: 'Now it is my turn to speak'. Be consistent from day one: 'Thank you kindly but I can't take gifts'.

- Peers and contacts: Plan plenty of time in sessions for introductions. Hint: Social events often reinforce isolation so manage them carefully to ensure a positive experience for all individuals.

Opportunity to engage with you

Opportunity is a simpler idea. Motive is like asking 'Will they (try to) be there?' Means is like asking 'If they come, how effective are they likely to be when they are there?' Opportunity is simply 'Can they be there at all?'

Compared with reflecting people's motives or means, it is relatively simple to keep improving the opportunities we create, although you will rarely get things exactly as you want them. Talk to refugees. Ask them about the various demands they are juggling and what works for them (Box 5.9). Monitor take-up – note sudden drops or increases. Follow up to find out why people didn't come. You probably can't find solutions that suit all individuals, but the more carefully you look at it, the better it will get.

Box 5.9 | **Snow or 'what seems impossible for one person is nothing at all to another'**

We organised a workshop and woke up to snow. None of the participants from hotter countries showed up. The Brits were wrapped up to the eyebrows in hats and scarves and walking boots. The Afghans, Poles and Ukrainians who strolled in wearing trainers thought it was really funny.

Timing. People with limited means have limited opportunities – if you have 15 minutes to get somewhere, you could make it by car, but you don't have a car so you end up not going. For some people, timing means working round school hours; for others, it is working round shift patterns or observing Ramadan. You have your own timing restrictions: part-time staff hours or the organisation's end-of-quarter reporting deadline. But fixed 'office hours' don't work – you will be wise to allow time in your plans each day for people dropping in.

Location. Within reach? Already familiar or easy to find? Accessible on public transport? How many buses? Is it seen to be a safe journey? You might need to choose convenience and familiarity for your refugee users over quality, especially as refugees often live in deprived areas. Ask primary schools. Ask a supportive local restaurant if you can use its dining space some mornings.

Venue. Does the venue seem welcoming when you arrive? Is there good physical access such as ramps or a lift? Is the building strongly associated with an ethnic or religious group? Is it a women-only space? Do they need ID or someone to sign them in?

Your awareness and space for refugees to make their own opportunities. Keep slack in the system so you can be opportunistic and make use of refugees' own approaches and initiatives. Leave space in your day or your session plan to respond to what refugees bring to you. Always plan time to stay on after a group or session for half an hour to see what happens. Make sure your team and volunteers have space to share and discuss issues they have learned about from refugees.

Initial opening/consolidating. Refugees need an opportunity to start engaging, something to create the possibility of a relationship. Then they need ways so they can take it forward; not because you want them to, but because they want to and they can. The rest of the chapter concentrates on this.

How to engage – initiating a relationship

So far this chapter has focussed on constraints that affect how likely refugees are to engage effectively with you. This section and the following two are about different aspects of what you can do about those constraints, and how you make engagement happen:

first, initiating a relationship

second, face-to-face engagement

third, developing a longer-term relationship and a deeper collaboration for your organisation's and refugees' mutual benefit.

A lot will be quite familiar as good practice to any hands-on practitioner, but it is about adapting to 'refugee' factors such as trust issues.

Information and publicity

If part of your role is publicity and outreach or recruitment, you have to think about getting information and publicity out that will overcome the risk of refugees being stuck in 'pre-gate' limbo, not even knowing you exist. Whether it is for ongoing services or one-off events, you need information where refugees will find it even when they aren't looking.

- ☑ It has to be where people will come across it.
- ☑ It has to be noticeable and understandable by the people you want to notice it and understand it.
- ☑ It has to leave them with the feeling that they want to get in touch with this activity or organisation.
- ☑ It has to be up to date.

Scrutinise your *hard-copy* leaflets, posters and letters, and *online* information and social media. Are they right for refugees? Are they clear with plain English or good translations? Are they something people can identify with, including photos or pictures of people they find familiar that will reassure them they are welcome? Are the dates (include the year somewhere), venue and postcode accurate?

The best way to get information out there is by getting out yourself and making direct contact, because it starts the possibility of a relationship with people who are stuck outside the gate (see Box 5.10). Humans are social animals. One face-to-face meeting outweighs a hundred fliers.

If you are trying to reach refugees from scratch, start by asking *where refugees live*. Usually where accommodation is cheaper. *Where do they go?* They shop for food, and might use shops where the shopkeeper speaks their language. Get the shopkeeper's support. They probably see the GP – ask the practice manager to tell the practice team. They take kids to primary school. Some attend faith services but many don't. Those who work have many jobs, but agencies, taxi companies and social care agencies are often where people get started.

Box 5.10 **Creating the possibility of a relationship – Case Studies J and K**

J A lawyer and mental health nurse go out with a central London soup run. They are taking 'the gate' to the people, giving initial information and then setting up referrals for anyone who needs more support.

K In my home area, diabetes awareness workers occasionally do on-the-spot pin-prick blood tests at the Muslim centre after Friday prayers.

Making contact via a credible third party

If you are in touch with a *credible third party*, they can use their direct and personal contact with refugees on your behalf. Distributing information via others works well if:

☑ they actually have direct contact with refugees

☑ they are keen on what you are doing

☑ they remember you are doing it, and

☑ they have the information to hand when they need it.

Send your third-party contacts updates by a mix of methods: post, text, email, phone. If your contacts use Facebook and Twitter, so should you. Best of all, drop in, go and see them face to face at their desk, not just at committee meetings. If you can, back it all up with links to a website which can be easily found online.

As well as refugee specialists and own-language organisations, many other hands-on workers in your area are probably finding themselves working with refugees – English as an Additional Language (EAL) coordinators in schools, community midwives, police community support officers. *Think broadly.* They might be grateful for a source to refer to and many people value networking (see Chapter 7). They might have events you could piggy-back on – fêtes and festivals, advice sessions.

One-off events

Your aim might be to engage refugees who are already part of your larger user-group, such as parents of children in a school, or heart patients, library-users or people living within a mile. One-off events or time-limited activities, such as a short course, can be very effective. They require a burst of effort rather than ongoing energy.

But it is pointless attracting people to a one-off event if that is where it ends – plan what you want to happen after the event as a way to the goals and framework for planning the event itself. We want women to get independent income through decent jobs? Let's put on a women's 'feel-good' day to recruit to a five-week self-esteem course linked to volunteering and work experience with a local employer.

There is no guaranteed topic that will always work, and it is important the event doesn't put migrants and refugees at a disadvantage. They might not know the rules of bingo or have cash to spend at fundraising events such as fêtes. Events are a risk. See them as experimental, evaluate afterwards and you will get better results over time.

Face-to-face engagement

Now that you have created the opportunity to engage, the refugee's first experience when contacting your organisation is crucial. It will be greatly affected by what happens in their first face-to-face encounter. If that encounter does not work, you are unlikely to see them again.

Points have been raised already about trust, clarity and practical issues such as cultural competence and having time for the unexpected. These are principles that underlie successful, productive encounters.

Safe and confidential encounters

SENSITIVITY

You will often need to know details about someone's life to be able to help them – regarding entitlements, for example. Don't be shy to ask for the information you need to know; just make sure they know why. Stop asking questions as soon as possible. You are talking to a fellow adult, and it is important to balance asking with listening. You want to build a positive relationship – not one that reminds them of their Home Office interview. But if people decide to tell you more than you asked, be ready to listen.

Presenting

It is likely someone will start to talk to you about something you didn't know
– they 'present' a new problem or something that is really worrying. Similar
principles apply whether someone starts to talk about trafficking, domestic
abuse or past traumas. Stay calm and listen without encouraging or challenging.
Explain about confidentiality. Ask them if they want you to do anything about
it. Are they willing to report it to the police? Find out if there is counselling or
other support available. You cannot act without their permission. Don't make
promises you can't keep.

Confidentiality

Remember how important confidentiality is in building trust, as well as being
good practice. Confidentiality is not the same as secrecy. Remind the person
you will keep what they say and their personal details ('identifiable' data)
confidential, and make sure they know what 'confidential' means, in 'plain
English'. Even native English speakers often think confidential means secret and
you won't tell anyone. Anonymity might also be important to people.

Box 5.11 Protecting confidentiality and anonymity

'You can feel confident and happy I will only talk to people who must know, not to my friends
or other people here, or anyone who knows you. I will talk to my manager or an expert to ask
them for professional advice. They only talk to the right professional people too.'

- Revisit your organisation's data protection and confidentiality policies and make
  sure the whole team is familiar with them.

- Generally, volunteers should not be able to access databases/files with personal
  data, but reliable volunteers could sign a confidentiality agreement.

- Only take notes if you must and don't recycle! Shred.

- Only take copies of personal documents, especially Home Office, identity, health
  records and passports, if you know you must, and ensure copies are kept securely
  and then shredded. It is better to note key numbers and dates and sign a written,
  dated note of what you have seen.

- People must give permission before you discuss their situation or refer their
  case to anyone outside the organisation. (Safeguarding may be an exception
  – follow your policy.) You can ask for advice if you are careful to keep the
  person anonymous.

- Always ask permission before taking photos (including group photos at socials),
  and also ask before publishing in print or online, even if you do not include people's
  names. Many refugees refuse to have their names or photographs online.

SAFEGUARDING

Safeguarding procedures must also be properly in place and there is a section about safeguarding in Chapter 11. As a minimum:

- You should know your organisation's safeguarding policy and procedures, and have had training.

- If someone does present to you with a safeguarding issue, or you are concerned about someone, stay calm.

- Remind them you will keep it confidential but not a secret.

- Confirm and clarify without encouraging further detail.

- As soon as you can, write down everything they said in their own words. Date and sign it.

- Report it to the correct person in your organisation, as given in the policy.

SAFETY

You need to be conscious of general safety, of course, and no doubt you have health and safety policies in place – check them. But also look at personal safety in any interaction and especially where participants or services users might be frustrated, unhappy, desperate. Think of your own vulnerability to harm, and that of the refugee, other staff, volunteers, service users and, at times, members of the public. Do assert your own views and keep colleagues informed if you are not happy with how an interaction is going – do not allow compassion to override your instincts or training. You might need an organisational line on giving lifts in cars, use of personal mobiles to ring 'clients', 'lone working' and certainly on home visits.

> Do not allow compassion to override your instincts or training.

Expanding engagement

In case work, engagement is more limited and your encounters are probably very focussed, but mutual trust is still just as important. If you are going to expand the number of people or parties involved in their case, they should understand why, should feel they can trust the new players and should have the chance to say no. To discuss their case with others, you need their permission, preferably in writing. If others will take over their case, consider whether and how you want to keep your working relationship with the refugee going, or build up new areas of engagement around other interests. There is discussion of referral in Chapter 7.

Where not dealing with confidential matters, it works well to start up engagement between a refugee and an individual at first but actively involve more people as you go along. To broaden that engagement, you need to find ways to increase how often you have contact, and different kinds of interaction that might serve other interests for the refugee. There are ideas in the rest of the chapter. As you become more familiar with each other, a wider range of issues will come into your exchanges, but remember: you are friendly, not friends.

A couple of hints:

- Keep in touch in small ways too – even a quick text is appreciated.

- You need to be quite organised if you are in touch with a lot of people, so that you don't get names mixed up and you remember their husband was ill.

- If you are making more regular contact, make sure you don't appear to be favouring anyone.

- Don't be slow to ask refugees to help – it shows you value them and that you see they have potential to do more than they are limited to at present.

Communication in English

Communication and language will usually be an issue in face-to-face engagement. Language has come up several times already, and also confidence to have a go, and use of language and the need for new conversational skills. A lack of English does not mean a refugee cannot engage with you, or you with them.

Before you think about *their* English, how is *your* English? Is it plain and clear? Can you slow down and use simpler vocabulary and shorter sentences? It is easier to communicate face to face than by phone, as you can both use so many visual cues, and it is easier to check people have understood. So face-to-face encounters are very important to refugees who aren't fluent.

Where you can't get the English to work well enough, and you both need to have a sound understanding, you need interpreters to bridge the gap. Not online translation, not someone's husband, but a trained and capable interpreter. Many practitioners don't make good use of them or think they will be too expensive. Communication in English and good practice are considered further in Chapter 6.

Longer-term relationships

In the longer term, the best engagement develops to the point at which individual users, and participants as a body, become influential forces in the organisation. You can strengthen relationships over time, evolving activities and reflecting wider interests, while refugees get better at accessing and making the most of opportunities.

Regular activities

If you can draw refugees into regular interaction, you have a real asset and so do they. You want people to come repeatedly over time, but this is often difficult for refugees. Coming often can be a drain on limited energy, cash and time – for example, finding £2 for buses not once, but every week. At £6/day to live off, this will be too much for some asylum seekers. Bear in mind also that set days, locations and times help some people set up a routine, but always rule some other people out.

The inescapable issue with regular activities is retaining participation – getting people to keep on coming and engaging. A great turnout in the first two weeks is wonderful, but you still want a good turnout eight weeks later and perhaps still a year later. Many people will give something new a go, but they are assessing and judging, comparing with other demands, coping with difficult, even chaotic lives. The 'law' of diminishing returns mean they will get more immediate benefit from the first few sessions than they get at each later session. To retain them you must make sure activities serve their interests and motivation. This means:

- ☑ Regular activities have to be high quality, delivering actual benefits so the refugee feels it is valuable to attend each and every session.

- ☑ Rewards are not just about enjoyment – friendship and pleasure might mean people want to come, but they won't be enough when other pressures arise, and refugees often have chaotic lives.

- ☑ If they have family demands and pressures, it is best if the family also sees their involvement as a good thing, so they will encourage and support your participant to come.

- ☑ Activities have to be reliable from your end, come snow or train strike.

- ☑ Participants' attendance is tracked, contact is followed up and they are reminded to keep coming, and know they matter as individuals.

- ☑ Activities stay fresh. There are easy re-entry points (e.g. a party, new term) for people who have stopped coming.

Any community development text book will also warn about group dynamics: pressures on individuals to conform and the risk of intolerance towards diversity. Many people are also wary or outright hostile to people who are not familiar or not similar, including, for example, people with mental health or behavioural difficulties or just body odour. Group activities often involve tensions over dominance, how to behave and group decisions. So a last addition to the list:

☑ You have to manage group dynamics *proactively*.

There are a couple of models with slightly different implications for your work.

Regular 'roll on, roll off' or drop in when it suits them – for example, conversation café, women's wellbeing drop-in coffee morning, Somali mothers' own-language toddler playgroup, free hot meal once a month. Many faith activities including times of worship fit this model.

It is flexible, so if people miss a few, they still feel they can come back. But it is hard work to retain numbers and you will constantly be recruiting and introducing new participants. New arrivals can find it hard to come in/fit in with people who already know each other. There is less of the helpful social glue that can build up in steady membership, and bad weather, festivals and holidays can leave you with more volunteers in the room than participants. (Few funders really understand this.)

On the other hand, you can't predict when you will go over numbers, which is a real problem with small rooms, handouts/equipment and if children are involved. If your numbers are limited and too many people turn up, you have a problem. It is hard to make waiting lists work with people who don't use IT or post, and have low language skills, confidence and little trust in authority – I generally assume that if I turn a refugee away, I won't ever see them again. Have a 'what if?' in place already to avoid turning people away if you possibly can. Have a standing agreement that you can use an overflow room if you need it, a 'stand-by volunteer' who lives nearby or an 'on-call' colleague who can run and join you; ask parents to take 15-minute turns helping in the crèche to keep ratios safe; ring for pizza to supplement the lunch.

Finite or fixed-term activities – for example, a men's talking therapy group for six weeks, or a one-term English course. This might involve buying in skilled input from outsiders (e.g. the therapist) and supervision costs. The sense of having only a limited time can intensify engagement and peer-building (Box 5.12).

Track participation closely – ring or text the same day if someone misses a session. It is nice to have some kind of recognition at the end – an extra hour for a shared meal, a group thank-you card to volunteers, group photo, certificates of attendance or special effort. Think in advance about how you will keep the relationship going when the current activities are complete, which might mean trying to keep the peer connections going too. Maybe a celebration later when results or qualifications arrive, or ask your first participants to support the new group members next time the course runs.

| **Box 5.12** | **More about making the most of fixed-term activities** |

Plan some lead-in time and 'lead-up' sessions, by which I mean sessions in the same place and time slot before the real work/course gets going. You could call them Orientation, Enrolment, a Taster Session. They are a way to get people coming in, publicise and get some word of mouth going, help refugees check if it is really going to be useful to them, get paperwork out of the way, and lay groundwork for the real thing by introducing vocabulary, principles, resources, and giving them time to prepare (e.g. realising they need to bring money, pen and paper, working out the route in advance and trying out child care). This lead-in should mean better value for everyone from the start, and fewer people dropping out.

Regular ongoing sessions with an element of progress or development – for example, English, children's health group for Afghan mothers, food bank with advice – that build up a group of repeat attendees or members who really should attend every week. Regular activities, especially where they build a group atmosphere (e.g. a choir), have a different mood and benefits. Habit and social glue can help retention. But motivation wavers, so quality and freshness really matter. It can help if people can see they are building towards longer-term achievable goals or markers along the way, such as a trip, a test, a performance, a qualification. Get participants taking responsibility for as much as possible – setting up, cleaning up, collecting money or attendance sheets, planning for social elements or how they want to thank volunteers, evaluation and steering or planning group.

Hosting another organisation's services

'Hosted' activities may be regular and group-based (e.g. health visitors), or for individuals (e.g. legal advice sessions), or one-off events that might happen a few times a year (e.g. public authority consultations). Make sure they are of *real* interest to the refugees you wish to engage, as many large bodies find refugees, ethnic minorities and other disadvantaged populations 'hard to reach' (although it can be seen as being the other way round). Some will see your organisation as a miracle cure without any sense of how much work it is to build up good engagement.[1] The wrong kind of event or garnering people to come to an event they find to be a waste of their time damages *your* credibility – not the outside organisation's.

People often start with dates, publicity, catering but stop there! Before you agree to anything, clarify with the representative right from the start…

☑ topic, content, their purpose, follow-up.

---

1 When this is highly paid consultancy firms, I get really cross – write and complain to the authority that has contracted them.

If you are satisfied that this will be of interest and value to your refugee contacts, and only if you are satisfied, go on to clarify...

☑ eligible participants and the evidence they require to prove eligibility, *in detail.*

If and only if you are satisfied, go on to clarify...

☑ who is responsible for publicity, costs of publicity, recruitment, 'did not attends', evaluation, data, participant expenses.

If and only if you are satisfied, go on to clarify...

☑ whether they will pay you, how much they will pay you and what they will pay for your overhead, volunteer and staff costs.

If and only if you are satisfied, go on to clarify...

☑ insurance/safety/safeguarding during their sessions.

If and only if you are satisfied, go on to clarify...

☑ a date to review the arrangements and who is the responsible decision-maker.

After all this is clear, *then* start talking about dates, details for fliers, rooms, refreshments, etc. (and can they do some free training for your volunteers, donate a box of paper and let you do a raffle on the day?).

Involving other individuals – involving refugees

It can work well if you choose to involve a few of your service users in the role of 'links', 'bridges', 'connectors', 'befrienders', 'core' group and steering group 'representatives', 'champions'. Their relationship with you is a kind of volunteer who is an informal part of your team (see Chapter 10 on volunteering).

'Connectors' or core members help the organisation to spread information and credibility outwards by word of mouth, to reach more people who are stuck pre-gate. They can encourage people to make contact – for example, accompanying someone the first time she or he comes in and helping with language. They offer people on the outside a familiar face who is not an authority figure, but who can answer questions about the organisation and reassure. They may also have knowledge and insight to contribute to your planning. It would be good if today's new refugee client was playing this role in a year or two. In the best case, they make the organisation something better than it was.

The downside is that newer contacts don't necessarily trust other migrants or refugees just because they are from the same country, ethnicity, language or religion. They may even trust them *less*. A 'connector' who has a strong relationship with a member of staff is in a position of power, and might be selective or unreliable; there is a risk to confidentiality, a risk of gossip or judgement, or they may just be unpopular. They may be seen as your favourites. Don't fall into the habit of relying on the views of a few helpful individuals or assuming that because you have agreed something with them, everyone feels the same. Nor that having told them something they will pass it on to everyone else in full or at all.

Summary and conclusion

Box 5.13 summarises the points in this chapter.

Box 5.13 Enabling refugees to engage – summary	
Stages of access	'pre-gate', gate, queue, encounter (Box 5.1)
Motive	resources, access, control
Means	money, time, to keep in touch, documents, English, knowledge, contacts, sense of agency
Opportunity	timing, location, venue, new space, your awareness
English	theirs, yours, checking understanding, plain English, bridge the gap, learning, interpreters
Regular activities	roll on, roll off/drop in, fixed-term, ongoing with progression, hosting others', individual 'connectors'

Seeing the refugee's view of your work is crucial. Without it you will waste a lot of time and effort.

Be strategic. Be clear on your aims and reasons for wanting to engage refugees. Try things out, and work towards a longer plan formed around learning from relationships.

Create ways refugees can gain and learn from positive experiences so they become more effective when engaging with organisations and in their new culture.

Create space for refugees to bring in their own issues and agendas. Those new ideas might not fit with projects and objectives put in writing at an earlier date. The spaces you create are opportunities for communication in the fuller sense, which will also change your work and your organisation. You are also a party in this dialogue, this praxis.

One last note: the message about the importance of relationships and responsiveness in this chapter is out of kilter with the dominant model of objective support, rule-bound, fragmented service provision via fixed-term, fixed-objective projects approved in advance by financial controllers sitting a long way away.

But engagement works with refugees when it is based on relationships of trust. So it also becomes the job of hands-on practitioners to interpret, mediate and advocate for refugees as they try to negotiate formal organisations and institutions, built on the objective model. After a short chapter about communicating in English, Chapter 7 will work through this challenge and some of the options and tools hands-on workers can use when advocating with and for refugees.

CHAPTER 6

Communicating in English – Plain English, Interpreters and Learning English

Introduction

When you find yourself working with refugees, you usually find yourself working with people who have little or no English, or if they speak English, they are still unfamiliar with the usage and communication habits they come across in their new country.

It is an issue shared by most migrants, and also an equality issue, because when communication and therefore knowledge and negotiation are constrained, it is harder to resist discrimination and make sure you have the same opportunities as other people (Chapter 3). The ability to communicate in English affects how effectively people engage (Chapter 5) and in some cases puts the hands-on worker in the role of mediator and advocate in relation to other formal organisations (Chapter 7) such as housing or health services providers, where someone able to communicate freely would be more independent.

You have a few paths you can take to cross the gap in skill. In summary, you can narrow it by adapting your use of language, bridge it with interpreters, enable refugees to learn by providing activities or facilitating their access to college. A number of non-formal and formal avenues for learning English are considered in Chapter 10 as well as an example of one approach included below.

Narrow the gap

Try to find out how good their English really is.

- Can they understand you OK, even if they don't have the skill or confidence or practice to reply?

- Can they read? Can they write English? Can they read and write in their first language?

- Can they use numbers in English? Is it the same script they know?

- Have they had their English assessed (most colleges will do this for free at various points in the year), or have they taken English/English as a Second Language/ESOL courses? Ask them what level they are (see Box 10.6).

- To get an initial idea, ask them to write their name, their address, their postcode and phone number. Give them a simple leaflet and ask them to read it to you.

Don't see these checks as an imposition; you need to know so you can adjust the way you communicate. Even without training, you can tell fairly quickly whether you'll have problems communicating, either face to face or at distance. If nothing else, you will know you can't rely on leaflets and letters but will have to arrange face-to-face meetings.

Don't confuse lack of English with lack of intelligence. People who can barely speak a word in English were teachers, business owners, musicians, civil servants before they had to leave.

What about *your* English? Is your English accurate, plain and clear? Do you finish your sentences? Do you use simple short sentences, take your time? You should pause between sentences for them to run through what you said and check they know what it means before you go on. Do you have a clear and reasonably loud voice and sound all your vowels and consonants?

Do you limit your vocabulary – avoid jargon, long words, complex tenses, double negatives, acronyms? You might need to compromise on precision to get the core part of a message across. 'I am the safeguarding officer' becomes 'I am the person who wants to know children are OK. If you have a problem, talk to me.'

> You might need to compromise on precision to get the core part of a message across.

If you are writing or printing anything, keep it short and aim for *plain English*. You could use standards set out by Plain English Campaign (plainenglish. co.uk). You could use 'Easy Read' standards and methods designed to improve communication with people who have learning difficulties. Some people find this patronising; I find it pragmatic and it works all right.

Check they understand. If you ask, 'Do you know what I mean?' you will get the reply, 'Yes.' Instead, ask them to summarise what you told them – if they didn't understand, start again from scratch. After checking they understand, write down the main points (can they read your handwriting?). They can take your summary with them and read it to check they understand, look up words and remember. It will help them explain to other staff elsewhere what you are doing for them. A leaflet doesn't achieve the same thing.

Bridge the gap

Bridge the gap (a bit). You may be able to bridge the language gap a bit if you find you have a mutual language such as French, German, Russian, Urdu, possibly Arabic.

As long as you start with plain English, smart phones and online translation packages can help for a few non-technical words or a very rough or 'gist' translation. Some digital translation is unintelligible and worryingly inaccurate, so don't rely on it.

Bridge the gap with interpreters. When their English isn't good enough or full understanding is especially important, *use an interpreter.*

Staff often start off by asking people to bring a family member. This is a bad idea. Obviously, school children should be doing other things. Adult children are also unhappy about it. I have a bilingual friend who had to tell her own mother she had cancer. It messes up family relationships – inverting care and authority structures, compromising confidentiality, preventing disclosure of family difficulties or control issues such as money problems, depression, violence. Husbands, sisters, friends rarely 'interpret' – they filter, summarise, reword, advocate and argue. It puts them in a strengthened and informed position, and your client in a weakened and ill-informed one.

There is the option to get training for staff from your organisation, or trained volunteers from your own contacts, or perhaps from a nearby ethnicity-based organisation or church/mosque. This can work when:

- it is not a highly confidential situation

- they are strangers to your client and there are no gender complications

- they understand and stick to fundamental principles and good practice

- their language skills are adequate in both languages (note that second-generation speakers, whose parents migrated here, don't usually speak their parents' language well enough)

- they are available and willing.

Or *use a professional interpreter.* In health, social, education, housing and advice work, you would usually use a 'community interpreter'. At first sight this might appear costly. If you have direct contact with self-employed, qualified, experienced professionals whom you can contact and book directly, this may be about £20–25/hour. An agency will charge £50 plus, of which the interpreter gets about £17. In theory, agencies have insurance, quality assurance, minimum standards for qualifications, DBS checks all in place, but in reality very few do this consistently. Charity- or local authority-based professional interpreting services probably have the best consistency and quality control.

Although £25/hour seems a lot, think about the potential cost to both the refugee and you of any misunderstandings. With a capable, professional interpreter in place, one meeting will be worth five meetings without interpreters. If you are a 'worthy cause', you might find even professional interpreters will waive their fee once or twice, but they do have to eat, so please don't ask too much of them.

Essential principles and good practice for community interpreters

The most important relationship in community interpreting is between the service provider and the service user – the 'community' interpreter's role is to facilitate communication and understanding between them.

There are fundamental principles community interpreters have to follow:

- Confidential – not secret.

- Always neutral, never take sides, never give advice, make no comment, have no influence.

- Be accurate, but interpret the meaning of what they say, not only the words.

- If in doubt, or the speaker is vague, ask for clarification. If they say things you don't understand, ask for explanation. If they speak too quietly, in unfinished sentences or for too long, interrupt politely and ask for clarity and time to interpret. If you have to interrupt or ask one party a question, make sure the other knows what you are doing.

- Be very clear about your role; clarify your role and principles to both parties before you start.

Normal practice consists of:

- Consecutive interpreting: The speaker stops after each sentence for the interpreter to interpret. Best in face-to-face encounters.

- Simultaneous interpreting: Interpreting into the other language at the same time as the first person speaks, without a break. Like TV voiceovers.

Interpreting qualifications. Profession community interpreters should have at least a Level 3 interpreting qualification (equivalent to A-Level standard but not an A Level). Ideally, they should have 30–50+ hours' experience and a DBS check.

Thank you to Oleg, Khalida, Ayo, Renu, Ayman.

Learning English to close the gap
Confidence to have a go

You can do a lot to help people gain the confidence to speak and improve their communication in English. There is the hope your refugee clients will gain confidence from their engagement with you. Most kinds of interaction with English speakers will help, so social, art and sports events where only English is spoken, visiting other organisations, participating in meetings or volunteering opportunities of almost any kind are all valuable.

Regular English groups

Chapter 5 talked about how to make regular group activities, such as English groups, work. Chapter 10 also looks at non-formal learning opportunities. Community or 'grass roots' English groups, conversation cafés, 'Speaking with Confidence' sessions add up to an informal approach that is neither coffee morning nor college course, but a ladder between them. They help many people gain confidence in their ability to speak and learn, as long as the group leaders take the role seriously and prepare well.

Community or 'grass roots' English emphasises people feeling more confident to speak English in daily life. They aren't usually formally structured or like an assessed or college ESOL course, and most groups strongly emphasise speaking over writing. They often have a social element, and might be flexible around babies and children, although that doesn't suit people who want to push on fast.

They can also help with more peripheral but important skills of punctuality, study skills, group and pair work, using IT. If the refugee is to go on to success in formal English courses and classes – at college, for example – they will need all this.

The model that follows is just one of dozens of community English models and approaches.

A 'grass roots' model for volunteer-led English group sessions

Thank you to REAP for permission to include the GREG model (REAP.org.uk).

This model, called Grass Roots English Groups, or 'GREG', works well for group leaders who are volunteers, backed up by a more formal organisation supporting them. It is designed to help people who have little experience of planning and teaching to deliver sessions that refugees (and other migrants) find valuable. It is only a suggested starting point to help you get going and very quickly you will develop your own approach and content to fit your group and resources.

The GREG model emphasises speaking and confidence to speak through a mix of activities including plenty of interaction. A good session should also include some work on:

- reading and writing

- numbers in English – for example, writing 1 and 7 in English format, saying 3.15pm and 3.50pm clearly

- local orientation, news, opportunities, contacts and visits

- practical vocabulary that adults will use in daily life (clinic and appointment, rather than zoo and zebra)

- helping people to 'progress' to future formal English courses at college.

It is best to design group activities on the basis of a full 10–13-week term in line with schools, including:

- weekly sessions

- two-hour sessions which can have a break

- 9.30–11.30 or 1.00–3.00 slots, which are often good times to fit around school hours

- adults with basic and beginner English (pre-entry, Entry 1–3), usually very mixed.

A basic term plan of 10–13 weeks includes:

- Group and session leader volunteers meeting to plan the term, what to include, who will do what and when. Start preparing a term plan and all session plans for the term, and handouts in group folders.

- 1–2 welcome and introduction sessions: new arrivals, welcomes, getting to know people and their standards, with time to help people who are too advanced to find something right for them. Perhaps 'Bring a Friend'.

- 6–8 sessions with lots of speaking and listening, and some reading/writing and other knowledge and skills, mixed in with...

- 1–2 sessions with visits, speakers, special themes (e.g. Eid, winter health).

- A session break at school half-term – although it is good to avoid this if possible.

- 1–2 outside events not in group time when people arrange to meet up somewhere local (e.g. college open day, visit to Citizens Advice office, a visit to another group).

- 1 final session with some kind of performance or party – invite guests! Give certificates.

To get started, try one term of two-hour sessions, each based on these sections:

1. Hello (20 minutes). Sign in, name badges, paperwork, homework, welcome/introduction phrases, ice-breakers, news.

2. Drills and Chains* (20 minutes). Check understanding, practise (mostly verbs and tenses) in full sentences as whole group then pair work and feedback.

3. Vocabulary work* and/or number work (10 minutes). They build up a glossary over time.

4. Three Quick Things (5 minutes) – for example, write out five postcodes, practice 'rrrr', find Hull on a map.

5. Practical English for Daily Life* (40 minutes). Ideally one theme with three to four activities – for example, Q&A phrases, role play, writing letters, reading, numbers, etc.

6. Poems and Songs* (10 minutes). Accent, flow, stress and love of English. Perform at end of term.

7. Finish and Farewell Recap. Homework – five words from the session. Praise, targets. Farewell phrase.

* Repeat and develop each theme and activities over two to three weeks.

Allow at least half an hour afterwards for individuals and holistic/case work.

Hints for groups with very basic beginners

- Don't leave very basic learners out. They might not even be able to say hello or write their name, but exposure to English, especially through interaction, will help them. Just make sure they feel welcome and that they matter. Make sure every session has lots of repeats and practice – good for everyone.

- Concentrate on getting basic beginners to speak, even if it's just words or half sentences. Social interaction (1. Hello and 7. Finish and Farewell) is good for this and quickly builds confidence to have a go. Also 6. Poems and Songs, which involves learning poems by heart and performing in front of an audience.

- Even if basic beginners don't understand the meaning of a sentence, encourage them to say the whole sentence loudly and clearly, then work on understanding again. This means 2. Drills and Chains and 3. Vocabulary can still work very well for basics even if the others in the group are more advanced.

- If you have several very basic beginners, try to have extra helpers or volunteers to work directly with them. For 5. Practical English it might be best to have simpler activities and material for them on the same theme, in a side group if you have enough volunteers to do this.

- Basic beginners often hardly write or write very slowly. Put 90% of your effort into speaking; writing can come later. For the glossary, you might need to write the words for them to take home.

Hints during the session

- Always do your speaking and listening first and don't start writing until later on. If you write things down too soon, people concentrate on copying and not on speaking and learning.

- Everyone needs lots and lots of practice – better one thing ten times than ten things once each, but put it in context and check understanding.

- Your participants are *not* children – use useful words, examples and themes (e.g. money, family, appointments), not things designed for children (e.g. discos and zoo animals). Give them responsibilities – they can collect money, do the attendance sheet, etc. (see Long Box 5.2, CS/5).

- Make sure everyone is involved and learning or they won't come back next week. Treat everyone as your equal. Don't let anyone dominate or talk over other participants, including volunteers.

Thank you to Ayo, Chhinder, Fatme, Ivone, Jamila, Jasmin, Kashmira, Marcin, Mari, Marimar, Poornima, Priya, Rachaporn, Rekha, Renu, Sharon, Stacey.

CHAPTER 7

Other Organisations, Networking and Advocating for Refugees

Introduction

The following chapters (8–11) will be centred around the entitlements and organisations that refugees *should* be able to access for support. 'Should' is not the same as 'can'. Being entitled is one thing; accessing what you are entitled to is another. Where Chapter 5 was about refugees engaging with organisations generally, and your organisation in particular, this chapter is about *you* having to engage with *other* organisations in order to support refugees properly.

Part of the reason this book exists is because so many refugee specialist bodies, resources and structures have been lost over the past decade that people who are specialists in their own, non-refugee fields are having to expand their specialisms and work with refugees directly. You need to be fairly aware and well informed to do the right thing by refugees.[1] But you probably can't know everything you need to know. Your best strategy is to know who knows already and where to find out what you need to know, when you need to know it.

> Know who knows already and where to find out what you need to know, when you need to know it.

The importance of networking

The key is networking – *forming direct contacts and getting to know people*. Google and directories simply don't give you what direct contact gives you. Good-quality networking means you get access to a wide range of good-quality information, advice and sources of help that other people don't know exists. You will do well if you can build connections by phone, email and social media, and sometimes this is the only option.

---

1   Remember, no matter how well informed you are, if you aren't licensed to give immigration advice, you must not do so – see Box 3.3).

But it is often direct, face-to-face interaction with people in the know that builds the most meaningful connections, even if subsequent contact is all done at distance. Nothing can compare with personal interaction if you want to find out what is really going on in your local area or region. Who are the 'friends within the system'? Whom do you trust and who should you not waste your breath on? This feels quite sociable, but it is work: people need to remember you too, trust you and respect you – or they won't return your phone calls. Mutual trust and respect can evolve into reciprocal support and real collaboration (Box 7.1).

Box 7.1 Appreciate and reciprocate

Please consider how a specialist refugee organisation feels when lots of different people who need advice and favours keep ringing up and demanding help, and then ring off – surely it has happened to you too. Check online and especially their website first and see what you can find out for yourself. Consider their capacity, what they invested to get that information, how they value their contacts and don't want you to mess them up. Appreciate the individual's time and consideration; they may have three people standing behind their shoulder waiting to talk to them while they talk to you. Don't ring at 5pm. Ask the person's name.

Give them a chance to gain something – for example, to tell you about an event they have coming up. Offer to send out their leaflets to your mailing list. Reciprocate: 'If I can ever offer ideas about children's health…' Send a thank-you. Send a nice quote they can use in a funders' report: 'It really helped and I was able to change what we do because of your advice. PS. You can quote me.'

Invest some time. Your time at any event or meeting is an investment – think of your time costing your organisation about £200/day (even if you aren't paid half that!). Don't just turn up and take part; double your winnings by actively seeking new contacts who have real potential to help you. Check the attendance list when you arrive, and make sure you are in time to hear the initial introductions so you can identify four to five people you want to talk to. Make sure you talk to them directly, not just in a group; check their role, check their attitude; discuss an issue of mutual concern (not the quality of the lunch). Get *their* contact card/leaflet with a direct email address (they will lose yours) (see Box 7.2 for where to start).

Box 7.2 Ideas for where to network

- Events: Go to Refugee Week/multicultural events, the AGM of any local refugee organisation or refugee project; International Women's Day or Holocaust Memorial events; BME Health Forum; White Ribbon Day events. Look out for what's on in the next town or city.

- Other people's meetings: If there are no meetings specifically about refugees, ask other meetings to add 'refugee mapping' as an item to the agenda and ask to share contacts to help your support to refugees. Try inter-faith groups, homelessness networks, advice networks and food bank meetings; join local mental health networks (e.g. Thrive), or ask to visit a health visitors' forum. More controversial are meetings around the 'Prevent Agenda' and offshoots. Go to local authority meetings such as Stronger Communities, Women in the Community. There are still BME, women's, disability, older age and other equality fora in some regions (e.g. West Midlands).

- Or you could set something up especially (see Box 7.3 for methods to help facilitate networking). Your AGM could take 'refuge' as a theme.

Follow up with an email within two days while you are still 'Sarah from...' and before you become 'you know, the one who...' – 'It was good to meet you. Here's that link I mentioned and please send me that report you wrote.' Be organised – add them to your database and circulation lists. Two good new contacts (about £50 each) isn't a bad afternoon's work.

Your networking doesn't only mean finding out where the refugee specialists are. You will find it necessary to connect with a combination of specialists in other fields (e.g. mental health, family law) even if you haven't done so before. You might find you are the one to bring people together (Box 7.3).

Box 7.3 Methods to facilitate networking

If you run an event with a refugee or migrant and refugee theme, there are certain participatory methods that will help. Ask for information about organisation/project/role and involvement with refugees as part of the process for registration; collate and make available on the day. Give out a full attendance list showing people's organisation to every participant and have name badges that clearly show their organisation. Use an arrival questionnaire for people to fill in while they wait for the event to start, asking questions like 'What organisations would you like to meet?', 'Can you recommend any organisations?', etc. Always have enough time for names and introductions, ideally with a question – for example, 'How many refugees contacted you last year?' Use methods like 'Find someone who...' and other ice-breakers, line-up, wheel activities and 'speed dating' methods where everyone talks to everyone for two minutes – very noisy!

Who is out there? If you are new in post or are feeling under pressure to develop your networks because you unexpectedly find yourself working with refugees, there are certain bodies or groups of bodies where you should be able to find useful contacts. This quick list gives an overview and more details are in Appendix A.

Local statutory and democratic bodies

- Local authority/council teams: housing and homelessness; social work – vulnerable adults, looked after children (LAC), domestic violence/violence against women and girls (VAWG); public health; other council teams –stronger/safer/cohesive communities, integration.

- Council services: libraries, children's and Sure Start centres, primary schools.

- NHS bodies: Clinical Commissioning Group (CCG); engagement and equality team; mental health; CSE (Child Sexual Exploitation/FGM/safeguarding nursing lead. Providers: community health – midwifery, health visitors, immunisation.

- Local MP, Assembly members, metropolitan authorities/mayor's teams for integration, equality, hate-crime, VAWG. Local councillors, district councillors.

In local areas: voluntary/community/faith

- Refugees' own community organisations (RCOs), Refugee Support, Refugees Welcome, City of Sanctuary, Student STAR, food banks.

- Citizens Advice (CAB), community law centres, advice services.

- Colleges: English and ESOL; employment teams.

- Equality bodies: women's centres, disability groups, mental health (e.g. local Mind), faith and inter-faith networks.

- Council/association/alliances of voluntary services where they still exist.

- Activist bodies: unions, campaign groups such as Amnesty International.

- Local businesses.

Regional and national specialists

- Refugee specialists: Refugee Council, Refugee Action, Freedom from Torture, Asylum Support Appeals Project (ASAP).

- Related: JCORE, British Institute of Human Rights (BIHR), Maternity Alliance.

- Federations: Law Centres Federation, Citizens Advice, Mind, Age UK, Children's Society.

- Smaller organisations with national significance: Bail for Immigration Detainees (BIDS), Yarl's Wood Befrienders, etc.

- Online networks: ASAN, Frontline, Refugee Support. Email for an invitation to join.

- Think tanks, policy organisations and universities: Runnymede, Rowntree, British Futures, Universities of Manchester, Birmingham, Oxford (Queen Elizabeth House), South Bank.

Referral and the 'One plus One' principle

The advantages of good referral are that you are brokering an arrangement that gives the refugee expert support and a range of inputs and options that is broader than you could offer. They gain experience of different organisations and a wider knowledge of what is available which boosts their means to engage in future.

You could just signpost someone by handing them a list or a name and wish them luck on their way. Or you might pass over all future responsibility for their support to another person or organisation. But the *best* referral respects your existing relationship with a refugee and all the work they have put into engaging with you, while expanding that relationship to include other useful parties.

When you refer someone to another organisation, you put them into a new relationship with a new organisation, and they have to make a success of it. To be sure you are taking the right approach, you need to have a realistic awareness of the refugee's own motives, means and agency at that moment to be sure they can make the most of the expertise and service you are connecting them to. You might consider accompanying your member or client initially, or facilitating access at the gate, queue, encounter in other ways. You can try to keep in touch with the refugee and/or the other professional to see how it's going, bearing in mind that confidentiality might limit what they can tell you.

A *bad referral* can do real damage, not least to your own relationship with the person you have been trying to support. Referral multiplies the cooks who are stirring the broth, and the number of faces and forms, competing suggestions and stakeholders. It can easily get confusing. Your refugee referee will be expending time and energy coping with multiple relationships. It might even be that the other organisation lets them down. Or maybe their expectations are too high. Disappointment can dampen people's enthusiasm to engage with formal organisations, not least yours.

It is about finding the *right body*. Your sense of the real quality and capacity of the organisation and even the individual professional you are referring them to is one issue. Simply finding the right expertise is another. Look at the issue they are facing first, and the fact they are a refugee second, if at all – remember, someone with toothache just needs a dentist.

It is not acceptable to deflect someone to a 'refugee' body simply because the person presenting is a refugee (see Box 1.1). Good referral adopts the 'One plus One' principle (WRC/REAP 2011) – in which any referral to a specialist refugee organisation or service is matched by at least one other referral to a service that has other relevant expertise but no special knowledge about refugees (Box 7.4).

For example, you would refer a female Iranian refugee who needs advice on housing to a housing advice service. You might also put her in touch with an Iranian women's association, but if so, you should make the extra effort to help her access another women's support organisation that has no refugee or ethnic focus.

A refugee male with a disability who wants to get some training for work may gain from being referred to a refugee community organisation that runs training, at the same time as a disability rights group that can explain his employment rights as a disabled person. But what he really wants is to be done with all those extra gates and queues and just get on to a good course from a high-quality training body that will respond to his needs as a unique individual, so that he can get on with building his future. If there isn't one, then the refugee organisation and the rights group might just have to do for now.

Box 7.4 **The 'One plus One' principle**

Each time you refer a refugee to a refugee specialist, project or group, you also refer her/him to at least one other non-refugee specialist, project or group.

Tackling third parties for your refugee clients – advocacy, complaints and influence

When your member or refugee client – let's call her Burtilla – is struggling with access to a service, you may be able to help the relationship along by helping *both* parties. Perhaps she has been turned away incorrectly at the gate or she is getting slow and poor service. The other organisation or individual staff member might be supportive but working within constraints. Or Burtilla may be meeting misinformation, denial and hostility. Start softly, with a gentle but firm 'nudge', although you might need to progress to a 'poke' and even a 'slap' (Box 7.6).

Advocacy

Don't take over. This isn't your problem; it's hers. Burtilla might not be keen on you getting involved and you must respect her wishes (although some people would prefer it if you did take over). You want her relationship with that organisation to work; you don't want to make it your relationship. Think of your role as improving the space within which this person is engaging the other body. Your aim is to clear away confusion and help to clarify what is expected of both parties. If you do this, your refugee client has a better chance of sorting out the relationship herself or himself.

To advocate in this situation, you must make sure the case is clear-cut. Check Burtilla's actual needs and what she hopes to achieve and whether she is realistic. Check entitlements carefully from authoritative sources (Appendix A). Get credible backup materials – for example, Freedom from Torture or ASAP briefings. Check she has the right evidence and documentation. Provide a credible, summary letter clearly laying out the facts and your sources (Box 7.5).

Ensure your client knows what the minimum is that the organisation has to comply with, and do not give optimistic reassurance that she will get more than that. Then Burtilla can try again.

Box 7.5 Letters of support and references – credible and effective

You will be asked or will decide to write many letters on behalf of refugees – supportive letters, informative and advocacy letters, personal and job references. Your credibility is as important as the message you are trying to get across.

- Look professional. Reply quickly, use letterhead, formal layout and correct grammar – also in emails and include an email 'signature'. Include a few words about your organisation and, if a charity, include the registration number. Include direct phone and email. Keep to one side of A4.

- Clarify your role and profession, qualifications; indicate your experience and expertise.

- Include relevant reference numbers and personal details from the refugee, which might include their Home Office asylum number, for example, but only include the details that are needed. Add how long you have known them and in what capacity and that you have their permission to write.

- Deal with one issue in one letter.

- Problem? State the situation, state what is wrong, what it should be, back up with evidence and preferably quotes from their organisation's own documentation on standards. State what you want them to do to put it right, by when.

- Reference? Think about what they want to know, be accurate on what you actually know, give reassurance rather than sales talk, don't emphasise friendship or friendliness – it might make you look less trustworthy.

- Don't plead.

- Follow up.

If Burtilla is still not successful, your next tactic is probably to accompany her to a face-to-face encounter, or ring, email or write on her behalf. Some organisations will want to see written and signed consent to speak on someone's behalf. (Interpreters might also need signed consent from the client.) Even though you are now acting directly and you are there to protect your refugee client's interests, your objective is still simply to facilitate the relationship between the two parties, by bringing clarity and perhaps some reassurance.

Make sure you fully understand the organisation's position and how staff are justifying that position – it may be logical or consistent with the information they have, but you have *better* information. Identify the points where there are inconsistencies (e.g. in their guidance regarding immigration status or suitable identity documents) or there are commitments or obligations outside normal practice that they aren't aware of (e.g. to register a patient even if they don't have proof of address). Show them the authoritative information you have gathered.

You may need assertiveness methods. You may need to involve a manager who has a broader overview and greater discretion to overrule the staff handbook.

Complaints

If this level of facilitative advocacy does not succeed, you need to change mode. Go from working alongside both parties to standing beside your client as you face the organisation together. In other words, you take this up a level, and now move to a potentially confrontational position to support your client.

This change in the nature of the relationship can easily provoke defensiveness, a closing of ranks and a search for ways in which you or your refugee client can be shown to be at fault. Make it clear that although you are taking her side, you are looking for resolution, not escalation. So it is usually best to start off calm, positive and polite – but calmly and positively and politely determined – rather than to bluster and demand.

Your next tactic is probably to let staff know that if there isn't a satisfactory resolution, you might, with regret, make a formal complaint.

- Assume it will go well. Act quickly, but only if you and your client both feel calm and have all the material you need.

- Keep a record of all communications with all relevant parties (date, name, role, notes of discussion, decisions, deadlines). Keep copies of everything, in one place, in order.

- Closely read the organisation's own policies such as a customer service charter, equality policy or complaints policy.

- If you have a 'friend within' the organisation, ask them *off the record* (phone or face to face, not by email!) if there is any context you need to know. Or you can contact someone more senior by phone or email to 'ask for advice'.

- Following their complaints policy, inform them, whether in writing, phone or face to face, that you are not satisfied and your concerns mean you are considering making a complaint. Explain what you hope will happen and by when. Provide copies of the materials from your authoritative source, having highlighted the key points.

- If this still doesn't work, help your refugee client to put in a written complaint following the organisation's complaints procedure to the letter. It should be in her/his own words. Add a letter which explains your role and your concerns as advocate. Keep copies.

- Follow up within a couple of days, to ask when you might hear something. If their eventual response is still not satisfactory, their complaints process should include details on how to appeal, and is likely to have a time limit.

At some point Burtilla and you have to decide whether to take it up a level or to give up. Your client will probably ask your view on this. If they don't want to go further, you must respect that. You are not obliged to help them take it further if you don't consider it reasonable. Either way, talk it through thoroughly to reduce the risk that it will damage your working relationship.

Formal complaint. If your refugee client isn't satisfied, follow the formal complaints process to the next step, which is probably an appeal to the next level up. You can write to the chief executive or even directors/governing board members/trustees. You may be able to write a 'Question from the Public' to a board meeting (e.g. CCGs/statutory bodies).

Third parties. When you get stuck, third parties might advise or advocate for your refugee client. Local advice bodies, CAB and law centres can advise. For NHS bodies, try PALS and Healthwatch, but especially Doctors of the World for asylum seekers, refused asylum seekers and refugees (see Chapter 9). Nationally, the Public Law Project might be interested in cases, especially if there is potential to make case law.

Newspapers. Local newspapers often like a personal story especially with a nice photo. But think carefully. What if they turn the story round? How sympathetic are most newspapers, especially local papers, to refugees?

Freedom of Information. If it is a state/statutory body and you need information about how it runs, budgets, waiting lists, guidance on prioritising and so on for your case, you can put in a Freedom of Information request. (For practical details, visit www.gov.uk.) To get the results you want, get some advice first; ACAS also has guidance.

Regulators. If you have a genuine concern about a failure of a legal duty such as safeguarding, misuse of data, or about misuse of public resources, institutional discrimination, etc., you can contact the relevant ombudsman (e.g. Ofsted, Care Quality Commission, Charity Commission), but get advice first. This is a big step – not the way to tackle a complaint about service delivery or a poorly thought-through policy.

Note that there are time limits on many complaints, appeals and judicial review processes – sometimes a matter of days. First try to resolve the problem, but quickly, and if you think it needs higher-level action, act quickly.

Box 7.6 | **'Nudge, poke, slap' – some tactics for practice and policy changes**

Nudge

- 'We would love you to talk to our steering group/give an interview for our newsletter about refugees' entitlements and access to your services. Can you come next month?'

- 'Here you are, I've brought you a flier from the EHRC about rights and eligibility. I hope it's helpful.'

- 'I always find working with your team very productive, but I have to have a bit of a grumble…'

Poke

- 'When I asked Doctors of the World about this yesterday…'

- 'Dear Head of Services, cc. Chair, I would appreciate your view on…'

- 'Sadly, I don't feel this is satisfactory and I am considering putting in a formal complaint.'

Slap

- 'Dear… With regret, my client wishes to make a formal complaint.'

- 'As, unfortunately, we have not been able to resolve this issue, if I have not had a more satisfactory response by the end of the day on Friday, I will be contacting the ombudsman, Ofsted, etc.'

Influencing practice and policy

In the long run, better opportunities and better access for refugees come from better policies and practice. You *can* influence other organisations, although it isn't guaranteed.

Changing the views of an individual staff member is probably more effective than filling in any number of surveys, as one person can be a strong influence on others in their organisation. There is an element of 'reflexivity' in any interaction – in other words, any new experience changes all the parties involved. Anyone who meets face to face with a woman or a man who has come all the way to the UK to escape danger and persecution will tend to become more aware of refugees. Maybe you can set up an opportunity for face-to-face interaction outside the staff member's normal working environment – an invitation to present certificates at a training day, for example. Heightened awareness now often means a person rethinking and changing what they do further down the line. Could this person become one of your good networking links? Even a 'friend within'?

Organisations often set up channels and activities exactly for your input, including input to policy and planning reviews. You can use feedback and suggestion boxes, of course, answer evaluation questionnaires, surveys, needs assessments, attend focus groups and consultations. Whether this makes any actual difference is outside your control. But most organisations do struggle to get decent input to evaluations and consultations; a concerted input by you and ideally also from refugees whom you are supporting could work.

If you feel there is a good chance of bringing about change, make a definite decision about whether to go for it or not. If you decide to lobby, select your issue wisely and invest real commitment and energy in it. A quick response dashed off between phone calls gives their consultation credibility but probably won't lever the changes you want.

Build a good case and provide credible evidence and solutions that they could almost 'copy and paste' directly into their policy and planning documentation. Whether you are replying to a survey, attending a public event or putting in an independent submission:

- establish your/your organisation's credibility – local expertise, history and track record, refugee involvement, number of refugee and other clients, quality and achievements (quantified if possible – otherwise, cases)

- it helps if you have respectable funders, good governance and a positive relationship with the body you are lobbying

- provide one or more detailed, relevant case study from actual work (anonymised)

- add data, views and quotes you have collected from refugee members or clients specifically for this case

- give a selection of solid, relevant statistics backed up with links to national research

- where possible, link your request for change to the organisation's constitution and strategic plans/mission statement, and also make the links to relevant legislation clear, which they can quote.

Decisions are often made by committees. If you can't manage the time to attend the right meetings, see if you can find a supportive voice who is there already and is sympathetic to the changes you want, and provide her/him with the data, case studies and so forth.

Sometimes, when reason and due process aren't working, you have to have a row (Box 7.7)

Box 7.7 '**Bang on the desk' tactics**

You might be the kind of person who is comfortable with good old 'bang on the desk' tactics, whether simply to ask, 'What about refugees?' or to lobby for a specific change: For example:

- Harass – turn up for everything, ideally accompanying a refugee member/client.

- Bombard – write letters (better than emails) to different layers in the organisation, asking for a response; get individual refugees and/or other members to write.

- 'Chain yourself to the railings' – simply don't take no for an answer; ask repeatedly for the same thing, asking what action has been taken since the last time you turned up.

- 'Bring in the cavalry' – your Chair writes to their Chair; involve your local councillors, MP, AM, MEP.

- Build alliances – try to persuade other local organisations round to your point of view so they will send the same message.

- 'Bus people in' – make sure several sympathetic members or friends of your organisation attend any open or public meetings; brief them first.

- But don't bluff – it is likely you will meet a counter-offensive and be invited to meet or asked to provide written recommendations, data and evidence, recruit people to respond to consultations, attend focus groups, sit on committees and other contributions that will demand your time – be ready to go and make a constructive input.

The great opportunity – the Public Sector Equality Duty

The Public Sector Equality Duty (PSED) really is too good to waste. It is discussed in some detail in Chapter 4, as an asset for the hands-on worker. Chapter 4 describes concepts and principles, protected characteristics, scope for positive action, and documents and processes that public authorities must fulfil under the PSED. It is designed to stop groups such as refugees getting pushed further and further behind in society. The PSED is there to make sure public authority staff think about disadvantaged groups such as refugees when they make decisions, design, deliver or commission other organisations to deliver services and activities.

This section revisits the documents and processes of the PSED and how they give you a chance to advocate for special attention to refugees in your area. These processes give you leverage.[2]

Public authorities must review the documents on this list at regular points. There should be an element of public consultation and public scrutiny, meaning there can be several opportunities to ask questions throughout a year, and to present evidence and arguments. Feed in questions and voices from refugees, send local data and add relevant reports from the Refugee Council, Women's Asylum Charter, King's Fund, Maternity Alliance. Hint: Resend the team doing the review a full range of evidence each time a review is done, as it is never exactly the same team and they will not remember or know about what you sent last time.

The relevant PSED documents should be in the public domain – they are normally on organisations' websites. Read them closely with a critical eye. You can quote them and refer to them when you argue for certain projects or challenge decisions.

There are strong opportunities where the Equality Evidence Review is the starting point and justification for Equality Objectives, annual Evidence Reviews or Reports and Equality Impact Assessments (each one is described in Chapter 4).

For greatest success, you will probably have to challenge the authority to increase the detail in its data, so that it makes refugees visible. It won't be enough if they look at the nine protected characteristics one by one (Box 4.4). You need them to identify sub-groups within protected groups – for example, within race, recognise certain nationalities that are likely to be refugees (e.g. Afghan):

e.g. race = ethnic minority – Asian – Afghan

...or identified a sub-group by national status:

e.g. race = not British/migrant – refugee.

Equality Objectives (based on Equality Evidence) are the five or ten priority areas public authorities have committed to tackling over two to three years. They create space and a framework for decisions and actions. Try to get refugees listed. But if you can't get refugees listed as a distinct group, make the case that they face multiple disadvantages as a sub-group of a group that is listed in the Objectives.

For example, if there is an objective to improve support to people with mental health difficulties, refugees have very high rates of mental health disability.

---

2   The Equality and Diversity Forum (EDF), which is a national network, Race on the Agenda (RoTA), a national race equality organisation, and also the Equality and Human Rights Commission (EHRC) have guidance, toolkits and training to support PSED lobbying.

If young mothers are a priority group and a special service is being commissioned to support them, many young refugee mothers will have additional needs, related to their experiences of flight and refuge.

e.g. sex = woman **+** age = young **+** maternity = with baby under six months

+ race = ethnic minority – Asian – Afghan **+** migrant (refugee)

+ disability = mental health

Equality Objectives create the space for action, but you will still need to push staff a bit to remember refugees when they design and fund services.

Equality Impact Assessments (EIA) with this kind of detail are of real value. Where the assessment shows some groups might not get the same full benefit (language 'barrier') or have additional needs (mental health and post-traumatic stress disorder), the EIA should trigger mitigating actions. Afghan mothers might need interpreters and specialist attention to mental health.

If you can feed into an EIA consultation and get your comments recorded, you can come back in a year and ask the authority what impact the service had on refugee mothers compared with other mothers. Did their mitigating actions work? Were there equal outcomes? Is their equality characteristic monitoring up to scratch? Does it make refugees visible? (See Box 4.11.) And if you have real-life real-time evidence from refugees that a new or changed service isn't working for them, the fact that you raise a flag at the original EIA gives you a strong footing to push for improvements.

Box 7.8 | **Ideas for adjustments and positive/ mitigating activities to request**

For example, you might lobby for:

- budget and proper standards for interpreters, letters in plain English, translated letters and information

- additional time in appointments to explain processes and give full information

- staff to have permission and resources to provide more holistic casework-style support

- training staff properly about refugees' documentation and entitlements so they don't discriminate, especially at the gate

- the organisation and staff to form links and communicate/collaborate with refugee support networks and have access to/be able to buy in relevant expertise

- scope for child care, transport costs, fee waivers and other cash-savers for refugee service users

- staff to run a special focus group with refugees as part of an Equality Impact Assessment review

- waiving a requirement – for example, two years' 'ordinary residence' – to be eligible for a service

- access to post-traumatic stress disorder (PTSD) counselling, even if it involves paying travel costs

- placement opportunities for young refugees who have no experience of British organisational culture.

Summary

Advocacy and lobbying is not only for refugee specialists. It is about children specialists with an expanding professional knowledge lobbying for refugee children as one of the special groups within their remit, disability groups to voice and argue for attention to disabled refugees, and so forth.

The practical focus of this book means we brush past wider issues about lobbying on British or international policy. It doesn't cover British democratic institutions, where helping refugees to understanding party politics, voting or standing for election would help them have a voice.[3]

And there is, regretfully, no space for the influential power of the arts, and, of course, comedy and satire in public awareness-raising. But that doesn't stop you enjoying yourself on YouTube/iPlayer with Alexi Sayle, Omid Djalili, Shappi Khorsandi; or satirists in print such as Steve Bell, the late great Ronald Searle, even Michael Bond and Paddington. There are more ideas in the footnotes.[4]

After this point Chapters 8 to 11 are about practical services and support that refugees and families should be able to depend on as they tackle daily life. You will be needed.

---

3   Operation Black Vote and parliamentary schemes exist to improve ethnic minority engagement in democratic processes.

4   The arts and creative expression are part of full and fulfilling lives. If you are interested in engaging refugees in art for art's sake – for creative expression and performance or aesthetic reasons rather than just functional wellbeing – look up groups such as Writers in Exile and engagement work by the British Museum. There are many highly skilled performers and teachers among refugees, whom you can meet performing at festivals and often contributing to Refugee Week events. No doubt they would be pleased to be offered a performance fee to add some zing to your AGM.

Spirituality is not my field, but St Ethelburga's in London does some very interesting work, and who could ignore the humanity of the late Rabbi Lionel Blue in the Radio 4 backlists?

If you are looking for sources for awareness-raising, there are powerful collections and archives held by the Imperial War Museum and Jewish Museum, some of which are available online. For school-age citizens, look up Benjamin Zephaniah's *Refugee Boy*, and Mary Hoffman's *The Colour of Home*.

Introduction to Practical
Chapters 8, 9, 10 and 11

Chapters 8 to 11 look at what you can do practically, by theme. Broadly speaking, these practical chapters go from supporting people to survive and recover to helping them build a future:

- Chapter 8: basic needs such as shelter, food and goods, money for essentials

- Chapter 9: physical and mental and emotional health and wellbeing and disability

- Chapter 10: learning English, education, training and employment

- Chapter 11: refugee children and young people, including unaccompanied children.

It is likely that, at some point, someone you find yourself working with will hit a bad patch. It could escalate into crisis. They/you will need to act fast to avoid disaster. Most of the time, though, you will meet people who are coping with a situation that is generally poor – never enough money, stuck in overcrowded housing, vulnerable to sudden changes and so forth. They might also be in touch with you because you are a resource for their longer-term strategies to build a decent future.

The **first aim** of these chapters is to *alert you to issues* that come up regularly when you find yourself giving practical support to refugees (Box 1). Introductions outline why and how certain issues are more likely to affect refugees and some of the kinds of tangle that people are likely to ask you to help them get through.

Box 1	Summary – some consequences of having to leave and seek refuge (see Chapter 2)

Many factors that are related to people's need to escape persecution and search for refuge have consequences that complicate refugees' potential to manage with the resources they have and access the resources and services they need:

- mistrust of authority, reluctance to engage

- difficulty negotiating access to British organisations and institutions (see also Chapter 5)

- poverty, insecurity, vulnerability and crises

- impaired physical, mental or emotional health

- struggles with language, skills and accessing opportunities and work.

The **second aim** is helping people to *identify entitlements*. Each chapter gives information about rights and state entitlements. You will need an adequate understanding of different kinds of immigration status relating to refugees, and when and how immigration status matters, as outlined in Chapter 3. Throughout these chapters, 'refugee' continues to be used in the subjective, inclusive sense, and 'asylum seeker', 'Convention refugee', 'refugee with Leave' and so forth are used only when necessary to differentiate between people with different immigration status and therefore entitlements defined by the Home Office. You can refresh your memory of the differences via Box 3.11 and the Glossary.

Refugees' entitlements may not vary as much from British citizens' entitlements as you expect, and each chapter explains what kind of mainstream state benefits and services – housing, health services, education – refugees are entitled to on the same footing as any British person. Where information on mainstream benefits is the same as for any British person and widely available, this book simply gives pointers to where you can find that information.

Be clear and confident in your knowledge about rights and entitlements. This is valuable when staff in other organisations are unsure about what they should do, but you can insist with visible confidence that refugees *are* entitled to their services. You don't need – and realistically probably could not gain – all the expertise it would take to answer every question or help in every unique situation. Just be realistic about gaps in your knowledge and know when to look for more expertise.

The **third aim** is to help you find *relevant services and sources of expertise and support*. There are sections in Appendix A giving important sources of specialist backup – statutory and voluntary – relating to the subjects in these chapters. Key organisations relevant throughout the practical chapters include:

- Scottish, Welsh and London-based Refugee Council, British Red Cross, Asylum Support Appeals Project (ASAP)

- local Citizens Advice and remaining community law centres, libraries.

Specialist help is not always easy to source, especially locally. Remember the 'One plus One' principle (Box 7.4) and start with the person's needs; their immigration status comes second. People are often very well served by bodies outside the refugee sector and any organisation offering support to people in need should be equally effective in supporting refugees.

The specialist services noted are also sources you can turn to yourself for expert advice as you build up your own knowledge and professional networks. Do make the most of your chances to network, and network well beyond the refugee sector.

The **fourth aim** is to suggest *ways you can help refugees cope with and improve their situation.* You or your organisation might be in a position to provide resources directly. Or you might end up diverting a lot of your energy into advocating for people just so they can access what they should be getting anyway. Alternatively, you might feel your most valuable role is to help individuals take more control of their own situation, by helping them strengthen assets such as knowledge, skills and their own contacts (Box 2). Chapter 5 described approaches you can use to facilitate refugees' engagement with your own organisation. Chapter 7 suggested strategies and tactics for advocacy in relation to other organisations. The following chapters build on ideas and recommendations in those chapters and add examples on each theme.

Box 2 | **Means and 'assets' refugees need to engage with formal organisations (see Chapter 5)**

- money and time

- the means to stay in touch

- documents

- English language literacy and confidence to speak

- knowledge skills and cultural competence

- contacts and networks

- a sense of agency.

Refugees are active agents of their own survival, but a part of this picture is 'the kindness of strangers', the generous responses of individuals when they meet face to face with a refugee in need, offering shelter, essentials and humanity.[1] Such kindness, however, is essentially random and no refugee can rely on it. You – in your hybrid role that is part stranger and part professional – are a critical asset for a refugee who is trying to find meaningful reliable support.

Do familiarise yourself with the content and layout of these four practical chapters. Any of the practical issues outlined might arrive with the refugee who walks through your door on Monday. Boxes contain additional details on

---

1   The kindness of strangers was the theme for Holocaust Memorial Day in 2013 when people across the world recognised the individuals who hid and smuggled Jews out of Germany and gave them refuge, sometimes being murdered by the persecutors in revenge.

subjects you might need in specific situations. The Table of Contents and List of Boxes at the start of the book give you an overview and the Index in the back of the book is your best tool for searching out specific topics.

All facts and details are accurate going into 2018, but be aware that some things change fast; remember to check, compare and record the date of any facts or figures you find in your research, especially if you have found things on the internet.

CHAPTER 8

Roof, Food, Money and Essential Goods

Introduction

It could be me.

Any one of us can end up destitute and struggling to find the basic essentials for life – shelter, warmth, food, clothing, money, social interaction. Perhaps things were OK, but a set of problems has turned into a crisis because a housemate stole your money or you got bad advice. Something like losing a job or the end of a relationship can turn anybody's life into chaos.

There are many ways a refugee in Britain can end up on the edge of destitution. Many exiles are already impoverished and dependent on others, with compromised health and restrictions on their movements and actions. There are difficulties with the official support systems. They might be caught between stages in asylum or immigration processes, bounced between multiple agencies with no progress or stuck on waiting lists. Mental ill health is often a contributing factor when people lose the means for a secure, decent life.

Asylum seekers can get some state support, but there are gaps and cracks. This person might still be waiting for a first asylum support payment. That one didn't comply with her NASS contract and the support was cut off. Refused asylum seekers may have to survive without any government support.

Even refugees with Leave are vulnerable to destitution. When they first get their Leave to Remain, refugees are caught by the '28 day' rule – 28 days after getting Leave to Remain all NASS support stops. By this time the refugee is meant to have obtained a National Insurance (NI) number, found new accommodation and have successfully registered for and be receiving mainstream benefits. If a refugee fails to achieve this, they can end up with no support at all coming in until the paperwork is sorted out. There are active campaigns challenging this and maybe by the time you read this it has changed (Refugee Council 2014).

Destitution is not just about money.

First, it is a *chronic insecurity* about the basic necessities in life such as personal safety, a secure, warm place to sleep and live, decent food and clothing, positive social interaction.

Second, it is a *lack of control* and *inability to access* structures and institutions – the food is there, the work is there, but you can't get to it. You are dependent on what others decide to do. A life on the edge of destitution is chaotic, and people are unable to manage, predict, plan, invest for the future.

Third, it is a *lived experience*, a struggle to ensure physical safety and dreading theft, abuse and violence. This is constant anxiety about yourself and others you care about, not just now but into the future. Destitution is an experience of failure and rejection or blame by authoritative bodies. There is deteriorating health, resources, loneliness, negative self-identity, lost aspiration. Such feelings and experiences are bad for anyone, and for refugees they could echo earlier experiences.

Fourth, it is has *consequences*. How deep is the impact of destitution? How long will it be before someone overcomes the damage to their financial situation or mental and emotional wellbeing? Some of the more dangerous strategies people adopt to survive have consequences too – borrowing, begging, stealing, trading sex and other commodities. Even the fear of destitution can have a long shadow.

This chapter starts with supporting people to survive. But 'refuge' is about more than surviving. It is surely about facilitating people to re-establish a *decent* life for themselves and their families. However, at present, you may have to sort out daily essentials before you can start discussing the future.

This chapter focusses first on shelter and housing, then food, clothes and basic goods and consumables, including the money to get them. Some necessary terms, defined earlier in the book, are in the Glossary. Useful organisations and all sources of expert advice and support mentioned are given in Appendix A. As well as Refugee Council, Red Cross, Citizens Advice and law centres mentioned in the introduction to these practical chapters, ASAP and the NRPF Network are important sources of advice relating to all of this chapter.

Outline of support

Although you give advice on immigration cases if you aren't licensed, you can work with someone on their claim or appeals for support. You just need sufficient knowledge or online access to information and advice, plus determination. If it is about state support, you will probably do better if you coordinate with their solicitor. Individual and family cases for support can get very complicated, so at times both you and your 'client' must get expert backup. There can be tight timescales and they/you might need to move fast.

There is limited **government or state support** from public funds for refugees via the National Asylum Support Service (NASS) or mainstream benefits. It includes accommodation and money for some asylum seekers via NASS, and for refugees with Leave to Remain via mainstream state welfare benefits.

Refused asylum seekers might have No Recourse to Public Funds (NRPF), although if they are taking 'all reasonable steps to leave the country' or the Home Office agrees they can't leave, NASS may continue to provide accommodation and money. Don't forget the different support and entitlements flagged up in Chapter 3, for disabled people (details in Chapter 9) and children (Chapter 11).

Voluntary, community and faith organisations also provide basic essentials. A lot of what asylum seekers and refugees draw on is what exists to protect any homeless, destitute or near-destitute person – for example, winter night shelters and food banks. There are often shortages and other restrictions and conditions, especially when services rely on governmental funds (e.g. Housing Benefit, European Social Fund), but sometimes because of the organisation's own policies. Check *before* you refer – a person who is on the edge cannot afford to waste time and energy.

Shelter and housing

What scale are we talking about here? With approximately 26,500 new asylum seekers in 2017–2018, NASS accommodated a total of 39,000 people (including dependants) dispersed across the UK (Refugee Council 2018). They are often housed in economically depressed areas, with the largest numbers going to the North West, Yorkshire and the Humber and the West Midlands, where there is vacant and 'hard-to-let' housing. The asylum seekers who are not accommodated by NASS find their own housing.

Others are in temporary hostel-style accommodation referred to as 'initial accommodation' while they wait to be allocated housing. People may share same-sex rooms in a mixed-sex unit. Families stay together unless adults are detained.

Because it is rare for hands-on workers to meet them or help them directly while in detention, detention is not covered in any depth in this book. If you are interested in visiting and supporting people in detention and want to know more about detention, see Association of Visitors to Immigration Detainees (AVID) and Bail for Immigration Detainees (BID); also Yarl's Wood Befrienders, working with the women's removal centre in the Midlands.

Once people are granted Leave to Remain or refused asylum, they mostly leave NASS accommodation. We have no statistics on the housing people find when they get Leave to Remain, whether sharing, renting privately, council, social housing or even buying property. But a substantial proportion of the approximately 25,000 people per year who get Leave are probably moving into the private rental or social housing market.[1]

---

1   In Chapter 2 I commented on debates about whether refugees are reducing the amount of social or other housing for British nationals.

At least initially, people looking for their own housing will find it in poorer urban areas. Many will be staying with existing contacts, with shared facilities, whether with extended family or others. They are possibly involved in some domestic or economic arrangement such as housekeeping, child care or other labour or exchange. They may be sharing space or a 'home in multiple occupancy' (where a single property is broken up into units or has rooms added) or even so-called 'beds in shed'.

Entitlements are summarised in Box 8.4 and some examples of support with resources, access to and control of accommodation are in Box 8.5. Prime contacts on any accommodation matter are community law centres, Homeless Link and the Shelter Helpline for advice. Networking is essential in preventing homelessness and supporting accommodation (Box 8.1). Your local authority will have a housing department with homelessness teams who may have or give information or referral, but they are very limited in what they can do.

Box 8.1 | **Network, build and change structures – Case Studies A–C**

A REAP runs an annual 'Refugees – Home and Homelessness' half-day event with a format designed so that practitioners and managers who work with refugees and asylum seekers can do some intensive networking, share knowledge and make useful contacts. There are no speakers, but different methods are used to optimise networking – for example, 'spotlights' by participants, peer-led discussion workshops, a detailed list of participants with project information and follow-up email listings.

B Frontline Workers Network is a highly accessible free, national peer-network of hands-on practitioners in housing and homelessness and related fields such as mental health and substance use. It facilitates workers to share experiences, information and questions.

C NRPF Network serves local authority and non-local authority staff and provides guidance particularly relating to people with care needs who have NRPF.

To find and access accommodation – now, soon, later

So what issues might people bring to you for your help?

(A) I NEED ACCOMMODATION TONIGHT

Rarely, but sometimes, an individual or even a family will ask for your help because they need to *find accommodation tonight* (see Box 8.2). Individuals might be sleeping on the streets already, or a parent and child could be on the point of physical eviction, or leaving a dangerous situation. They haven't been sitting around passively up to this point – they will have been actively seeking out solutions, so find out if they already have contact with homelessness bodies.

They might be seeking your view as an alternative to other views they have already gathered, in the hope that you can give them better news. However, unless you can provide them directly with accommodation, they will probably do better at this critical moment to be listening to specialists who know the exact local options available to avoid sleeping on the streets.

Start by ringing the local authority as soon as possible for advice. You will need to know the person's immigration status. Even if the local authority cannot or will not help, they may have suggestions or contacts you can follow up.

You might find there is a local homelessness organisation that has access to a 'clearing'-type system to find the nearest shelter with space that night. Many overnight shelters are only open in midwinter. Many shelters and also women's refuges are funded via Housing Benefit and may not be able to accommodate asylum seekers and people with NRPF.

The person you are assisting will be expected to take up any options they still have – staying on in their previous accommodation, paying for a hotel – before any state or homelessness charity will house them. If they are running away from violence, it is in their interests to contact the police.

The local authority might give a person with Leave to Remain an appointment as soon as the next day to assess their case, but this might only mean they get a list of contacts. If the person has Leave to Remain, their situation is similar to any British resident. Broadly, single males are unlikely to get immediate help from most local authorities, although pregnant women or women escaping violence should get some help which might mean bed-and-breakfast or help to get space in a refuge if anything is available. The local authority has a legal duty to safeguard and protect children if the family is homeless (Chapter 10).

Some voluntary hosting organisations exist where people give asylum seekers or refugees a home in their own house for the night or for longer (e.g. Refugees at Home, Housing Justice). Most are set up for short- to mid-term stays. There are usually some screening processes such as any criminal record or references. If asked for a reference, you need to consider carefully if you really are in a position to give assurances to the potential host.

Box 8.2 Should we let them sleep in our side room tonight?

Giving a roof, even for a night, is, of course, of real, immediate value to someone who has nowhere. But be clear on what you expect of them and what they should expect of you.

How long can they stay? What about food and washing? Fire and hygiene? Smoking and rubbish? What about obligations to other users, safeguarding, security within the building, security from the outside? Who will be cleaning up if there is a mess?

What is your legal position? Will this be a problem with your current insurance, licence or landlord? Will you need extra insurance?

Prepare yourself for someone who is having a hard time. Be 'friendly but not a friend'. Consider what giving (and then possibly later refusing) direct support does to the nature of your and your organisation's relationship with the person involved. No one can stay living as a 'guest' for long.

What if others hear and ask for accommodation too? Can you help with a longer-term solution?

(B) I NEED ACCOMMODATION TOMORROW OR VERY SOON: ASYLUM SEEKERS AND REFUSED ASYLUM SEEKERS

If an asylum seeker asks for your assistance, they might not need accommodation tonight, but ask you to support them to find somewhere new or better to stay very soon.

This might be because they had their own accommodation but can't stay any longer because of poverty, worsening relationships or a risk such as violence. It may have been a temporary arrangement anyway, sofa-surfing or subletting from contacts. If they can no longer stay where they are, and can show they are destitute, they can apply (or reapply) for NASS accommodation, but there will be a wait.

Or they:

- are in NASS accommodation but their asylum application or appeal has been rejected, and they have 21 days to leave the property. They can ask to stay there if:

  - their solicitor is going to submit a new claim for asylum

  - they can show they are taking 'all reasonable steps' to leave the UK or

  - they can't return to their country of origin (see Chapter 3 and ASAP Factsheets)

- are being evicted from NASS accommodation because they are accused of being absent for extended periods, or subletting, or there are complaints about violence towards staff or other residents

- are finding the conditions utterly intolerable perhaps because of their own mental ill health, and have a strong case to move (e.g. rape survivors requiring single-sex accommodation, ground-floor accommodation for someone who has impaired mobility)

- or they are being placed in other accommodation but want to stay where they are (Box 8.3).

In many circumstances, they and you need to act fast. They get 21 or 28 days' notice to leave and then the landlord or landlord's agents can removed them, backed up by police. This is *different* to standard eviction processes for private tenants which you may be more familiar with and which can take months.

Box 8.3 **If they are being dispersed, or moved out of your area**

To resist the move, write to NASS immediately. Get other letters of support. Write to the refugee's MP.

If the move is unavoidable, you might be able to help them prepare for the move.

Talk about the new town; look at pictures and maps together. Search online for local organisations (sports, arts, cooking, refugee support or mental health groups – remember the 'One plus One' principle).

Ring around until you find a group that seems interested and friendly. Explain the situation, and pass the phone to your client so she or he can speak direct to someone in the new organisation and start to establish new contacts before getting there.

If they are learning English or studying, help them contact a college in the new area and try to arrange a transfer, instead of them having to start again. You may need to ring as an advocate to sort out an application.

Find out what the cheapest fare is from that place back to your area, and how long it takes, so they can see they won't be completely cut off.

(C) I NEED ACCOMMODATION TOMORROW OR VERY
SOON: REFUGEES WITH LEAVE TO REMAIN

Refugees with Leave could be asking for help with accommodation because they:

- have just received Leave to Remain and are now several days into the 28-day period and must leave NASS accommodation

- had their own accommodation but can't afford it for similar reasons to asylum seekers or

    - have rent arrears because their past and current circumstances mean they are in debt and have irregular income

    - face delays in benefit payments resulting in a risk of or notice of eviction

- are looking for something cheaper, better or more convenient

- hope to get social housing.

People with Leave to Remain in some dispersal areas might be able to stay in their NASS housing by arrangement with the local authority, paid for with Housing Benefit/Universal Credit. They can apply to the local authority for housing. They must show they are homeless, but not intentionally homeless, and that they have a 'local connection' – that they have been resident in the area and/or have important contacts and attachments there. The area where NASS housed them will usually be seen as their local connection. If they had a choice of staying in previous accommodation but left, they might be considered intentionally homeless.

However, people often have unrealistic hopes and waste a lot of time because they believe rumours and misinformation about being given social housing. They might wait months or years before they realise a better option is to find a private landlord who will accept them as a tenant. If they aren't earning enough, they need to find a landlord who will accept benefits.

Finding private accommodation can be harder for refugees (and other migrants) as landlords may be wary of housing refugees even if they have Leave because of 'Right to Rent' requirements from 2016, obliging landlords to check people are in the country legally.[2] Most landlords have no idea what different documentation means and may wrongly reject asylum seekers and refugees with Leave.

You could write a letter for the refugee to carry with them, explaining the law and documentation and reassuring potential landlords that the person you are supporting is eligible and that the landlord will not be fined or get into trouble. You may be asked to write a reference or to act as a guarantor. Consider carefully what you and your organisation will do if it goes wrong.

There are a few other possibilities for refugees who need housing soon:

- Longer-term hosting arrangements – for examples, Refugees at Home (Box 8.5, CS/D).

- Charities and churches that have registered schemes or registered as social landlords in order to provide accommodation, which often has a specialist or therapeutic element such as Birmingham Hope (also CS/E).

- Deposit loan schemes (CS/F).

- Case workers in some organisations help individuals find and manage accommodation – for example, at Freedom from Torture, Room to Heal (also CS/G).

- If someone does get Housing Association housing, there is usually a support worker or team who helps new tenants learn how to manage a property, so they don't lose the tenancy (also CS/I).

- Activist members of voluntary networks such as the range of Refugees Welcome groups that have grown across the country will sometimes take up individual cases.

---

2   Search www.gov.uk for 'Right to Rent' for official guidance leaflets that refugees can give landlords.

I need to improve on my existing accommodation

Refugees and asylum seekers might be in touch with you to help them improve their current accommodation. Whether they are in NASS, social or private accommodation, refugees may be finding it hard to maintain a decent standard of living and sense of wellbeing in crowded, shared facilities or poorly maintained properties. They might be concerned about safety, cleanliness, space, heating, facilities and bills. Some people have co-residents who are also in distress, with difficult behaviour or coping strategies, or who may be aggressive or discriminatory.

A tenant who wants improvements in their accommodation should check (or ask you to check) their contract first. Residents should record dates and details of conditions and incidents. Then contact the manager or landlord. If you are going to contact the manager or landlord for the tenant, you need to have permission, preferably in writing. They should keep records of contact or attempts to contact managers/landlords, keep photos and copies of correspondence/texts.

If they are in NASS hostels or housing, they will have a named accommodation manager who is usually non-resident. There is talk of expanding the manager's role, but their role at present is more to run the property rather than promote asylum seekers' welfare. Some are more helpful than others. NASS housing is run by commercial companies on behalf of the Home Office. They have sub-contracts with private landlords. If the NASS landlord or direct accommodation manager does not help, you contact the commercial contractor. You might need to involve the local authority – environmental or public health – to pressure the NASS contractor, or other landlords, into action.

There are cases of criminals targeting asylum accommodation or housing because they know vulnerable people are staying there, attempting fraud or trying to involve people in activities such as illegal forms of trade and working, false papers, loan-sharking, or because of other kinds of intimidation or acts of asylum-hate. If your contact fears for their safety, it is best also to contact the police, but it is quite possible asylum seekers or refugees will not want to involve the police. Residents should keep the manager/landlord informed. Landlords might be able to fit CCTV, alarms, panic buttons or new locks, or contact the police themselves if they are also concerned.

There are also obligations on tenants to maintain the property and not compromise safety (e.g. not smoking indoors). Being new to the UK, there might be unfamiliar problems, such as condensation and damp, drains, gardening, fire alarm systems. Tenants usually risk eviction if they sublet.

Box 8.4 Entitlements to shelter and accommodation for people with different immigration status

	State/social accommodation	Shelters/hostels, refuges	Private rental
Asylum seeker	If NASS approves their application for support, they are likely to be dispersed outside London/major areas; may be moved several times. Single or joint (same-sex) room, often in shared accommodation. Prime contractors sub-contract to smaller organisations and landlords. Accommodation manager visits. Contract includes not being absent for long periods, not subletting. NASS will not pay for accommodation they find themselves. Family or parents with children – see Chapter 10.	A few hostels, charitable organisations, etc. will accommodate asylum seekers but not hostels that are contracted by local authority or other government-sourced funding. May accommodate from one night to longer e.g. three to six months. Also see voluntary 'hosting' schemes e.g. Housing Justice.	Allowed. No financial support. Landlords are required to check immigration status for 'Right to Rent', and might be wary but asylum seekers are allowed to rent. Might need deposit, references. Often via extended family networks, sublets. Often rent directly from contacts without a tenancy agreement. Might include exchange of labour or other exchanges.
Refused asylum seeker/ NRPF	Only if agree to leave or can't leave and successful application, in which case NASS accommodation as above.	As asylum seeker.	As asylum seeker.
Refugees with Leave to Remain	They can apply for social housing on grounds of homelessness when first granted, or for other needs. They need to show a 'local connection' which includes having been accommodated there by NASS. They might be able to remain in the same accommodation. Local connection might also be close family or a new job. Financial support via Universal Credit (previously Housing Benefit) or pay rent themselves if earning. Temporary accommodation still paid via Housing Benefit.	As for British national. Shelters/hostels/ refuges mostly rely on being able to claim costs from Housing Benefit (Universal Credit has been problematic). There may be waiting lists, eligibility questions e.g. normal residence in a local authority area. Only 'verified rough' sleepers' with a 'CHAIN' number access some services, and might get additional services.	As for British national. Allowed. Financial support through Universal Credit (previously Housing Benefit) with UC rates and process and Council Tax relief as for a British national. Ownership, also as for British national.

For organisations offering specialist advice, see Appendix A.

Box 8.5	Examples of support for refugees' resources, access to and control of accommodation – Case Studies D–I

Providing resources:

D   Refugees at Home, Room for Refugees, Housing Justice: hosting schemes. They coordinate and support people to give room in their own houses to asylum seekers and refugees.

E   Micro Rainbow: an international human rights charity that supports lesbians and gay men who are being persecuted around the world. It set up its first 'safe space' hostel for lesbian and gay asylum seekers in London in 2017.

Assisting refugees to access accommodation:

F   Wycombe Refugee Partnership finds a property for a refugee family with Leave, and pays the deposit from donations. Universal Credit/Housing Benefit pays the rent. If or when the refugee can pay it back, the deposit is used to secure another refugee family's home.

G   Glasgow Housing Association has a migrant support worker who helps new refugees negotiate access routes into social housing in Glasgow.

H   ASAN (Asylum Support Appeals Network) is run by ASAP. It is a highly active national network of support and appeals advice workers taking on NASS cases where something isn't right. Members can email out a question about the specific issue they are tackling that day, and almost instantly get expert responses from other members.

Refugees take control:

I   Crisis 'Skylight' is more than a training programme, with 'turn up and start' options from ESOL and 'ready to rent' classes, to employment and wellbeing activities open to anyone who has been homeless recently or is at risk.

Money to live, food, clothing and other goods

This section looks at essentials such as food, clothes, basic consumables and the money to get them. Employment in order to earn a living is covered in Chapter 10. Entitlements are summarised in Box 8.8.

People need certain resources to meet the *basic functions of life*: food to eat, money to pay rent and electricity bills. Health and medicines are mostly free; details are in Chapter 9. Your interaction with a refugee might start by getting enough food or money to buy food for the next few days. It might be for 'private' goods such as underwear, paracetamol and tampons that aren't available from donations or charity shops. Some money is required to manage your asylum claims – photocopying, post, special delivery, travel to interviews and solicitors, and larger expenses such as £500 to instruct a new solicitor.

Money to live a *decent* life – rather than just surviving – means accessing and managing a wider range and quality of food, suitable clothing for all weathers, glasses so you can read, bus fares to see your counsellor. Some assets increase a person's agency and ability to manage things efficiently for themselves: a charging cable, a smart phone. There are longer-term needs such as saucepans, a vacuum cleaner, home broadband. Many courses are not free and student fees can be in the hundreds. At some point the person who has nothing today might need clothes for a job interview or a wedding.

People's needs go beyond the immediately functional – they also need to relax, get exercise, to socialise and keep in touch with distant family. Don't underestimate how important it is to have enough money to give birthday presents or feel good about yourself in the presence of peers, whether that is about putting on deodorant or lipstick.

People get into problems. *Urgent cash problems* happen for many reasons, some already noted above. Suddenly, your asylum-seeking volunteer needs £18.60 for travel to a Home Office interview – a travel voucher is due but has not arrived so they must pay up front and apply for a refund. With very low cash flow, it is not easy to budget or save for unexpected costs like a breakage or a theft or a £25 fine for dropping litter that will double if it isn't paid by Friday.

Refugees rarely have any capital, struggle to get bank accounts, have no safe source of credit, especially in their first years in the UK. Many of us are so used to managing our money with a bit of capital, bank accounts or credit that we hardly notice. I have course fees due? Put it on the credit card. Dentist wants proof of address? Show them a bank statement. We don't realise how critical (or convenient) banking is to our lives.

Refugees get into debt. When people are just coping, they can start to slip; borrowing £5 this week but paying back £3 before the money runs out again. Many people in the UK are struggling with debt, and refugees are especially vulnerable because they have low and erratic incomes that they can't improve (unless allowed to work), and no ways to spread costs. If you need £500 to instruct a new solicitor, you have to get it some way. There can also be problems with repaying smugglers and traffickers. See Box 8.6.

Box 8.6 Dealing with debt

Debt – often hidden debt – is a big problem for refugees. Once someone is in trouble with debt, the first evidence to hands-on workers is often problems with utility bills and rent, where people have prioritised other demands on their money over bills, although the actual debt problem may be bigger and more complex than household bills.

Rent, tax or 'pay-day' lenders with extreme interest rates should be prioritised. If someone comes to you with a final demand on rent, tax or utilities, you can contact the creditor and ask for time, or a repayment plan.

Contact National Debt Line for one-to-one advice by phone that can help people over several months. They may not have interpreters, so you might make the initial call. Their video tutorials do have language options. The Debt Line is linked with Citizens Advice where the refugee can get face-to-face advice and they might book interpreters if you ask in advance.

Many people send or 'remit' money back home to parents even if it leaves them short.

Some people make bad decisions. Some people drink.

The Joseph Rowntree Foundation talks about a 'poverty premium': the poorer you are, the higher the prices you are probably paying for heat, food and so forth (JRF 2014). Should we talk about refugees paying a 'non-resident' premium? Besides bank accounts, many asylum seekers or refused applicants can't get a local authority residents' card, for example, which gives other people free access to libraries, discounts for leisure centres, adult education, etc. And also a 'new resident' premium –when they are new to the country, with a low level of English and little familiarity with British bureaucracy and commerce, it is easy to misunderstand costs, deadlines and penalties. When people are new to your area, they won't know about the library, travel passes and cheap shops, and won't have peers with whom they can buy rice in bulk, or to help smooth out shortages (see Box 8.12, CS/M).

What money can refugees get?

People may have left their home country with savings, and even had some still when they arrived in the UK. Distant family can sometimes send money. After this has all run out and they are destitute, asylum seekers can apply for NASS (Box 8.13).

Between 2012 and 2017 the numbers receiving asylum support roughly doubled: by the end of April 2018 more than 42,000 asylum seekers (including dependants) were receiving NASS money for subsistence. They receive under £38 per head per week – less than £6 per day. They receive the money via an 'Aspen' payment card (Box 8.7). All members of a family get the same allowance, just less than £6/day, although children may get free school lunches (worth about £2 a day) in term time. If you are an asylum seeker, you can request NASS subsistence without requesting accommodation. ASAP Factsheets are your first stop as details change often.

Pregnant women or babies under three get £3–5 per week extra. Parents can apply for a one-off Maternity Payment of £300 or £250 if they have been refused asylum. Maternity Action are the experts here.

Aspen cards for asylum seekers' NASS
Box 8.7 subsistence (living costs) support

An asylum seeker or refused asylum seeker receiving NASS subsistence support has an Aspen card which is charged weekly with their asylum support money. It can be used as a payment or debit card in shops. Asylum seekers (not refused) can draw cash from it at bank machines (not the ones in shops which might debit the card but not give the money!).

Some individuals have made a direct arrangement with refused asylum seekers who have Aspen cards and can't get cash. They go shopping together. The supporter chooses items they need at shops that take the Aspen card. The refused asylum seeker pays for them with the card. The supporter pays them back in cash.

On receiving Leave to Remain, refugees can legally start paid work.

In the 28 days after getting Leave, the Job Centre/Jobcentre Plus is the main focus of activity in order to get the mainstream benefits they are entitled to:

- Their National Insurance (NI) number should arrive in the post, but if it doesn't their benefits might be delayed too. They should ask staff at the Job Centre to sort out problems with NI numbers, or you can ring the NI application line for them.

- They should go and start the process of applying for Universal Credit or other mainstream benefits straight away, taking all evidence, documentation and Home Office letters with them.

- The Job Centre might help them find a job or get on employment-related training.

- They will need a 'basic bank account' which payments can go into and from which they can withdraw the money, but will have no overdraft or cheque facility. This can be difficult to open as banks require proof of identity and address, which is difficult if refugees are in the middle of leaving NASS accommodation. (You might be able to write a letter to help – see Box 7.5.) A 'Change Account' (thechangeaccount.com) might be an alternative although they need an email and residential address.

- While they wait for their advance or first payment, handouts and food banks might be their only safety net.

	State support/benefits/relief	Private income
	Entitlements to subsistence and money for people with different immigration status	
Asylum seeker	NASS (main source for asylum seekers) c. £37–38/head via Aspen card which acts as a cash card (banks only) and debit card.	Not permitted to work for money
	Pregnant women or women with a baby under three get £3–5/week extra.	
	Once-only maternity grant £300 or £600 with twins.	
Refused	No Recourse to Public Funds (NRPF).	Not permitted to work for money
	Or, if approved for NASS, c. £36–37/head via Aspen card acting as debit card only, but not cash.	
	Maternity grant £250.	
Refugee with Leave to Remain	As British national, Universal Credit (previously JSA, IS, ESA, Housing Benefit and Council Tax, Family Tax Credit).	[AQ] Not permitted to work for money
	Child Benefit, maternity grant, etc. as British national.	

Box 8.8 — Entitlements to subsistence and money for people with different immigration status

Providing money and goods to refugees

So what can you do? (See Box 8.12.)

Can I give them cash?

Most people reading this book probably don't feel comfortable giving out cash. If a stranger arrives in your centre asking for money, the response is usually no. When there is already familiarity and mutual trust, you may feel more inclined to go to your treasurer or even get out your own purse. Do you make it a gift? A loan? What if they tell others who then turn up asking for money? (See Box 8.9.)

Box 8.9 Cash contributions to individuals or a small cash fund

It seems nice for people to pass the hat around or even sub someone from their own pocket. Staff or other members might pay someone to fix a computer or to clean. But consider how this looks to outside observers. Your board could authorise you to set up a small cash fund that you can use to support people in crisis. You can make it up from a special appeal, skimmed from income or reserves.

To be fair, and to avoid unmanageable expectations, you must set clear criteria on eligibility, deciding who and why and how much to give them, and who decides and how you will report to your donors, if any, or to the public.

Rather than giving cash, you could pay the fare or purchase the necessary item directly. Some local refugee partnerships or welcome groups pay money for house deposits directly to the landlord.

Even small organisations can set up emergency grants or loans. You must set rules which you stick to and be able to justify your decisions if challenged. Your trustees are accountable. Make sure everyone in the organisation understands and accepts the responsibility and the risks. If you give loans, make sure it won't cause a problem if they can't or don't pay it back.

It might seem a wonderful solution simply to give money to a refugee who has been especially helpful during an event or assisted with office work, but it would be seen badly by the Home Office and NASS, not to mention the Inland Revenue, Charity Commission and your employer's public liability insurance provider. A gift? Yes. A prize? Yes. A reward for contributions to...? Best not. You also need to be careful about expenses, which should clearly be only *actual expenses* in return for *original* receipts. Some possibilities you can consider for offering paid work are presented in Chapter 10.

Giving or lending money changes a relationship; it confirms how unequal your positions are and introduces new tensions

Cash from other bodies. There are small grants available for 'relief of poverty' or 'prevention of destitution' – for example, the Vicar's Relief Fund handled by the Frontline Network. Many larger organisations such as colleges have small funds to help members or students. These funds often pay for something specific and practical, like a fridge or a part of course fees. There may not be anything official, or publicised, but it is always worth ringing up to ask in a crisis.

Ask local libraries, local councillors, the local council and inter-faith networks whether they know of anything in the area. There are grant-search packages by NCVO 'Funding Central' and Directory of Social Change 'GrantsforIndividuals' which you pay subscriptions to use directly, but local voluntary sector support bodies and even councils and libraries may have subscriptions to these search packages, and will often help you search.

You might consider making links with a credit union where people can save via your organisation and borrow against what they have saved. Credit unions are not used by large numbers of British people, especially the majority of us who have access to credit. But many cultures across the world have forms of savings societies where people put in money regularly and all pay towards any one member's major costs – whether it is a house, an operation or a funeral. So the concept of a credit union (if not the language) will often be more familiar to your refugee contact than it is to you (www.findyourcreditunion.co.uk).

Can I collect donations of goods for refugees?

Perhaps your organisation already runs a food bank satellite, or you take part in a regular community lunch, or you know someone who volunteers in a charity shop. These are important access routes for refugees to source food and items they need – hot meals, groceries and goods, clothes, books, bedding. And don't forget the value of what you take for granted in your office every day – photocopying, broadband, electricity or surplus stationery – just check with the boss first!

If you and your organisation are inclined to collect donations of cash or goods, *start small* and learn as you go along.

Whether cash or items of any value, *keep proper records*. The good news is that with proper records you can claim Gift Aid on cash donations, though not on goods (unless you run a charity shop). Be honest and clear: if you say to donors that the donation is for 'refugee children', then you can't legally use it for adults or any other migrant children (Box 8.10).

Think whom to ask. Your members, suppliers and local businesses or strangers?

Box 8.10 **Know your donors and everyone will be happier**

Are they...

- regular supporters or members who might not have much, but who will help over and over again in small ways, including giving their time?

- reasonably well informed, and will want to know about your organisation and whether you will use their contributions intelligently?

- strangers attracted by the idea of doing something nice for someone, and don't much mind what as long as it isn't too inconvenient?

- other local organisations like the school or Muslim centre, who can use their networks to channel goods to you, probably as part of a longer-term exchange of information and ideas?

Acknowledge with thanks and appreciation, get permission to keep contact details, protect people's data, maintain relationships.

Make sure you get good items that people need (Box 8.11). It works well if you:

- mobilise supporters, donors and volunteers to build up to a date or event that acts as a deadline (Refugee Week? Eid? Your AGM?). Most people prefer a finite commitment.

- ask for specific things – such as winter coats – not 'clothes' or you will get bin liners full of stretched bikinis.

- only appeal when someone has a specific need – we were asked if we could provide a second-hand baby buggy. We put the word out, and a few days later one of our members brought one in from a friend of hers.

Don't underestimate how easy it can be to get donated goods and clothes, nor how difficult it can be to manage, store and distribute them properly. I worked in a small two-desk office at one point and had to talk someone out of bringing in a double bed they wanted to donate, without appearing ungrateful.

Who gets what and how will you get it to them? You can give donations out 'first come, first served', which is simple and fairly quick. But first-comers will not necessarily be the people in most need. Alternatively, set priorities and criteria. Only people who use the services already? Only asylum seekers? Or will you judge by some level of need? This puts you in the position of judging between people – a responsibility you must face up to, including the risk of getting it wrong.

Can you reach out to other organisations for referrals? Or pass what you can't distribute to other charities?[3] One way out of complications with quality, storage and distribution is to collect donations on behalf of other organisations – for example, asking for food to pass to a food bank. We were once asked to collect winter coats for detainees in an Immigration Removal Centre – we had the networks to collect from; they had the people in need to distribute to. It was very satisfactory.

Success is not measured by how much you collect but whether you get the things people need and get them to the people who need them, when they need them.

Box 8.11 Hints on handling donations

- Don't ask for more than you can handle. Donations need handling and might need cleaning. Are you going to wash those eight bags of clothes that just arrived?

- If you receive food, you need to consider hygiene, refrigeration, vermin and the sheer bulk that demands space and transport. Even tinned food goes out of date.

- If you can't pass donations on straight away, they have to be logged and labelled and stored. If you end up not knowing what is in those boxes in the cellar, you might as well throw the whole lot away.

- Staff time is expensive, so do you have volunteers you can rely on to label and organise efficiently without supervision?

---

3   I persuaded the bed-donor to kindly dismantle the bed and take it to a community furniture store which we used to refer refugees to if they needed furniture, so we were all happy in the end.

Help refugees access other services that have goods and resources

You can multiply refugees' access to resources by finding out and forming connections with other activities and organisations in advance. Look for:

- Weekly or monthly refugee or homelessness drop-ins where there may be food, clothes, nappies, toiletries, as well as haircuts, health care, advice, friendly company and central heating. There may be showers (Box 8.12, CS/J).

- Gurdhwaras (Sikh temples) and Salvation Army halls often provide free hot foot. Mosques and Muslim centres may have donations to give during Ramadan and Eid celebrations.

- Permanent services that have been mentioned already, such as libraries and children's centres.

In addition to the usual benefits of networking, you can make direct links with other organisations. For example:

- Food banks partner – where you refer refugees in need to collect a week's worth of food and perhaps have a hot meal and advice check at the same time. One model is the Trussell Trust approach, and you can search for food banks across the UK on their website (CS/K).

- Get a wholesaler trade card (e.g. Costco) for your organisation and let groups of people shop together (there is often a minimum spend and only named people can use the card).

You might assist refugees to learn ways to manage in the UK:

- Volunteering opportunities can give refugees access to practical resources as well as other benefits.

- Opportunities for building local peer contacts so they can swap news and information and lend/borrow/pool/share resources and knowledge.

You might channel services or relevant training from other organisations:

- Training and advice from a local 'financial capability' network, where different organisations can provide training and information on managing money, credit, household savings and benefits (CS/L).

- You can find opportunities to gain life skills for a tight budget such as healthy cooking classes, riding bikes, allotment projects:

    - search for 'community furniture' projects (try British Heart Foundation, YMCA shops, Sue Ryder), including environmental 'upcycling' charities and projects; also municipal dump or 'reuse' shops, where you probably need transport but can get household goods and furniture and even sports gear, electronic goods, gardening equipment for virtually nothing – just a bit of luck on the day

- free or bargain make-up, hairdressing, meals, even fitness coaching from colleges and gyms that need practice opportunities for their students

- in big cities there may be dentistry schools which need practical opportunities for students to do work that would costs hundreds of pounds otherwise.

Box 8.12 | **Examples of projects and services relating to money, food and goods for refugees: Case Studies J–M**

J The New North London Synagogue has made running volunteer-based drop-ins for asylum seekers into an art form, with themed collections, drop-off deadlines and a rota for volunteers to prepare items before the day.

K A Foodbank Voucher Partner – the director can sign a voucher for a refugee in need, who takes it on the right day to the nearest satellite distribution point that hosts a 'touring' food bank. You can contact the food bank administrator in advance if there are special dietary needs.

L Energy Best Deal Scheme (now ended) provided speakers to groups, including English-learning and migrant groups, to give a one-hour talk about saving money on fuel bills.

M All-languages women's welcome groups were put on by a women's centre to draw attention from a mix of women – those who wanted to learn English, those who wanted to support refugee and migrant women. The women's centre's idea was to bring women from all walks of life together to form friendships and mutual solidarity as a valuable commodity for many aspects of life.

Summary and conclusion

There is no doubt that refugees' anxiety and distress is worsened by experiences of negotiating the NASS system. (Some of the impact of this is picked up by health services which are the subject of the next chapter.) Destitution is a reality for refugees in Britain, and some would say the government is deliberately using impoverishment as a tool (weapon?) to create a 'hostile environment' for 'illegal immigrants' as a way to reduce 'demand' for asylum.

Even within Parliament there is widespread criticism of the way immigration support is run.

One must also surely be concerned about what this all means in the long term for British society, as people who could easily have started contributing to society, not to mention to the economy, take years to recover from the hardship and distress that living on the edge of destitution has caused them.

As a practitioner, you may have already been a little surprised to find yourself working with refugees. Many people who never expected to become knowledgeable about homelessness or poverty are finding they have to become specialists in these as well.

People don't only need a room or a house. They need a home, where they can have some kind of life that isn't just survival.

Long Box 8.13 | **How to apply to National Asylum Support Service (NASS) for subsistence and accommodation**

- Ring the Refugee Council or Migrant Helpline to find out whom to ring. Migrant Helpline has multilingual advisers and you dial a different direct number for different languages. The applicant may have to wait a long time. If the number is 0800, this is a free call – it is only a question of how long their battery will hold out. But it can be expensive if someone is not on a contract, so let them use your landline if possible.

- NASS will ask for Home Office reference numbers and specific questions about existing support to check if the claim is eligible. They will tell the applicant how to prove they are destitute.

- They will send application forms and information about what the asylum seeker needs to do. The applicant will need to explain how they supported themselves to that point – for example, they were helped by friends. They must give details of all bank accounts here and in other countries, any savings or assets, and bank statements showing there is no money left.

- Then the applicant needs to explain why that is no longer possible – perhaps their friends can't afford it any more or the relationship has broken down. They will need a letter from the friends to confirm this is true.

- Copy everything.

- Post the documents as soon as you have everything together. It is best to get at least proof of postage.

- They are likely to request further evidence and confirmation on certain points.

- Expect to wait a month or more. Act fast if refused – the asylum seeker may have only days to notify their intention to appeal.

- Note: It is easy to get confused about addresses and reference numbers so be very careful. If letters are handwritten, check for legibility, especially numbers as 1 and 7 are often confused in handwriting.

- Problems? Contact Citizens Advice or the local law centre.

CHAPTER 9

Health, Mental Health and Disability

Introduction

Physical, mental and emotional ill health and disabilities are big issues for refugees and anyone who works with them – more so than for the main UK population at random. Refugees are ordinary people but some have been through extraordinary and damaging experiences. They have faced loss and prolonged stress. Even after arrival, poor living conditions, poverty and stress can further compromise health and wellbeing and compound disabilities.

Long Box 9.1 at the end of this introductory section looks at refugees' experiences in more depth, and possible consequences for health.

It is important that we think about refugees' health in terms that go beyond illness and medical treatment. We shouldn't pathologise depression as if it is a failure of some bodily or mental system, when it is a normal response to what someone has been through. We mustn't perceive disability as a problem inherent to that person; it is a contemporary situation in which current social and bureaucratic norms make life harder than it should be. Refugees are actively pursuing their and their families' health, wellbeing and ability to shape life ahead.

Resources are stretched, but they exist, and refugees are entitled to care and support. In outline:

- Asylum seekers, refugees with Leave and to some extent refused asylum seekers get free health and mental health treatment and care on the NHS. (This is not the case for all migrants.)

- All disabled people can ask their local authorities for support to address care and wellbeing needs related to their disability, regardless of immigration status, although they need to be 'ordinarily resident' in the area.

- Some charities have specialist support for refugees, especially relating to mental health.

But do refugees engage effectively with health, mental health and social work professionals? Refugees, as with all migrants, have to learn about the NHS and local authority social services – what exists, their rights and entitlements, who does what, where to go first and how to take things up a level.

Language is an issue. Even if they speak some English, they may not understand the vocabulary of health and social care services, let alone the flow of acronyms: A&E, UCC, UTC, MIU and so on.[1] They might lack details or ways to express physical feelings or pain.

Some find it hard to trust clinicians and social workers. They may worry about confidentiality. They may fear Home Office surveillance (unfortunately, in 2016–2018 NHS Digital provided the Home Office with data on patients' name, date of birth, GP and last known address, although even within Parliament criticism was fierce). They may find treatment approaches unfamiliar.

There are without doubt failures and errors in the overstretched system and people share stories about poor treatment or perceived rudeness.

This chapter looks at issues, entitlements, sources of support and ideas for action when you find yourself working with refugees around health, mental health and disability. The information on entitlements as always comes with a 'health warning' that laws and policies change. If you are dealing with a complex or critical matter, or if you are moving from 'poke' towards 'slap', you need to get up-to-date advice from expert sources (see Appendix A).

Refugees might come to you directly with health questions, but their initial contact is more likely to be about training or some such interest (unless you are a health professional, of course). Health issues tend to emerge while you are discussing other things. They might ask you for reassurance about processes or what to expect before, during or after an encounter with a health or social care professional, to help them judge the value of what the professionals told them.

This chapter is not about you stepping into the shoes of a clinician or therapist (unless you are one!). Please don't attempt to therapise if you are not qualified to do so. Our health system is stretched, and long waiting lists for counselling and other treatments are frustrating. Even so, the best support you can give a refugee is to smooth out access to the clinical and professional support that is right for her or him, and offer wider opportunities for self-help and a healthy, enabled life.

Long Box 9.1	**Seeking refuge and refugees' health, mental health and disabilities**

Being discriminated against over a number of years, possibly including exclusion from services, could have affected people's long-term nutrition and resulted in inadequate treatment of conditions, including lack of preventative care such as immunisations. Across the world, people with a diverse range of physical, learning, mental health and other

---

1   Accident and Emergency, Urgent Care Centre, Urgent Treatment Centre, Minor Injuries Unit.

disabilities are neglected, abused and persecuted in many ways. Poor living conditions means higher levels of infection and disease with long-term impact.

Abuse, violence and torture or the effects of war on military or civilian populations will cause physical injury, including head, back and joint injuries, and long-term harm which might still need treatment. Or it can result in mental and emotional trauma and other disabilities such as impaired movement and mobility, sensory damage such as hearing loss, or chronic pain, disfigurement and other health issues. Abuse and its physical and emotional consequences are often gendered; both males and females may have been sexually assaulted and raped, resulting in sexual and reproductive complications.

Transit from town to town and country to country in poor conditions, with little access to hygiene or health care, will often mean higher levels of infection, disease and illness, compromised immune systems, under-diagnosis and under-treatment with longer-term consequences and worsening impairments. Illnesses such as HIV, TB and other infections spread fast in camps and crowded conditions. People get problems with teeth and feet.

Once in the UK, pressures within the asylum process create and heighten mental distress, increasing both physical and mental ill health, and contribute to refugees becoming disabled in the longer term. Poor housing, food, unhealthy coping strategies (e.g. drugs, alcohol) and unregulated employment continue to be factors in nutrition, infection and injuries through accidents or violence.

Migrants generally have a low take-up of preventative and screening services, so there is a problem of people presenting late with cancer and heart disease, making treatment harder and often less effective, or simply, for example, not knowing they have diabetes until it has already done them permanent harm that could have been avoided.

On a lighter note, younger couples and families quite often have babies in the first few years after they first arrive.

Physical ill health and wellness

Some of the physical impact of past experiences is described in the Long Box 9.1.

For refugees, the NHS system is not always easy to understand. The General Practitioner (GP) system is unusual and will not be familiar to people from most countries in the world. People often have certain expectations of treatment, formed in their original country, where health care might have been private or hospital-based, or methods such as injections or X-rays used routinely. They may doubt the competence of UK clinicians who follow different pathways.

Their health and best chance of full recovery depend on getting to the right service via the shortest route, first time. People who are used to getting health care at hospitals and don't understand the system, or for whom the system isn't working well, are more like to go to A&E when a GP would have served them better.

There are many positive reasons for the hands-on worker to put in some effort to help them get this right. It improves their care and speeds up any recovery. It saves them time, effort and anxiety. It also saves the NHS and the taxpayer money, and none of us can afford to watch NHS resources being wasted.[2]

Entitlements and access

Advocacy is again often necessary, but entitlements are simple at first sight. Project London, part of Doctors of the World, has up-to-the-minute guidance.

Asylum seekers, refused asylum seekers and refugees with Leave have access to all primary, community and acute/emergency services for free.

In Wales and Scotland, they all have free urgent and secondary care.

In England, asylum seekers and refugees with Leave get free urgent and secondary care

In England, refused asylum seekers do not get free urgent and secondary care, unless they are still receiving NASS support because they are taking steps to leave or because the Home Office has recognised they cannot leave or be deported at present. The situation of refused asylum seekers in England is described more fully in Box 9.3.

Entitlements are summarised in Box 9.2 below.

What does this mean in practice? As a starting point…

- ☑ Everyone can (and should) register with a GP who will see them for free. You can help a great deal just by encouraging and helping people to get registered as soon as possible.

- ☑ Everyone will be treated free in a life-threatening emergency.

- ☑ Anyone can ring 111 free across the UK, for health advice and clarification.

- ☑ Anyone can attend walk-in family planning and sexual health clinics, including HIV testing and treatment and termination of pregnancies.

> Everyone can (and should) register with a GP who will see them for free…
> Everyone will be treated free in a life-threatening emergency.

This is what should happen when someone arrives in the UK:

- • A person who has claimed asylum registers with a GP wherever they are staying and gets an NHS number and an initial health check. It might include being checked for tuberculosis and giving a medical history

---

2   The NHS Right Care, Right Place public education campaign has some very useful, plain-English resources that are also helpful for handouts in English groups.

including immunisations. The GP will use an interpreter – probably by phone – if needed.

- The GP treats them or refers them for secondary, specialist treatment for any existing conditions. They fill in an HC1 form (this has lots of pages – they might need help) and should get an HC2 certificate that they show to the pharmacist for free prescriptions, free dental treatment, optician appointment and more. They get an appointment to see the GP for any new condition they want attention to and so on.

- They register with an NHS dentist and have a new patient dental check and the dentist starts any work that needs doing.

- If they move or are moved by NASS, they register with a new GP, but they don't need a new health check each time as their records should be transferred. If and when their status changes, and even if they become homeless, they can still always register and be seen by a GP for free. Even if their claim is rejected and they lose part of their entitlements, they will continue and complete any course of treatment that has already started.

- They can take up screening opportunities, smoking cessation, diabetes testing and self-care training.

Box 9.2 | **Entitlements to health care for people with different immigration status**

	Primary care (planned)	Community care (also see Box 9.3 (planned)	Secondary care (planned)	Emergency/ urgent (unplanned)
All	GP temporary or permanent registration, family planning, sexual health, immunisation, TB, HIV. NHS 111, NHS Choices (online). Free prescriptions if they have a means-tested HC2 certificate.	Clinical care for home-based nursing care, child development, podiatry, speech and language therapy, health visiting (families with babies under five), occupational therapy, diabetes, dentistry, optometry, community pharmacy.	Public health e.g. support and education on healthy eating, smoking cessation.	Free A&E, ambulance in emergency, emergency treatment for life-threatening condition, plus continuing treatment resulting from the life-threatening emergency treatment. Acute mental health.

cont.

	Primary care (planned)	Community care (also see Box 9.3 (planned)	Secondary care (planned)	Emergency/ urgent (unplanned)
Asylum seekers and Refugees with Leave to Remain	Same as resident British nationals.	Same as resident British nationals.	Same as resident British nationals.	Same as resident British nationals.
Refused asylum seeker NRPF	Yes, free England NRPF must pay full price for prescriptions. Scotland and Wales free prescriptions.	Yes, check if a service 'in the community' is considered secondary, e.g. hospital providing clinic.	Wales and Scotland secondary treatment and care free. In England, a course of treatment that has started will be completed free. Can access secondary care but not free. See Exceptions.	If an ambulance is used but it is not an emergency, NRPF may be charged. Urgent/immediate treatment and care including treatment to protect human rights will be given immediately but may be charged later. See Exceptions.

*Exceptions on secondary care. Refused asylum seekers who were trafficked, those receiving NASS (if making efforts to return/cannot be returned) and disabled people receiving care from their local authority have same entitlements as asylum seekers and refugees with Leave. Trafficked people who are NRPF will be treated for urgent conditions resulting from their trafficking, but not other conditions.

Sources: HEAREquality.org.uk; Public Health England 'NHS entitlements: migrant health guide'; Doctors of the World; NHS England leaflet 'How to Register with a GP – asylum seekers and refugees'.

There are some other opportunities for free access to health care and alternatives for some free treatment and care easily available to all.

- 111 is a free telephone service staffed by teams including nurses and doctors, giving advice on treatment and the correct service for your condition. Interpreters are available.

- NHS Choices website has information about a wide range of conditions, prevention and self-help treatment, and local services. There are online apps and ways of asking GPs for advice using smart phones.

- Pharmacists in the UK are highly qualified. They are largely private businesses although they handle NHS services as well as prescriptions. They give high-quality advice and can treat a wide range of conditions including giving some medicines that GPs might also prescribe. They will advise whether or not to see the GP or get more urgent care.

- In London, Doctors of the World run walk-in clinics that don't require any identity or immigration papers, with qualified paid and unpaid medics. Project London will also advocate strongly and effectively at distance to get individuals access to free NHS services, including secondary care.

- Faith organisations and homelessness bodies may run weekly or monthly 'drop-ins' and also street outreach with medics.

- Fairs, shopping centres, even supermarkets host NHS screening services. Patients will probably need NHS numbers and/or proof of name and address, but not always.

- Health visitors (specialist nurses) run sessions and groups at children's centres where mothers can get health care for themselves as well as for their babies, but they might need paperwork.

- Health charities provide advice and help with lifestyle and healthy living around specific conditions, both small local charities (e.g. community cancer centre), and branches of national charities (e.g. British Heart Foundation) and therapeutic support and expertise like Maggie's Centres.

Some alternative routes are less reliable and may be dangerous to the person's health:

- buying antibiotics, medicines, etc. from abroad via family or on the internet from people who aren't licensed in the UK, or being given partial packs from friends who haven't finished medicines they got on prescription

- seeing unregistered clinicians such as doctors from the person's home country who are practising in the UK without a licence

- using homeopathic or folk and cultural or popular remedies, including faith healing

- discharging themselves, refusing treatment or delaying looking for treatment because of money.

The most basic access issue for health care is *registering with a GP*. You might think the GP practice would be the expert in access entitlements but you would be wrong. Many asylum seekers and refugees with Leave are turned away at 'the gate'. This is despite NHS guidance and sometimes even after the local Healthwatch[3] or even Doctors of the World has tried to help right the situation. GP receptionists do not always have sufficient or accurate training on this. The most common reasons given seem to be that they think the person is not entitled to register, or that they don't have proof that they are 'ordinarily' resident in the area, or proof of address.

- They are entitled. Everyone is entitled.

- Although the practice can ask for proof of residence or address and photo identity, they cannot insist on them, and cannot refuse to register someone who can't provide them. (They *can* refuse to register someone if their lists are full.)

- They have to give you the reason for refusing to register you in writing. Insisting on this usually improves the situation as staff will check before committing themselves on paper.

In England, there is an NHS England leaflet, 'How to Register with a GP – asylum seekers and refugees', that you can give the refugee. And add a letter from your organisation to the practice, offering your help to clarify. Or accompany the refugee as she or he speaks to the receptionist or practice manager directly (glance through Chapter 7 for hints on effective communication). You will be most useful in this situation if you are confident in your knowledge. People usually want to do the right thing; they don't want a fight.

If it doesn't work, you can complain, or talk to Healthwatch, the local NHS Clinical Commissioning Group (CCG), NHS England, your councillor, your MP and campaigning groups such as Doctors of the World. Realistically, though, most refugees prefer to walk away and try another practice.

Perhaps the second most immediate issue is having *adequate interpreting at appointments*. Interpreting is an essential aid to communication in English (see Chapter 6). Having appropriate interpreting counts as 'ensuring equal opportunity' and 'positive action' under the Public Sector Equality Duty (Chapter 4). If someone doesn't have good English, they should make sure the receptionist writes down that they need interpreters in appointments and put it on their computerised patient record. They might get telephone interpreting using a conference call or hands-free or Skype-style system. But face-to-face interpreters are better for longer appointments such as initial health checks, health visitors on home visits, physiotherapy, complex or sensitive situations such as abortions. Many non-English-speakers find 'tele' interpreting alienating where a good face-to-face interpreter can be reassuring.

---

3   Healthwatch is an independent statutory body that exists in every local authority area, backed up by National Healthwatch, that has powers to acts as an independent 'champion' or watchdog for local people, checking on health and social care commissioning and providers.

The third most common thing people ask for help with is understanding letters about appointments, especially being confused and worried by cancellation letters when their appointment is moved. Confusion often leads to them not turning up or turning up at the wrong time or place, wasting everyone's resources.

	Entitlements to health and mental health care
Long Box 9.3	**of refused asylum seekers in England**

Refused asylum seekers who have NRPF still get free primary, community and emergency treatment and care, including emergency mental health care. Several services are available free to everyone, such as family planning.

But in England refused asylum seekers do not get free urgent and secondary care, unless:

1. they are supported by the local authority in relation to disabilities

2. they are still receiving NASS support

3. they started treatment before receiving their refusal (they complete the treatment free)

4. they were trafficked, in which case they may continue getting free secondary care relating to their experiences and treatment during trafficking, including secondary mental health care, but not for other needs or mental health issues if they are not related to the trafficking or abuse.

If they are receiving NASS, it is probably because they have proved they are taking steps to leave the UK, or the Home Office recognises they cannot be deported at present. They may have made a successful human rights case to stay, which could be on the grounds that they are receiving ongoing treatment for a serious health condition, or care relating to a disability, and stopping the care would amount to degrading and inhumane treatment.

If they need secondary (elective) or urgent (immediate, unplanned) care, it will not be refused but they will probably be sent a bill for payment, for example:

- for antenatal care, delivery and postnatal care, if it is not a matter of life and death

- if they attend for emergency services but it is considered their need is not an emergency and they are diverted to urgent care

- they pay for medicines.

Take a few minutes to consider if you are clear on the differences between primary, NHS community, emergency care (999, A&E) and secondary care and immediate care. Confusion could result in a *large* bill.

- Generally speaking, *secondary* care is elective, more specialist or advanced diagnosis or treatment. It is often delivered in a hospital, but this is no longer always the case as the NHS moves secondary services into the community. People can agree a payment plan in advance.

- *Urgent* care is something to address an immediate problem, such as stitching a flesh wound, which has to be done now but is not life-threatening.

To be sure, ring 111 or ask Healthwatch or the doctor or nurse. They might not know straight away – they aren't accountants. But they are in the best position to find out. Receptionists may not be clear on details.

If they can't pay, they might be able to challenge the decision to charge them or the amount charged. The NHS might pursue the debt, although they don't tend to be aggressive. The NHS can arrange a payment plan as low as £5 per week or write it off. If people leave the UK without paying, it will probably reduce the chance of getting permission to return to the UK in the future.

Pregnancy and birth – Selna's birth-plan

Refused asylum-seeking women in England, like the fictional Selna, have to pay for at least some of their care around childbirth.

- Family planning is free to everyone.

- Antenatal care – care, screening and monitoring and education during pregnancy, before the baby comes – is secondary care, so Selna can arrange a payment plan in advance to pay the costs of between £1500 and £4000. If she had already started antenatal care before her claim was refused, treatment is free.

- Emergency care: if Selna has to go to emergency services (A&E) because the situation has become life-threatening, emergency care is free but she may have to pay for follow-up treatment later on.

- Delivery is immediate care and immediate care will always be given, but she will be billed for at least £2000.

- Postnatal/health visiting is community care and Selna will be invoiced depending on the amount of care she requires (upwards from £300).

See Maternity Alliance.

Mental and emotional health and wellbeing

Without being clinically trained in any sense, anyone who comes into contact with refugees can hardly avoid being concerned about their mental and emotional health and wellbeing. Any ordinary person who has been discriminated against to the point of persecution because of their sex, gender, ethnicity, sexuality, beliefs, etc., and any person who has gone through experiences of violence, departure and transit and losses, will probably end up dealing with painful memories and complex, difficult emotions. Such difficult feelings are not the same as mental illnesses, but it is reasonable to expect that a substantial proportion of the refugees with whom you come into contact will struggle with mental ill health at some point, or repeatedly over time.

You may also meet refugees who:

- had to seek refuge in the first place because they had mental health issues and would have been discriminated against, degraded and persecuted

- had pre-existing conditions that were triggered or worsened by their flight for safety

- are traumatised by their experiences of detention in the UK, while in the asylum process

- are refused but allowed to remain temporarily because their mental health is so poor that to remove them would amount to degrading treatment or torture

- are caring for a family member or others who have more or less severe mental illnesses

- are facing mental health difficulties for other reasons (e.g. postnatal depression).

Feeling sad and unhappy, or grieving because of bereavements and losses, or suffering loneliness and homesickness are not the same as mental illness. No matter how intense and painful these feelings are, they are normal responses to what people have gone through. These feelings are part of a bigger picture of mental and emotional health. Depression or PTSD, however, are treated as mental illnesses. Some might call it mental ill health, mental health issues or challenges – people use different language according to their view of what is appropriate and useful. A high proportion of refugees must deal with PTSD, but the proportion of British soldiers returning from active duty, or people involved in serious accidents or incidents are similar.

What indicators might you see that someone is struggling? It might be one of your refugee volunteers, a group member or a parent of one of your students. They probably aren't going to approach you for help with their mental health.

You might notice someone demonstrating or expressing difficult feelings through their actions or how they dress and behave in relationships. You might see signs of self-harm or dangerous coping strategies. A person might constantly suffer from physical aches, pains, headaches or sleeplessness. People receiving treatment might be taking medicine which affects their concentration and memory or ability to express themselves.

Feelings and symptoms come and go. If you aren't a qualified clinician, don't try to diagnose, don't prod or try to treat. If you are concerned, look up the website of Mind and NHS Choices. For better understanding, consider taking 'Mental Health First Aid' courses (mhfaengland.org) and become your organisation's 'mental health first aider'.

What is the *scale* of mental health issues among asylum seekers and refugees? Estimates range as high as 50 per cent of asylum seekers having mental health needs at any one time. Even people who get through the asylum process reasonably well may have a serious mental health crisis some time later, even after years.

The consequences can be far-reaching. Not only do people often suffer when they are mentally ill, but their illness can have an impact on their future as people find it harder to take back control of their lives and rebuild a fulfilling life. People may neglect their health, family needs and relationships, threatening any job they have or their accommodation, bringing them nearer to homelessness and destitution. Carers and families are also affected.

There are all the usual difficulties 'pre-gate' before people access support for mental health difficulties, such as doubts about authority, lack of knowledge, etc. With mental health, there are other questions. Do people believe their feelings or illness can be relieved or treated? Do they have to and can they accept the label 'mentally ill'? How will peers treat them if they find out?

But most people recover or learn to manage their mental health. Experiences and memories don't go away, but with support and access to good care, the personal and wider impact can be reduced.

Entitlements and access

Everyone gets mental health services and emergency services free (with the exception in England of refused asylum seekers, covered in Long Box 9.3).

Box 9.4 Entitlements to NHS mental health care and treatment for people with different immigration status

	Primary	Community	Secondary	Acute plus 'emergency' (A&E)
Asylum seeker	Yes, mostly via GP	Yes, including community teams	Yes	Yes
Refused	Also voluntary sector commissioned by CCG/LA		Restricted and conditional in England, as Box 9.2	
Refugee with Leave to Remain			Yes	

Services available to refugees from the NHS

The NHS concentrates resources on patients with fairly intense needs, although this varies by area. Concerns about scale, availability and quality of resources for adult mental health generally have been in the news for years. There are few specialist refugee services in the NHS, although there are specialist mental health teams, for example, in community health, PTSD and acute specialisms who might find themselves working with refugees as part of their case load. Capacity is a real problem and the majority of refugees will need to access general NHS mental health services.

NHS Choices and 111 have information, with some translation and interpreting available. Otherwise, the first point of access is the GP, who can provide some treatments directly such as medication, and is the key to referral to NHS counselling services and to approved charities and private counsellors providing talking therapies, which people might be asked to pay for. Parents with children under five can also start the process of getting help through family health visitors. As an alternative to GP and health visitor routes, other professionals, including you, can contact the local community mental health team directly (ring 111). In some areas there is now a 'Single Point of Access' (SPA) system that connects enquirers, including professionals in other fields, with the right service for them or their clients. The refugee will usually be offered an assessment, although they may have to wait many months, then wait again for the treatment. If they do not attend their appointment, it could delay getting treatment by weeks – so make sure they go!

Treatments are outlined usefully on the NHS Choices website. They are often provided in the community, and can include group therapy, talking therapies including cognitive behaviour therapy (CBT), and inpatient/residential treatments, although these are rare.

If a person gets to a crisis point, and especially if they are a danger to themselves or others, the routes are a little different, although they can still start by visiting their GP. If they are actively suicidal, they can go/you can take them/you can call the police/the police might take them to A&E. This might involve restraint if they are a danger to themselves or others.

They will be assessed at A&E – sometimes in a separate unit designed both for security and to provide a better environment for the person in crisis. They may be detained or 'sectioned' for hours, days or months. An independent mental health advocate should be available to the person in need at this point (contact your local Healthwatch). When people come out of residential or sectioned care, they should receive support to remain stable or recover, such as regular contact from a community psychiatric nurse. Mental ill health is considered a disability, and the local authority can be requested to do a community care assessment with a mental health advocate involved, which might give the refugee a level of ongoing support; this is discussed in the next section.

The NHS does not provide much treatment for mild to moderate mental health needs. Lower-level support is often provided by or via the voluntary and community sector (VCS), sometimes having been commissioned by the local NHS Clinical Commissioning Group or local authority, but often relying on grants or public fundraising and therefore not bound by immigration rules in the same way that physical health care is.

Highly specialist regional and national charities such as the Helen Bamber Foundation and Freedom from Torture[4] care specifically for refugees with mental and emotional health difficulties. Your local Mind, Rethink and some disability and carers' organisations, bereavement support organisations, arts or gardening therapy projects and similar can often provide services with few restrictions.

Other specialist bodies and some smaller local organisations provide holistic, 'wrap round' and therapeutic case work for refugees that combine care at many levels, sometimes tackling case work such as housing and money at the same time. One example worth noting is the Baobab Centre for Young Survivors in Exile – very small, but expert.

Disability

One way to define disability is the way it is described in the Equality Act 2010: 'a physical or mental impairment' that has 'a substantial and long-term adverse effect' on your ability 'to carry out normal day-to-day activities'.

Definitions aside, what the hands-on worker needs to focus on at this point is whether and how and why a person finds it harder to take the best care of her or his daily needs and interests, including communication and learning. If getting on with the normal business of life is harder for one person than it is for someone else, who has different physical, visual, learning capabilities or better mental health, then as a decent society we should try to change the way we do things so the person or people who are finding life harder can find it less hard. Disability is not about medical problems; it is about self-determination.

Many people look at disability as society's problem, a 'social model', believing lives are being wasted, and unnecessary and avoidable difficulties are being caused by ignorance and poorly thought-through attitudes and policies. They argue that unhelpful assumptions throughout political, economic, educational and social systems in Britain underpin decisions that fail to reflect the fact that everyone has different needs. If you support this view, one implication is that we all need to put our houses in order.

(As an aside, although this argument about 'the social model' is led by disability rights campaigners, it can also be applied to age, gender, sexuality, for example, and also to the way refugees are rendered less capable by attitudes and policies in the UK.)

In places across the world, people with physical, learning, mental health and other disabilities are neglected, abused and persecuted in many ways. People's

---

4   Previously known as the Medical Foundation for the Care of Victims of Torture or just 'the Medical Foundation'.

physical or other impairments may be caused or worsened by persecution or in war or transit, or in the continuing struggle for survival once in the UK.

It is difficult to get a sense of scale regarding disabled refugees. Neither Home Office nor local authorities nor NASS keep relevant statistics. The way 'disability' is defined varies across different sectors in the UK, so any statistics that do exist are hard to compare (see, for example, Box 9.8). But the average proportion of disabled people in the general British working-age population, given in government census data from 2011, is 16 per cent. You will come across a high proportion of refugees with learning, physical, sight or hearing impairments, facial disfigurements or other disabilities. When you factor in levels of mental ill health noted among refuges, in the region of half the refugees you meet are disabled, using the definition above.

Disabled asylum seekers need reasonable adjustments to be able to manage their lives even on a par with other asylum seekers. If data is not gathered, their needs will not be identified, recognised or addressed under the PSED, either individually or as a group.

Entitlements and access

Disability, social care and equality laws protecting disabled people are more significant in shaping their entitlements than immigration status. Entitlements are summarised in Box 9.7.

- Disabled people who are supported by a local authority are entitled to free secondary care even if they have NRPF.

- The NHS has a duty to provide accessible information and communication, primarily to make sure the NHS communicates effectively with people who have learning difficulties, but this is relevant also to refugees.

- NASS, like any public authority, must make reasonable adjustments. Therefore, they might reasonably allocate someone a ground-floor room if they have mobility problems, or case workers can argue for a single room if someone's mental health difficulties make this reasonable.

- The Equality Act 2010 protects all disabled people in Britain from discrimination. The PSED requires authorities to ensure that disabled people have equal opportunities to those who are not disabled.

Community care assessments. It is the responsibility of the local authority where someone is 'ordinarily' resident to assess adults' needs for (non-medical) special care if asked to do so, or if they appear to require care and support (Care Act 2014). The person requesting an assessment may be asked to show they have a 'local connection' (See Chapter 8). The local authority where NASS houses an asylum seeker is where they are 'ordinarily' resident; or if a refugee has found their own accommodation, it is the area where they are living now, even if they are in temporary accommodation such as shelters or sofa-surfing.

Local authorities differ. The person whose needs are being assessed can and should have an independent advocate present, and if their disability is related to mental health, an independent mental health advocate. If the assessment concludes that the disabled refugee needs support and care, the local authority has an obligation to provide or fund appropriate support. There is no set minimum for this support and it should include not only health and hygiene but wellbeing (Box 9.5). It might include:

- counselling

- support to deal with bureaucracy and entitlements, information and advocacy

- equipment and aids (e.g. hearing aids, mobility aids such as wheelchairs, household aids for independence)

- a Freedom Pass or free local travel

- adapted housing, including residential accommodation

- a carer/personal assistant should also be assessed on need, even if they are NRPF, under the Care Act, although they are not entitled to Carer's Allowance.

Box 9.5 Wellbeing in the Care Act 2014

The Care Act 2014 (www.legislation.gov.uk) introduced a 'general duty' on local authorities to promote an individual's 'wellbeing' when making decisions about them or planning services. Wellbeing can relate to:

- personal dignity (including treatment of the individual with respect)

- physical and mental health and emotional wellbeing

- protection from abuse and neglect

- control by the individual over day-to-day life (including care and support)

- participation in work, education, training or recreation

- social and economic wellbeing

- domestic, family and personal relationships

- suitability of living accommodation

- the individual's contribution to society.

Although care may be arranged, it is means-tested and will *not* necessarily be free.

A copy of the assessment and decision should be given to the individual in writing. A refugee may need your help to understand this document and any actions arising from it, or to correspond with the authority if there are errors or they disagree with any aspect and want to appeal.

There are a number of reasons why what should happen does not always happen. These include:

- Some local authorities have introduced 'pre-assessment' or forms of screening and on that basis may refuse to do a care assessment.

- Staff think asylum seekers or people with NRPF aren't eligible for care assessments, or imagine that the assessment is done by the Home Office or NASS or sub-contractors.

- The work is poorly done.

Several organisations across the UK have now successfully appealed on behalf of clients against 'pre-assessment screenings' that led to refusing a 'full' assessment. Staff of one organisation I spoke to felt that having been successful with one appeal had made it far easier to insist on proper care assessments ever since. They felt it had been well worth the frustrations and effort involved.

Do not confuse NHS 'community care' which is free (including nursing care at home and 'nursing homes') with 'social care' at home such as washing and dressing, or 'home care' or care in a 'care home' which are not NHS services and are not free. The latter are provided by the local authority and are usually means-tested.

There are some other useful entitlements. UK nationals and permanent residents can ask to register as disabled with their local authority often without needing to request a community care assessment. This gives them access to various additional services such as community transport, free public transport (Box 9.6) or free adult learning classes which might include English or British Sign Language.

Refugees with Leave can access mainstream benefits including the benefits available to disabled people who are British nationals, such as Carer's Allowance and Access to Work funds when in employment. Once they have registered with the Job Centre, this process should move along routinely, but they will be subject to the same further assessment process regarding potential employment and benefits as other disabled people in the UK, with the same controversies and inadequacies.

> **Box 9.6** **HEAR briefing – transport for disabled asylum seekers and refugees**
>
> 'Disabled and older people are also entitled to free and concessionary travel from their Local Authorities and public transport providers. Every local authority has different eligibility (some include mental health service users and others) but concessionary transport must be provided to all people with sensory impairments, mobility issues and learning difficulties regardless of immigration status under the Transport Act.' (HEAR.org.uk)

Besides local authority services, alternative sources of support include:

- Colleges of further education, which provide the majority of ESOL for adults in the UK, have welfare teams and often include a specialist support worker for disabled learners.

- Trades unions support workers' rights and often have peer-based sub-sections for disabled workers, who will advise people to some extent even if they aren't in the union, although they will get full support if they join.

- Deaf and disabled people's organisations (DDPO) are 'user-led' and 'expert by experience' groups run by and for people and carers who have direct experience of being disabled and struggles with bureaucracy. They are often local, but good at networking, and there are many 'user-led' networks that connect groups such as the National Survivor User Network. DDPOs sometimes include all disabled people, sometimes only people with specific characteristics, such as HIV.

- Older people's organisations often have expertise on disability.

- Organisations supporting people with all disabilities can often be found working within one or a few local authority areas, partly because of funds from local authorities' commissioning advice services and social care. There are also larger-scale (e.g. Scope) and national specialists (e.g. Terrence Higgins Trust). Some, such as Freedom from Torture and the Helen Bamber Foundation, have been mentioned already.

There is a definite problem in the arena of disability rights and support. Although many refugee and many disability organisations claim to have a 'we help everyone equally' approach, they don't consider it necessary to have the knowledge to 'do' disabled refugees:

People and organisations who 'do refugees' often 'don't do disability'.

People and organisations that 'do disability' often 'don't do refugees'.

Many disability bodies assume asylum seekers and refugees are not entitled to the support British nationals can get, and I have heard more than my fair share of activists express doubts that refugees should be entitled to the same. If you are looking to refer someone, check carefully first.

Given the scale of disability among refugees, this is a worrying problem. HEAR (HEAR 2018) has a Googlegroup trying to connect people who work with disabled refugees, to build up a collaborative network of people, with enough members to improve the situation.

Box 9.7	Entitlements to services and support for disabled people with different immigration status		
Disabled	**NHS**	**Local authority**	**NASS and mainstream benefits system**
All disabled people in UK, regardless of immigration	All 'public authorities' have duties of care for safeguarding and health and safety, and are bound by the Human Rights Act 1998 and Public Sector Equality Duty under the Equality Act 2010 to make reasonable adjustments to ensure that disabled people are not further disadvantaged by the planning and delivery of their services and design of their physical facilities.		
Asylum seeker	Yes.	The Care Act 2014 requires a community care assessment on request for anyone 'ordinarily resident' to determine the person's needs, which the local authority must then provide.	Standard NASS financial support. No additional amounts from NASS.
Refused asylum seeker/ NRPF	As Box 9.2 (health care) and Box 9.4 (mental health care) except people who have had a care assessment and were found to have care needs which are being provided by the local authority and who are entitled to free secondary care.		NASS accommodation with 'reasonable adjustments'.
Refugee with Leave to Remain	As Box 9.4 (health care) and 9.6 (mental health care).	For mental health, an independent mental health advocate should be involved. If they are found necessary, this can include additional financial support and adapted accommodation. Also Freedom Pass, equipment, personal assistant, etc.	As British national/ permanent resident. Includes, potentially, Disability Living Allowance (DLA), Carer's Allowance, Personal Independence Payments (PIP) and Employment Support Allowance (ESA) (also Universal Credit). DWP Access to Work funding via employer.

Box 9.8 **'Deaf', 'deaf' and deafened refugees**

It seems hearing impairments and hearing loss are more common with refugees than the general population, especially for younger people, particularly where refugees have been caught in military conflicts, but also through long-term under-treated infections.

In Britain the body of people who use British Sign Language (BSL) as a shared language, often from birth or early childhood, often identify as Deaf and part of a 'Deaf Community'. People who are deaf or hearing-impaired but do not speak BSL – whether they did not grow up in the UK or were deafened at some later point in their life – are not generally considered to be part of the 'Deaf Community' in the sense that there is no shared language. People from other countries may speak national versions of sign language (e.g. Lebanese Sign Language) or a simpler international sign language.

In many countries, people who are deaf from birth have not had access to any form of education and language – spoken or sign – and if they arrive in the UK as adults, language acquisition of any kind is more difficult. They may always struggle to master more advanced forms of language, beyond vocabulary. People who were deafened but did first speak a language need to learn English as well as BSL, but do at least have a base of language to work from.

What can you do?

When asking people what I should put in this book the answer that came back to me most often was:

'Don't poke.'

You can't and *mustn't* take over the clinician or psychologist's role and seek to diagnose and treat from your good will and general knowledge. But there is a lot you *can* do to facilitate refugees as they try to manage their own health, mental health and disabilities. This section picks up from points from Chapters 5 and 7.

Engaging – a resource for refugees' health and wellbeing strategies

You want refugees to engage with you as a resource for their own health and wellbeing strategies. You don't want to add unhealthy or disabling pressures, so check your own house is in order. Refugees may be just outside your metaphorical 'gate', but if they have health and mental health difficulties and are already coping with disabling environments and rules on various fronts, they might not come through.

For people to trust you, they need to feel it is a safe space – where they won't be judged for their condition and will meet only acceptance and thoughtfulness. We don't know if the man drinking tea in our office has decided life isn't worth living, or the woman who rather annoyingly keeps missing appointments is only able to cope because of medication. Does your job allow you flexibility to adapt around people who are not functioning quickly and efficiently? If not, you might need to raise this with managers.

> A safe space – where they won't be judged for their condition and will meet only acceptance and thoughtfulness.

You have your own limits too: supporting someone as she or he copes with traumatic experiences could bring you or colleagues close to your own tipping point. Know the boundaries and keep to them.

Build trust, listen and acknowledge their experiences of injury, illness or mental difficulties – some might call it witnessing. Whatever you do, don't tell people to 'go home and have a nice cup of tea and try to think positively'. You are denying their experiences, you are rejecting their attempt to engage with you, you are belittling and criticising their efforts to cope with their difficulty. They will agree, smile and leave.

Quite modest practical activities can become an asset for refugees' health and wellbeing strategies and be an alternative to other structures that disable them. Without doubt, any work you do that lessens someone's housing or financial problems will help take off the pressure and free them up to work on their health and agency. Helping to register with a GP and understand letters from the hospital protects their practical access. You might put on activities that people use for their health and mental health benefits directly, but avoid the stigma that would result from labelling them as 'refugee' or 'mental health'. For example:

- Put on free exercise classes, yoga or 'family wellbeing' days.

- Work with local faith bodies to lobby for a women-only swimming session.

- Give out screening kits for bowel cancer.

Chapter 5 described the potential of hosting professionals from other services. Also, for example:

- Many organisations arrange 'drop-in' opportunities at a lunch or a summer fete, when NHS community health staff give advice, check blood pressure, etc.

- Offer free space to an outreach counselling service.

- Fix a fortnightly slot for a job advice service run for people with disabilities.

- Invite a speaker from the local carers' wellbeing charity to your English group (you might have to find someone to interpret what she or he says).

Without necessarily being health-focussed, any activities that break down isolation and enable people to interact with peers are positive for wellbeing: writing courses, team sports, a monthly 'bring your own' lunch. The Refugee Council runs a bread-making group called 'Just Bread' for just this purpose – people find kneading bread soothing and rewarding.

Opportunities for self-expression in a safe space are good: read about Freedom from Torture's 'Write to Life' groups. I have known of dance, drama, writing groups, gardening, a scrapbook project, even flower arranging for refugees, but you have to have backup structures in place. Schemes like mentoring and befriending are valuable, but you must know what you are doing. British Red Cross and many local Minds have experience here and collaboration may be your best route.

Networking and advocacy – a mesh of support

Finding and networking with contacts, good referral and advocacy, and tackling failures in services were the themes of Chapter 7. Some people need more specialist health, mental health or disability services than you can provide. Normal good practice on referrals and 'One plus One' apply (Box 7.4).

You could look at ways to help refugees step it up, to start engaging with practice and policy-makers directly. For example, encourage them to:

- take up opportunities to train in health improvement so they can play the role of Health Champions, Health Connectors and other voluntary and potentially paid positions for the local NHS, or as interpreters

- become members of Healthwatch, where they can get involved in getting patients' voices heard, train to do 'Enter and View' visits and perhaps join the Healthwatch board in future

- train in health or mental health advocacy.

I noted under difficulties with GP registration that you can escalate from service provider to manager and upwards. There are multiple feedback mechanisms, starting with evaluation and feedback forms and complaints processes in each and every statutory service. You can talk to PALs services in the NHS, approach Healthwatch or the relatively new GP Patient Participation Groups. Contact campaigning groups such as Doctors of the World or Disability Law Service; or go direct to the CCG or local authority, perhaps putting in 'written questions from the public' (see Box 9.9), or to NHS England/Local Government and Social Care Ombudsman/Care Quality Commission. There is your local councillor and your MP if you want to raise a case to illustrate a wider issue.

Remember, as well as needing to meet – and be seen to meet – their PSED/ equality duty, the NHS wants asylum seekers and refugees to get the right treatment at the right place, which gives you a positive lever for suggestions that would improve communication and access for them.

Box 9.9	Challenging authorities on issues known to be important to refugee access to health

Where there are gaps in health services, you may consider using consultation opportunities and the PSED channels mentioned in Chapter 7 to ask questions on specific topics known to be frequent problems for refugees in access to health, such as:

- Do you have performance data on GP registration of newly arrived asylum seekers?

- How many PTSD-trained counsellors are there in the borough?

- What services have you commissioned to support survivors of torture?

- What is your policy on using interpreters?

- How many disabled refugees use your service?

Conclusion

Refugees' health, mental health issues and disabilities are interconnected. They affect what refugees can do as they try to get by. Helping them access treatment and care is part of the picture, but should end at some point. What we should aim to be supporting instead is their good health, wellbeing and ability to get on with life.

Each of us can only do so much, but we can see our role alongside clinical, social work and legal professionals as filling some of the gaps so that refugees can gain strength and support in the context of a much larger mesh of wide-ranging services.

CHAPTER 10

Learning English, Training, Employability and into Work

Introduction

Acquiring decent English, learning new skills and obtaining useful qualifications are necessary and positive steps for a person as she or he takes back control, and starts to build a new life in the UK. Refugees who lost careers when they went into exile have mixed emotions about starting from scratch, but the sooner a refugee can function in British society, the sooner she or he becomes employable. Perhaps after a couple of courses and 'transition' jobs, your contact will get into a decent job with a reasonable salary and be able to re-establish a career. This chapter is all about the future.

There are risks in taking on the challenges of study and work: investing time and money but failing the final exam; extra pressures on fragile mental health; bad advice, bad courses, bad employers; unrealistic expectations. Some people struggle to bend to unfamiliar educational, economic and authority structures as well as the social dynamics within them. These things can set people back. But in the daily hubbub of finding the right room or lending someone a pen, people gain confidence and new skills to act and interact within this diverse society. As they progress through and beyond 'English for Speakers of Other Languages' (ESOL) and casual contracts, people broaden their experience, knowledge, support networks and contacts, and some find a new British identity.

There are a few points to bear in mind as you support refugees along this road.

Respond to individual diversity. What people are capable of doing will change with time. There are many factors:

- the consequences of the past, present realities and how they are coping

- their current 'motive, means and opportunity' (see Chapter 5) which influence how effectively people 'engage' in education or the job market – their sense of agency will be significant

- their existing means, knowledge and skills, and also, regarding employment, English, level of previous education, qualifications, working experience, training, volunteering, working in the UK to date

- other 'equality' characteristics including age, gender pressures, undiagnosed learning disabilities such as dyslexia, cultural expectations about teachers or bosses

- immigration status – people face different restrictions, described below.

Explore possibilities. There are hundreds of options.

Be aware that training providers/employers can be flexible. Unlike asylum support or acute mental health services, training providers and even employers have a good deal of flexibility if they choose to respond to an individual refugee. Managers can often use discretion and squeeze in a few extra students who don't fit the funders' criteria, or find room for a placement. Teaching especially is highly vocational and teachers don't like turning people away if they want to learn, although admissions staff might be less sympathetic.

Think strategically towards realistic goals. You and the person you are supporting will do well to think and talk about longer-term life and career goals before setting things in motion. People have to have money to live, and many schemes are designed to get people a job. Being employed is a good thing. It improves income and stability and has other advantages such as learning to handle pay slips and the tax system, or feeling part of a team.

But some jobs are dead ends. For example, work as a security guard has few opportunities for promotion; social care can lead into caring professions such as nursing, but can also drain people's physical and emotional resources; changing shift patterns make it hard to follow a course; bad jobs undermine confidence. To quote a discussion I was party to: 'The risk is that they will get somewhere but be going nowhere.'

> The risk is that they will get somewhere but be going nowhere.

Goals motivate a person and give a sense of identity. Some people still need to hold on to dreams to get through today. But there is a risk that an individual will waste time, even years, turning down opportunities while they wait for the perfect break. They may burn up energy proactively applying for courses, degrees and jobs that they stand no chance of getting. The price can be humiliation and cynicism, even debt (Box 10.1, CS/A).

Reasonable goals help people make strategic choices about how to invest their time and energy today. When someone has a clear and reasonable goal, they can see a low-skilled job as a step towards what they really want, and accepting the job offer becomes a positive tactic rather than a negative compromise (CS/B and CS/C). Being strategic helps people face setbacks with determination and might help mental and emotional resilience (CS/D).

Do remember you are not the architect of their strategies, but one of their strategic assets. Refugees have to do what they feel is best for them and their families. They value your knowledge, your help and advocacy, your encouragement and advice in bad patches. They may fully appreciate the effort you put in to finding them a good course, but if it doesn't fit *their* priorities, they will probably walk away (Box 10.1).

Box 10.1 | **Refugees making their own choices about progress to work – Case Studies A–D**

A   was a secondary school teacher in the Middle East who took a one-year postgraduate course to teach in the UK. However, he could not make the cultural shift to cope with student behaviour in British schools. He left one and then another teaching job, then turned his back on teaching and got work in a food factory. He had to quit because he couldn't cope with the physically demanding work. The last time we spoke he was still unemployed.

B   was a plumber before he came to the UK. He started training as an interpreter, but quit as he didn't feel comfortable or believe it would provide a full-time income. Despite being in his late 50s, he joined a utilities company at a junior grade, rapidly got accreditation and promotion through their internal scheme, and became a Corgi-registered gas engineer, making a good, reliable living in his own trade.

C   was a refugee doctor who spent more than five years unemployed while he repeatedly failed the English tests needed to start requalifying as a doctor in the UK. After five years, under pressure from the Job Centre, he took a job as a porter in the NHS. Within a month he had been trained and moved to phlebotomy (bloods); within three months the NHS made him an offer of a funded place on a full-time degree in a therapeutic field, which he took.

D   had been stopped from working as a nurse because of discrimination against his religion. Now in the UK as an asylum seeker, he is not allowed to work or requalify unless he can pay private fees, which he can't. So he goes on every free first aid course, health and safety course, health improvement course we can find him, plus every free English group he can get to, so he is ready to restart his career should he ever get Leave to Remain.

Know about entitlements and eligibility. There are a few common restrictions that affect education, volunteering and employment opportunities (restrictions that relate only to non-formal or formal training are described in the training sections):

- Immigration status (for a reminder of definitions, see Box 3.11 or the Glossary): asylum seekers, refused asylum seekers and people who have No Recourse to Public Funds (NRPF) can't legally work. Therefore, they have limited access to free or subsidised training funded by government, most of which is related to employment, from ESOL to professional qualifications. Some support is further restricted to Convention refugees.

- At present if an asylum seeker has been in the asylum process for more than six months, they can access slightly more ESOL, but changes to immigration bail in 2018 mean an asylum seeker can be prevented from studying any course that could lead to a qualification, including English-language ESOL courses.

- Asylum/NRPF status restricts volunteering that might be seen as 'unpaid work' – for example, a former teacher offering to teach for free.

- The time remaining on visas and permits: even refugees with Leave to Remain may not be able to get places on longer-term schemes or employment opportunities (e.g. three-year courses, apprenticeships or permanent contracts).

- Voluntary sector projects and programmes may have eligibility restrictions if they are funded from governmental sources, plus the constant confusion over entitlements and 'we don't do refugees' attitudes mentioned in several chapters are still an issue.

- Clumsy criteria for shortlisting: staff recruiting for courses and jobs often have a set list of qualifications, experience, continuity of employment, residency, which disadvantage refugees – for example, requiring a GCSE in English or a reference from your most recent employer.

- Evidence: whether people have credible evidence of status, ID, address, qualifications and proof of address (Appendix B).

Do look out for public authorities using the PSED to justify 'positive action' schemes that give extra help to people who are recovering from mental ill health or who are disabled, carers, young people, women, Tamils or Bangladeshis and many more ethnic groups, plus combinations (e.g. Bangladeshi women). It is not common to find one specifically aimed at refugees, but it does happen.

Put these points together and your role starts to emerge. Refugees are diverse, and are active agents of their own futures – you need to respond to the individual. Be aware but make no assumptions. Network and be informed – you can help with accurate knowledge and up-to-date information. Listen and create space for people to think and act – where they can articulate their goals and analyse their chances. You can talk strategy and tactics, work out alternative routes and help them to negotiate access.

This chapter covers issues and entitlements, opportunities and ideas for action in your work with refugees. It does not look at teaching methods and resources, or at practical advice such as how to do a job interview or access 'in work' benefits, as that information is widely available. Chapter 11 will look at education and training for children/young people. Appendix A has sources of further advice and expertise.

Daily English and other non-formal learning

Building on what has already been said in Chapter 5, and with reference to the 'GREG' model in Chapter 6, this section looks at 'non-formal' learning opportunities set up outside formal settings (some say 'community', 'grass roots', 'informal' learning).

These are activities that are not usually matched to fixed standards such as ESOL levels or exam board assessments. They tend to focus on daily life. English is what most people put on for refugees, although the focus of activities might be job seeking, better parenting, managing money, health, learning to cook or how to do beauty treatments, or many others, often with a wellbeing element. Don't forget that through your organisation, refugee 'volunteers' can access a wide range of free non-formal training put on by and for the voluntary sector, from first aid to Freedom of Information. All of these – plus activities that go alongside such as summer picnics and helping with publicity – help people to learn, to gain British experiences and look to the future.

Non-formal learning activities tend to be led by volunteers and local activists, identity-based groups such as an Iraqi association or women's group, or by/supported by charities and faith bodies (see also Box 10.2). Schools, mental health bodies, the NHS, local authority or the police might give a 'community outreach' brief to staff to run non-formal sessions, courses or groups as a way to establish a bridge with the wider public. Often there are no eligibility criteria, but when activities are funded or aim for a specific result, eligibility may still be restricted to certain social groups – for example, families with children under five (most children's centres) – or by postcode.

Box 10.2 **Gender and the single-sex dilemma**

You might be asked to segregate males and females, on the grounds that:

1. You will get a higher turnout from people who avoid mixed-sex groups, in particular when families disapprove or where women have faced sexual assault or domestic abuse.

2. Some people learn better in single-sex groups, although the opposite is also true.

3. Men often dominate discussion in mixed-sex groups.

Before you decide, remember that a good facilitator mediates group dynamics; that this is an integrated country and women and men need to learn to interact as equals for a healthy society; and that exposure to new experiences builds confidence to tackle similar situations in future.

If you set up single-sex activities, ensure the quality and benefits to men and women are equivalent, or you risk consolidating inequality.

Non-formal does not mean unimportant. Someone who has means and assets has plenty of choices and will probably see non-formal learning as a form of leisure. But this kind of 'community' opportunity may be the only structured learning available to asylum seekers and people with NRPF, and even people with Leave to Remain who have other constraints or disadvantages.

Those who need non-formal learning need to guard their resources carefully. They can't afford the costs or risks or demands of more formal options. In the best non-formal learning, they gain skills, knowledge, experience and confidence, social interaction and perhaps a shared identity, acceptance and holistic backup. But even in relatively low-cost, low-risk, non-formal learning, if they feel their investment is not helping them get where they want to go, they will cut their losses and stop coming. Socialising is not enough. Quality and relevance matter; without them, you'll have no participants.

> In the best non-formal learning, they gain skills, knowledge, experience and confidence, social interaction and perhaps a shared identity, acceptance and holistic backup... Quality and relevance matter.

You usually find some people who are stuck in non-formal groups (Box 10.3). They would prefer to be elsewhere – in college, for example, or working – and they are capable of more demanding activities. But college arrangements, immigration status, money, caring roles, family pressure and health mean they have nowhere else they can go. Their only 'investment option' is the non-formal group, even if they feel it gives a 'poor return'. They can be frustrated and even disruptive as they try to gain what they need rather than what you intend the group to provide.

Box 10.3 People get stuck outside formal learning

Although some choose non-formal learning over formal, a distinct group of people are stuck in non-formal activities but would rather be moving faster in their lives. Perhaps...

- Courses are full. There are no courses at their level. They have been excluded for poor attendance or inadequate progress. They are newly arrived or have just moved to the area, or their circumstances have recently changed. Courses often start once a year and they just have to wait.

- Their immigration status restricts them. They don't have the necessary evidence. Accommodation is temporary or insecure and means they aren't eligible for courses. They can't get free places and they can't afford to pay.

- They care for children or others, are pregnant or just gave birth, or have demanding families. There is no suitable or affordable transport from their accommodation, taking into account disabilities or other constraints on time such as school pick-up. Paid work prevents formal learning.

- They are avoiding people who go to the college who might be a danger to them.

Non-formal learning is not better or worse than formal learning – it is different. Refugees might be making use of non-formal opportunities before, during or after other, formal training (Box 10.4). As with wellbeing-focussed activities considered at the end of Chapter 9, the best non-formal learning complements the formal. If you are creating non-formal opportunities, you will be most effective when you work alongside formal providers to create a good mesh of services and support so that individuals can step across the gaps (Box 10.4, CS/E and CS/F).

Box 10.4	Refugees mixing formal and non-formal learning – Case Studies E and F

E   has attended informal English groups for some years. She also attends formal college two days per week under an employability programme, a regular women's group that runs a range of learning and mental wellbeing activities, and NHS physiotherapy sessions teaching and encouraging self-care for chronic back pain.

F   attends two colleges which both offer him part-time study for free, plus a 'grass roots' English group that also runs social lunches, and one-to-one mentoring by a specialist refugee charity.

In current social policy, non-formal learning is largely invisible. You might also come across some qualified teachers who are inclined to dismiss 'community' English and 'barefoot' teachers. (None of this addresses the fact that formal education excludes many of these learners.) Non-formal learning is seen as fuzzy and unproductive, and this can be true. It tends to gets little serious attention and sporadic, small-grant funding if any. It has become part of the 'new role' for hands-on workers who are not refugee specialists. Longevity and effectiveness usually hinge on the commitment of key individuals acting on their own initiative. They may have limited training or backup, but a sharp eye for what can disable people and a knowledge of possibilities (Box 10.5).

Box 10.5	Examples of volunteers, activists and organisations offering non-formal learning for English – Case Studies G–K

G is a qualified, unpaid English teacher who runs her own 'English with Confidence' class in a community centre, and offers one-to-one lessons to women with babies in their own homes.

H is a charity that supports young adults who are mostly full-time at college. A volunteer runs several study sessions per week where refugee students do homework together, with his help.

I and her friends run an own-language-based group with support from a children's centre. Each week their three-hour session combines a two-hour crèche with an hour of English run by her next-door neighbour, a one-hour slot for topics such as parenting or weaning delivered by professionals over three to five weeks, and an hour of everyone sharing food and socialising.

J is a school that asks Somali-speaking bilingual parents to interpret so that other Somali parents can attend sessions where they learn about their children's school work, phonics, maths methods, homework and school trips.

K could not manage the demand for English, so set up a listing service for other English groups and volunteers, plus numeracy and conversation-related activities within a five-mile radius, to help people find groups across the area.

See also the example of a model for 'Grass Roots English' in Chapter 6.

Formal English, ESOL, training, formal education and qualifications

Formal learning is education and training with set standards, learner assessment and qualifications, usually with outside scrutiny and run by a mix of non-profit and profit-making bodies as well as statutory providers. Learners are in classes separated by topic, level of skill and knowledge, and by the qualification they are aiming for. For refugees, formal education often includes support to get a job or move closer to the job market by becoming more 'employable'.

A good-sized college may have cheap food, warm rooms, free IT and sports facilities, even 'access' funds, plus supportive staff, welfare and advice teams, tutoring, mentoring, even counselling. There might be celebrations, clubs or volunteering schemes. There should be help for disabled refugees and somewhere to turn to in crisis.

Access to formal learning is likely to be restricted by funders' requirements. In addition to restrictions noted in the introduction, you will often find refugees are limited by:

- How long they have been in the country (e.g. less than six months, at least three years).

- Where they live or are 'ordinarily resident': usually based on local authority areas, although some institutions might defined catchment areas based on postcodes or distance.

- For refugees with Leave, whether they are 'economically active' (available for work, actively seeking work) and/or on employment-related benefits (e.g. Jobseeker's Allowance or Universal Credit). Some courses are aimed at groups who are 'economically *inactive*' to try to move them 'nearer to work'.

- Nationality: asylum seekers and recent refugees are mostly 'non-EU', although some will have British or EU passports gained in recent years, but this may all change with Brexit.

- Evidence: for example, someone who is the spouse or dependant of a refugee may need evidence to prove the relationship, such as marriage and birth certificates (see Appendix B).

Refugees depend a lot on personal recommendation when it comes to choosing courses and colleges. If someone asks your opinion, they have several decisions to make.

SUBJECT

There is an incredible array of subjects, courses and facilities, especially with the current phenomenon of colleges merging. Refugees who are keen to get on might look at the following.

Topics to function in daily life:

- ESOL and other English (e.g. literacy). You might find English as an Additional Language (EAL), as a Foreign Language (EFL) (e.g. Teaching EFL or TEFL)

- other functional and 'skills for life' (e.g. numeracy)

- wider relevance (e.g. driving theory, first aid, life in the United Kingdom)

- wellbeing and resilience (e.g. positive thinking, arts, health).

Related to getting into a job:

- courses that link ESOL and job skills (e.g. ESOL and beauty, entry-level health and social care)

- entry-level 'into work' training (e.g. Level 1 and 2 health and social care, lifting, chemicals handling, security, forklift driving, food hygiene, catering, hospitality, safeguarding)

- functional skills for employability and getting into work (e.g. basic IT, job interviews)

- the above combined with later 'on the job' study (e.g. apprenticeships, structured study with assessed work experience element).

Looking strategically towards a career or profession:

- into work but also creating routes to higher qualifications and careers (e.g. Level 2 and 3 health and social care, child development, interpreting, teaching assistant, catering and nutrition, advice work, book-keeping, IT skills, business studies, self-employment)

- occupational/professional (e.g. nursing, accountancy, law, IT)

- requalification (e.g. engineering, teaching, medical, nursing, including IELTS (see next paragraph)

- academic (e.g. GCSE or A-level English, maths, history, psychology, 'access to university' courses).

LEVEL (BOX 10.6)

There are regulated scales for assessments and qualifications across the UK that almost all British education and exam boards can be mapped to. In ESOL, new English learners will be at one of the 'Entry' levels, from 'Pre-entry' (no English at all) to 'Entry 3' which was once described to me as 'good enough for a job in an all-night garage'. There are also international testing levels that refugees might have or want to get:

- IELTS – International English Language Testing System (people say 'I-Yelts') ranging from 1 to 9, where 5+ would be needed for entrance to a British university and 7.5 for refugee doctors and dentists wanting to requalify and practise in the UK.

- TOEFL – Test of English as a Foreign Language, scored out of 120, where 90–100 would be adequate for a place at most universities.

- SELT – the Secure English Language Test, taken at approved centres only and the candidate must prove their identity. It is required for visa applications.

Box 10.6	ESOL levels and how well someone can communicate in English
Pre-entry	Not even hello
Entry 1	Personal information, name
Entry 2	Simple questions and answers
Entry 3	Basic functional, sufficient for 'a job in an all-night garage'

Level 1	Conversation
Level 2	Conversation: GCSE pass
Level 3	Discussion and debate, sufficient to start training as a community interpreter: A Level, International Baccalaureate, Scottish Highers
Level 4	Teaching English to migrant adults: approximately second-year undergraduate
Level 5	Fully fluent: honours degree
Level 6	Sufficient for international interpreting, and teaching English language and literature in schools: Master's

DURATION AND FORMAT

There are many options that people new to Britain might not know about. The right choice will probably mean a better result.

- **Duration.** From one week to three years. To avoid losing everything if you have to drop out and for flexibility, learners often study a combination of separate units or modules to earn credits for a full qualification.

- **Part-time.** Part-time might be certain days only, or evenings and weekends. Learners lose some of the benefits of peer support that can build up with daily interaction. It can be hard to keep up momentum over a long period with gaps. Part-time courses spread the costs although they are often more expensive over their full term than full-time courses, and some learners can sign on for benefits or work while studying.

- **Full-time.** The learner is expected to spend at least 35 hours per week on study, although this includes placements and private study time. Learners on full-time courses can focus more intensively on the subject, and some prefer to struggle financially for a short time but make progress fast. Full-time courses are not usually possible for people who rely on benefits.

- **Online courses.** Many courses can be found online but learners need to check the site is real and their qualification will be recognised. Some courses combine online study and assignments with webinars and face-to-face time with tutors or seminar sessions. It can be hard to keep going on an online course over time, especially with no peer support. People expect online courses to be cheap but they usually are about the same as 'classroom-based' training, although there are fewer travel costs. Subsidised online courses at lower levels are increasingly available through the voluntary sector.

- **Start dates.** Most courses (not online) are still usually based on three terms per year, and by far the largest choice of full-time courses and others will be those starting in September, with the second largest choice starting in January. Shorter and part-time courses and apprenticeships can start around the year, and even practical degree programmes such as nursing sometimes start at other times of the year.

PROVIDERS

The nature and size of different providers means they can and do offer different things. The refugee, with your support, needs to check quality. Try the Ofsted website and use your local contacts but make sure they/you are up to date. For example, where some bodies will provide placements, less good providers might leave the student to find their own.

- 'Adult learning' is run by the local council, usually aimed at local residents, with a scale of fees including subsidised places for people on benefits who are ordinarily resident in the area, but not usually people who have NRPF.

- Colleges of Further Education (FE) are independent non-profit bodies, with funding from multiple governmental sources and various related restrictions on eligibility and fees. Academic and vocational courses mingle in FE, usually with considerable emphasis on employability and often links with local employers.

- Private training companies might be linked to national or international corporations, providing, for example, Secure English Language Tests (SELTs)/International English Language Testing System (IELTS) and 'Life in the UK' tests, and handling contracts for the Job Centre. Many have a strong public ethos; others are profit-driven. Some are very good and some are not. Some providers push eligible learners on to unsuitable courses in order to meet quotas for the Job Centre. Some courses are only internally assessed, leaving students without a recognised qualification. Some providers are more focussed on getting migrants to take out loans for fees than on the quality of teaching. Unfortunately, refugees and migrants are targeted by companies that sell qualifications.

COST

Money matters, but the cheapest course is not always the best investment.

- Fee structures can be confusing and may be negotiable. Don't rely on brochures and websites – talk to someone. Encourage the refugee to start finding out about fees at the very beginning and well before the course starts.

- Add on travel costs. (Can they walk? Cycle? Bike locks and safety gear?)

- Allow for extras such as Student Union subscriptions, cost of identity cards and replacements if lost, exam fees, decent IT access, photocopying and printing tokens, books and equipment, placement costs, extra costs for trips and opportunities outside their course.

- Compare the total with net income over this period, and then compare it with likely increased income after the course.

- Can they pay in instalments? (They might not be allowed to have their final results if they haven't paid by then.) Can they get benefits or work at the same time? Is a grant or access funding possible? (Hint: They should get an offer of a place *before* they apply for grants.) What about a career or student loan (also ask the college)?

Once your refugee contact has made these decisions and come up with a shortlist of their best options, there is still the process of applying. I have known people miss out for a whole year because they didn't start this process in time. For a full-time course, ideally start to apply six months before – popular courses will be full well before the term starts. Apply now. You can always turn the place down later.

Inevitably, there are forms to fill and they can be surprisingly difficult, even for ESOL courses. Most are online and people often need help. A few hints:

- At open days, perhaps with your help, people can check the course is right for them, confirm they are eligible and show evidence, get an on-the-spot assessment of their English if necessary, and usually apply there and then, saving months as well as the risk of wasting time and effort.

- When filling in the application, make sure the refugee includes:

  - qualifications or experience from *before* the UK – many people don't realise it all counts. Help them include the British equivalent if possible (see Box 10.7)

  - a list of non-formal training in the UK (easier if they have attendance certificates)

  - a recommendation letter from you – it might encourage the provider to take a risk on a borderline candidate

  - your phone number and direct email in case the provider has trouble communicating with them.

- Keep in touch and make sure they are following up their application:

  - Have they heard anything? Should they ring to check?

  - Do they have an interview? Do they have the right date and place? Do they need to rearrange?

- Have they accepted any offer in writing?

- If they have a conditional offer, do they understand what they need to do next?

- If they are on a waiting list, they will probably still get on the course as a lot of people drop out. Have they rung up to show they are still keen?

- Do they know they must attend an enrolment day before the course starts, and do they have the right date and place? Do they have everything they need – photos, evidence, cash, etc.?

• Help with the mini-crisis of getting started: your council has a list of childcare providers, get a recycled computer from a green project, a bike from a bike project…perhaps you can donate pens and paper.

Box 10.7 | **UK NARIC (National Academic Recognition Information Centre)**

NARIC uses an extensive database to provide an informed opinion of the equivalence of British and overseas qualifications. They provide an equivalent national qualification name but don't compare specific institutions or provide an equivalent grade. Most universities pay for access to the NARIC database in order to assess overseas qualifications. A growing number of employers know about it.

With thanks to Sheila Heard, Transitions.

People often drop out in the first few weeks when time, financial, physical and emotional demands are higher than expected and the reality of classroom life including peer dynamics becomes clear. You can continue to help your contacts after they start. Poor study skills or time management can mean missed deadlines and disappointing results, even when people have worked hard. Poor punctuality or attendance under 85% can result in being excluded. Ring and encourage them, organise a study group for the first half-term, book in a couple of one-to-one sessions. The provider will usually be working hard to keep people's attendance, behaviour and progress up to scratch. Encourage the refugee to make use of help within the system:

• teachers and tutors for subject and content

• staff such as 'learning mentors' for study skills, including time management

• less formal 'buddy' and peer-support systems or welfare and disability support services, pastoral staff, counselling service and more specialist referral to outside services

- financial support which might be available mid-course if it is a question of helping a good student stay on a course – teaching and welfare staff will bend over backwards to help students who are doing their best.

Employability, volunteering and into employment

Earning a living can mean so many things – plaiting hair or building nuclear reactors. No one doubts the significance of starting employment and gaining control over your income, being active, interaction, experience. Getting into work is one problem; poor employment and poor employers, under-employment, drudgery and low pay are others.

Entitlement to work is fairly simple as already described: asylum seekers can't work, nor can refused asylum seekers. Adult refugees with Leave to Remain can. There are a very few exceptions where asylum seekers who are highly skilled in IT and 'shortage' professions are permitted work, and there has been campaign after campaign since asylum seekers were banned from paid work in 2002 to reverse the ban – so far all unsuccessful.

This final section is about how you can help refugees' strategies to get decent work.

Helping refugees make themselves more attractive to employers

Employers are all different: statutory bureaucracies must recruit staff who will reliably help them work towards set standards; private businesses are driven by profit calculations; agencies want people who will turn up where and when needed and send in timesheets on time. To get employed, you have to persuade an employer to employ you. Employers only look for staff when they need a job done, so they only want someone who will do that job. Refugees need to see themselves through employers' eyes.

> Refugees need to see themselves through employers' eyes.

Refugees will almost always need to adapt, if not requalify. Some skills that refugees bring are more immediately transferable and useful to UK employers than others (Box 10.8, CS/L). Work in catering, retail, music, many building skills or academic research, for example, are fairly global and easy to adapt. Engineering, medicine and agricultural practice have core principles, although practical application will differ in the UK.

Other professions such as teaching, journalism, public relations or law might not transfer as easily as you'd expect, because they are more cultural (see Box 10.1, CS/A). Lawyers need to 'convert' their knowledge to English/ Welsh or Scottish law, and might start with a law 'conversion' course if they can fund it, or work upwards by entering advice work – for example, getting an OISC licence (Box 3.3) to start working their way in through immigration law.

Computing and IT skills are transferable but change very fast, and people who were stuck in transit or asylum fall behind. Even if refugees have something similar on paper, it is from another country and possibly some years out of date.

Box 10.8 | **People have very different skills – Case Studies L and M**

L   was a veterinary specialist in his 60s who couldn't get a job in Britain. His special field was camels. Eventually, he found a small charity with a London office that raised funds for rural projects in his region of Africa and became an expert adviser, although up until we lost contact, I don't think he ever got paid work.

M   was a young man I interviewed for a job. He promised that no matter what, we would always be laughing if we employed him. With some regret, I gave the job to the more boring and experienced candidate, thinking that we would probably get more work done that way.

Employers also want people who can line-manage, think ahead, make decisions, understand money, monitor standards and engage well with the public. They value organisational skills such as planning, logistics, handling data and IT. These are skills that many people bring from work in earlier countries, and from real-life experiences, including parenthood, and don't necessarily rely on training. Employers are also looking for a new colleague – a person they will have to spend days and months with. But they are not looking for a friend – they want someone who will add to the effectiveness of the team and who will make their working life a bit easier, not harder (Box 10.8, CS/M).

Legitimate employers need evidence. They need formal and paper-based evidence of entitlement to work. They might need your advice or reassurance on what immigration paperwork means.[1] They want proof of identity, address, NI numbers and bank accounts as evidence the person is legitimate.

They might want original certificates for formal qualifications. You could ask someone independent, whom you trust, to read the refugee's own-language certificates and letters, or ask someone credible, such as a teacher, to do an informal assessment and give their written feedback which you quote on your letterhead.

They also want evidence in the sense of being able to see that someone is genuinely capable. A reference is a powerful tool for this, especially where it is clearly from a credible person and organisation (see Box 7.5 and Box 10.9). When other evidence is missing, you can help by offering your own assessment, but acknowledge this is informal and state its limitations.

---

1   The Refugee Council's Guidance for Employers, *Employing Refugees* (2014), is good and due an update as this book goes to press.

Box 10.9 A reference for a refugee

Box 7.5 on writing letters for refugees spells out how important your credibility is. Regarding job references, there are further points:

- In references, the employer or course convener is looking for reassurance, not a sales pitch.

- Give dates and details: when you first met them, dates of trainings or volunteering tasks, responsibilities and duration.

- Think about what the employer wants to read, not about all the things you could say.

- Help them see that the person has the skills and aptitude they want. Ask for the job description and person specification and go through these carefully, giving examples of something the refugee has done with your organisation that demonstrates the right skills. Remember other organisational assets: she is a fast learner, team player, thinks ahead, has good judgement. If you would employ them, say so.

Employability

Supporting a refugee's 'employability' includes helping them access training – largely covered in the sections above. Non-formal learning also plays its part, which includes helping with cultural competence. You can also help people access specialist schemes.

REQUALIFICATION SCHEMES

- Requalification schemes are for people who have already worked in skilled professions before coming to the UK (e.g. medicine, engineering) – see Box 10.10. These tend to be focussed on refugees, because other skilled migrants had to sort out accreditation before they got a visa. Most schemes were decimated by short-sighted funding cuts from 2010 onwards, and requalification can take several years, so those schemes that remain are nearly overwhelmed by demand.

- Examples of providers: Refugee Council, Transitions, Refugee Assessment and Guidance Unit (RAGU), BMA Refugee Doctors Initiative.

- Eligibility: refugees might need Leave to Remain or be 'permitted to work' and there might be restrictions based on length of time in the UK. Some schemes have a minimum English requirement, because they are designed to finish off the process of requalification that may have started some years earlier.

- Support provided: includes one-to-one and group and career guidance, study groups and seminars, applications for grants to help study or pay exam fees, work experience and searching opportunities for supervised placements, support during placements and help with job search, application, interview and sustaining employment for the first six months.

Box 10.10 | Joining professional bodies

Another way to give UK employers confidence in overseas qualification is to join a UK Professional Body as a graduate member. Professional bodies will often use NARIC (Box 10.7) as part of that process. Graduate membership is seen by employers as an evaluation of graduate-level professional knowledge and skills.

With thanks to Sheila Heard, Transitions.

EMPLOYABILITY SCHEMES

- Employability schemes are open to a wider public, although a few might have funders that guarantee places for refugees, possibly for Convention refugees, or positive action schemes – for example, increasing the chance for Somali women to enter the labour market.

- Examples of providers: Jobcentre Plus (Department of Work and Pensions, DWP) includes Job Coaches and referral to providers. Also colleges of FE, non-profit bodies including social enterprises.

- Eligibility: as above, except English as ESOL might be provided.

- Support provided: usually short-term or up to 18 months, classroom and online, practical IT, book-keeping, office practice and skills, mentoring, job search, CVs, applications and interview skills in the context of equal opportunities. Might include preparing people for self-employment and setting up small businesses. Some bodies have direct links with local employers who can give workshops, work experience placements and guaranteed interviews. Some schemes follow up after someone gets into paid work to help them manage the practical, financial and emotional pressures of transition into work, and might mediate if there are difficulties between the employer and employee.

SELF-EMPLOYMENT SCHEMES

- Self-employment schemes prepare people, including refugees, to set up their own businesses. Many 'mid-life' refugees have run businesses but need help converting their experience to the British context with its strict financial, tax/NI/pension, employment, health and safety regulations.

- Eligibility: as above, though excluding ESOL.

- Examples of providers: Tern, Chaigaram.

- Support provided: goal-setting, business planning, book-keeping, support on regulations and finding help with resources and premises, credit and subsidies.

Schemes that support disabled people/refugees into work

- These include people with mental health issues or recovering from mental ill health.

- Examples of providers: voluntary sector, DWP funding through 'Access to Work'.

- Eligibility: varies but may include postcode.

- Support provided: DWP will assess an individual's needs such as IT equipment, and pay up to 100 per cent of what is required for them to be able to maintain their job. Other schemes include personal planning, volunteering, one-to-one support, phased start to work, ongoing support in employment.

Relevant networks and sources of peer support and expertise and campaigning

- For refugees: Council for At-Risk Academics (CARA).

- For career and other advisers: RCAN in London, Refugee Employment Network, Career Development Institute, Women's Resource Centre, Age Concern.

Volunteering and helping refugees towards work

Helping people make themselves more employable especially means finding them opportunities for work-related experience. It is essential that asylum seekers are not seen to be doing 'unpaid work' and that the Job Centre knows people with Leave to Remain are still 'available for work'. Volunteering such as befriending or gardening don't look like work and might not seem to provide work skills directly, but they do provide a chance for team work, receiving and giving instructions, time management and so forth.

Volunteering might be just helping out here and there, or a particular task over time, or in some cases a formal arrangement including job description, interviews and volunteer 'contract', often for more than six months. This is generally considered good practice, but for asylum seekers it could look like 'unpaid work'. It probably isn't the style best suited to refugees with demanding lives, who are treading several paths at once towards paid work.

Try contacting other organisations that use volunteers:

- Volunteer bureaux: there are still some bodies, associations of voluntary services and local authorities that run agency-style brokerage that matches would-be volunteers to organisations that need them. Other brokerage points include libraries, local authority magazines, online sources such as *The Guardian* voluntary work and volunteer support jobs.

- Direct contact to organisations that use a lot of volunteers and unpaid time. For example:

  - A range of one-off activities, usually unstructured: Women's Institute, churches, parents at schools, even local campaigning groups such as Amnesty International or 38 Degrees.

  - Can someone shadow you for a day? Attend a public event for you? Be your representative at a regular meeting?

  - Ongoing but less formal, although there should still be an orientation at least: food banks, English groups, charity shops, sometimes libraries.

  - Formal with training and a commitment of at least six months: hospitals, Age Concern visitors, Age Concern advisers, Citizens Advice (one year+), Scouts and Guides with a 'career'-type ladder of increasing responsibility. Some have application processes and might require evidence.

  - Persuading organisations such as a community centre to create a volunteering or 'work experience' opportunity specifically to give a refugee a chance. There are commercial organisations that do this for schools.

You can set up volunteering opportunities. But don't rush into it. It is not as simple as you might think. Discuss and plan before you start. Like many things, when volunteering works well, it's great. But both sides lose if you don't manage it well. Be clear in your own mind whether you are doing this because you want to help the refugee or because you need extra help to manage your own workload. You have little control over volunteers, who have demanding lives and can't always be reliable. At the same time, they can't make decisions without you. So when volunteers are doing something, you usually need to be there, which could make you less productive in other ways.

Get the blessing of more and less senior staff, as they will feel the effect if a volunteer has problems or if you do. Remember other service users. Will group members be happy with the volunteer's style of leadership? You are responsible and liable for volunteers' behaviour, wellbeing and safety. You have a duty of care to keep the organisation and all its staff and members safe. DBS checks are essential if anyone in contact with your organisation is vulnerable.

If you are setting something up from scratch, an agreement on a task-by-task basis within a well-organised environment (Box 10.11) is a more manageable approach for you at first, and for refugees as it allows for their daily realities and gives you and the refugee clarity on what is expected and what to expect, plus a chance to do it differently next time. Remember to keep a record of what they do over time, including training and responsibilities, so you can write meaningful references in the future.

Box 10.11 **Necessary policies for volunteering and employment**

Make them aware of your existing policies and procedures, and make sure you comply with them yourself. Key policies are likely to be:

- safeguarding including DBS checks, confidentiality, data protection, health and safety including daily and more irregular safety procedures, fire drills and security

- expenses

- equality and diversity

- supervision, discipline and grievance, bullying and harassment, whistleblowing

- IT and financial security

- task description, code of conduct, complaints for the volunteer's own reference.

If you can invest a little time up front, you improve their experience and opportunities to learn, and reduce the risk of disruption later.

- Allow a proper training and orientation (also Box 10.11). Be realistic in what you ask volunteers to do with or without training; even photocopying confuses people who aren't used to doing it.

- If your system relies on volunteers (e.g. asking them to lead regular activities), build in time for ongoing recruiting. Have routine backup plans in place for when someone rings in ill.

- Make your volunteer expenses policy clear and stick to it consistently. And note: expenses can really add up, just £4 per day two to three times a week is £250+ over six months, so give a monthly deadline for claiming expenses and avoid nasty surprises.

- Be sure that thank-you gifts can't be interpreted as a substitute for payment – by the Home Office or the Tax Man (or by the refugee).

Even gift cards could be problematic, but a nicely presented bag of stationery or a basket of food treats is usually appreciated.

And check your insurance – it will only cover a certain number of people per year.

Going up a notch from volunteering, you may consider something more substantial such as offering refugees **structured work experience, a part-time placement, career-oriented internships or apprenticeships**. You might recruit from your own contacts and participants, but it is a very good idea to host trainees from requalification or employability schemes that specialise in supporting refugees. A good scheme will usually support you to set up something appropriate including selection, task and supervision structures, and will provide ongoing external supervision and support. There is an initial cost implication in staff time and possible insurance, IT and so forth, but most schemes will pay people's travel expenses at least, and some degree-level schemes give a small fee to organisations that host placements.

A placement that is set up properly in advance can be an asset to your work, and after the first placement it will be less work to set up each time, but the benefit to refugee trainees remains extremely high. Be honest and thorough in your feedback – trainees are there to learn.

For increasingly direct access to employment, you can try to build links with local employers (look out for guidance from the Refugee Employment Network). Remember: few organisations will employ someone just to help that person out, or to do you a favour. But employers do have discretion. It helps if they know and trust you. If you want to encourage a local employer to facilitate refugees into work, you will need to make a commitment yourself, and be organised and efficient.

- Maybe you can find a 'friend within' the company (ideally at executive level). Some managers or bosses have experienced migration or refuge themselves, although that doesn't necessarily make them sympathetic.

- Make sure employers are confident that refugees are allowed to work and that they are familiar with the paperwork that proves someone can work.

- Ask employers if their staff can provide coaching, mock interviews or hands-on 'work tasters' or introductory training (Box 10.12, CS/N); or work together to design and manage work experience or work placements (CS/O).

- Offer to help advertise their vacancies and send to all the refugee contacts you have built up. Then invite people to the office to work on applications and interview skills.

- Discuss how they shortlist. Can they avoid requiring UK qualifications and UK experience that rule out very capable refugees? They can choose to interview all refugees who apply, but they have to be careful not to discriminate either against or in favour of refugees when they appoint.

Box 10.12	Examples of refugee service/employer collaboration – Case Studies N and O

N   In 2017 a major chain linked up with the Refugee Council to provide four days of training and one-to-one job coaching, plus guaranteed interviews to refugees. Over half the refugees who completed the first set of courses were offered jobs by the chain.

O   Transitions is a non-profit social enterprise in the model of a commercial recruitment agency, which works with large employers to set up placement schemes for suitably skilled and qualified refugees in engineering, IT and other fields. The aim is to 'convert' the placement to full employment if the refugee adapts and progresses well.

To give themselves the best chance of a decent job sooner rather than later, refugees need to understand British recruitment approaches. Whether you use group discussion or mock interviews where refugees play the employer, find ways to help people understand that they should:

☑ not apply for jobs they stand no chance of getting

☑ recognise this *is* a competition

☑ take up strategic opportunities of all sorts to make themselves more attractive to employers

☑ show off their full range of experience, including UK/elsewhere, paid/unpaid, plus community and family life

☑ present themselves in a way that the employer sees what she or he is looking for

☑ make the equal opportunities system work for them:

   – answer the specific questions fresh each time

   – make sure they score something for every single part of the person specification, including drawing on family or voluntary experience

☑ review their expectations of working relationships with bosses and colleagues

☑ not see a refusal letter as a measure of their worth

☑ hope for just a little bit of luck.

Employing a refugee

Can you employ a refugee?

A small warning before you start. If you give one person a job, remember how other members might feel. People who have been committed to the organisation for a long time often feel that they deserved something back. It is worse if they applied but weren't appointed. To avoid losing them, you need to tackle this head on: talk to each individual directly about how they will feel if they aren't successful. In addition, have outside involvement in decisions, and inform the whole organisation and membership about all processes and decisions. You could involve members in the selection and interview panels. People passed over still won't be happy but it *will* be worse if you ignore the problem.

If you already recruit and employ staff, a few adaptations might be enough to make it more likely that a refugee can successfully apply for your next vacancy. Recruiting and employing a refugee is like recruiting and employing anyone. You are still bound by the laws against discrimination which forbid 'positive discrimination', so you can't employ someone just because she or he is a refugee, or Syrian or Sudanese, for example, as that would be race discrimination. But you can take positive action to encourage refugees to apply: you can state in adverts that your organisation is keen to encourage refugees to apply, you can send job adverts to refugee charities and employability projects, and you can guarantee interviews to all refugees who apply. But when you appoint, you have to do so on the basis of equal opportunities, for reasons based on merit, not on race, disability or other personal characteristics.

You might need to adapt your selection processes.

- Edit your person specification (Box 10.13) and application form so it is really clear and explains the equal opportunities process, including how people's answers will be scored for shortlisting.

- Under 'Employment History' make it clear people should include time and skills from other countries, volunteering, community activities and skills they have gained in other contexts.

- Rather than a blank 'Personal Statement' section, lay out a series of questions that echo the person specification.

- Do not judge the application by the handwriting or quality of the grammar and presentation (unless writing and presentation are relevant to the job and in the person specification).

- Their interview skills will not be honed for British culture, so include a series of practical tasks related to the job. You could ask them to teach you something, complete a spreadsheet, write one page about a 'what would you do if' scenario. Tasks reveal skills and abilities that people might not know how to express in English.

Box 10.13 Making person specifications more refugee-friendly

Standard person specification	Refugee-friendly person specification
GCSE English	Or the equivalent of Level 3 (GCSE standard) English
Safeguarding training at Level 2	Or willing to complete Level 2 safeguarding training within the probation period
Knowledge of local authority structures and opportunities for influencing the commissioning cycle	Or understanding of bureaucratic organisations, and keen to learn about local authority structures and identify opportunities to influence commissioning

Make good use of probation, because it lets you take a risk on someone. It gives the person time to prove their potential. Make it clear from the start that you will *only* confirm them in post at the end of probation if they meet reasonable goals and conditions which you have laid out clearly. It is likely to be about training or skilling up so they can clearly do the full job properly by the end of probation. You might even make the job offer *conditional* on passing a certain qualification or English test, for example. You should have substantial additional supervision to support them to develop as quickly as possible, achieving the understanding, skills and performance you need from them.[2] Be in constant communication about what is working and what isn't working. If it doesn't work, say goodbye, and start a new recruitment.

Look at it from a step further back. You might consider *adapting existing or potential opportunities* in the organisation to be more accessible and suitable for refugees. One possibility is to revisit job descriptions and pay scales and therefore the person specification. If they are currently based on people already having skills when they come into post, you can review them so that someone with potential who is short on experience and qualifications can apply. This might mean slightly lower salary costs, but will also mean a greater commitment on the organisation's part to good-quality, effective supervision and access to training. It might be worth exploring apprenticeships – information is widely available.

You have a number of options regarding job structure and contracts:

- **Temporary contracts.** If the job on offer is for less than one year, you can appoint anyone, without full equal opportunities recruitment (although check the conditions from your funders), but you can't extend the contract over one year. If you decide to continue the job over one year, you have to start a proper equal opportunities recruitment from scratch, and at that point the post holder has to apply for the job in open and fair competition.

---

2   Usually, when people reach the end of probation having met any conditions and so can take on their full responsibilities, they should have a proportionate pay increase to reflect their greater value to the organisation.

- **Part-time contracts for set hours or variable hours**, usually with a maximum or minimum. You might take a full-time job and split it into two or more jobs. Coordinating roles and work can be an issue. Part-time hours might allow people to continue studying.

- **Casual or 'zero hours' contracts.** These have been controversial in the 'gig economy' because they are open to misuse, but, when used well, they are flexible and effective for both employer and worker. If there is no work one week, you don't have to offer the person work. If you offer work, they don't have to take it. But if they do, the casual contract defines the terms and conditions. The employer pays the worker's tax and NI. Casual workers still have annual leave and other rights. If the work becomes regular, it should change to a normal employment contract.

  Another advantage of casual contracts is that you can split one job and give three or four people an opportunity for some work experience. But beware of management costs, and the risk that it clashes with benefits rules, or that the little income might be eaten up by commuting costs. If this is primarily about giving experience, make it time-limited and be sure people know that and keep looking elsewhere. After six months, give another four people a chance.

- **Self-employed.** 'Gig economy' employers have been in the courts to determine whether their drivers, cleaners, plumbers, etc. are 'self-employed', especially because self-employment means people have fewer rights than employed workers. Arrangements with self-employed refugees can work well, perhaps as interpreters or caterers. But be sure they really have self-employed status with Inland Revenue. If not, you might be accused of avoiding tax or NI. They must invoice you for payment. Although you are not obliged to check, for their sake make sure they understand that they still have to pay tax, but they pay it themselves and must keep paperwork and do tax returns. Self-employment messes up benefits and makes it harder to get loans or a mortgage. If people aren't self-employed already, I would advise caution and obtaining outside advice.

You might also consider making a job flexible to allow for the pressures some refugees are under with mental health difficulties and multiple pressures from the other demands of rebuilding a life. Remember that you are required to make reasonable adjustments by law so as not to discriminate against disabled people, and mental health is a disability. Phasing in from part-time to full-time might help people make the adjustment. Every job should have a probation period, and if you are employing someone who is recovering from mental ill health, you should have sufficient supervision to support them as they develop their confidence and resilience.

Even if you are taking positive action to employ refugees, you are still bound by normal regulations on terms and conditions. Trying to do a decent thing does not mean you can downgrade terms and conditions, even if that would tip the balance towards making something financially viable. So bear in mind that part-time or temporary employees cannot be treated less well than full-time or permanent staff, so you still need to include annual leave and, in due course, statutory maternity and parental leave, pension contributions and potentially redundancy pay.[3]

Once a person is in post, they are (and you treat them as) just another colleague, even if they are getting additional training and support. As described in Chapter 1, refugees are just normal people, not angels. There is no guarantee they are nice or that you will like them. Nor will they necessarily be grateful, even if you have gone to considerable lengths to create this opportunity. You never know if anyone you recruit – refugee or not – will turn out to be the right choice. They might turn out not to have the potential you thought, or to be unable to do the job for other reasons. You should already have suitable probation and employment/employee policies in place so just apply them consistently and make sure all colleagues – refugee or not – are treated fairly and equally.

To help protect refugees once they are in work

Other than jobs via friends and family, when refugees first get paid work, it is often through agencies, such as catering and waiting, warehouse and security, health and social care, cleaning plus 'self-employed' options in the gig economy such as driving taxis, food delivery and interpreting. Many get work through peers in small businesses which might be cash in hand. Also there are entry points into direct employment in schools, supermarkets, shops and the NHS (www.jobs.nhs.uk, for example, as porters – see Box 10.1, CS/C – and healthcare assistants).

When they start, you might need to give a little extra support. There's a lot to adjust to and crises that refugees are prone to, such as ill health, caring responsibilities and time to see their lawyer, might compromise their value to the employer.

Refugees might find it difficult to cope with the new pressures of employment: travel, timings, urgency to learn and perform, physical demands, life outside their 'comfort zone' and not necessarily in a 'safe space' (Box 10.14). They will have intense interaction with new people who may have no idea about – or empathy with – their life experiences. People's aspirations and hopes shift as daily working realities blur longer-term goals (Box 10.14, CS/P).

---

3   Information on employment rights is widely available and not specific to refugees; see, for example, www.gov.uk, ACAS or Citizens Advice. See also www.redundancycalculator.gov.uk.

Refugees are vulnerable to poor treatment at work: they have little knowledge of norms and rights, and may not communicate well in English. As their whole family might depend on their wage, they may not be able to walk away from an opportunity to earn. For those working outside the law, the cash their employer puts in their hand is the only food and roof they have.

Not all poor treatment is cynical exploitation. Often employers or managers just don't pay enough attention to their staff's rights and needs (CS/P). Employees who don't know what good practice is, or are nervous about asking questions, are likely to lose out. But there are employers who deliberately underpay, pay late or don't pay at all (CS/Q), or who ignore safety and welfare, or bully and intimidate staff, pushing them into dangerous situations (CS/S).

Box 10.14	Refugees and dealing with the new pressures of finding decent jobs – Case Studies P–S

P   was one of three refugees who all trialled for a job. One calculated the travel was too expensive for the pay. One worked during the pilot stage but found the long shifts exhausting. P stuck in the job for ten months but ultimately left because she found the stress level and tensions between staff in the department intolerable.

Q   another interpreter, lost in the region of £500 pounds she was owed when the agency she worked for went into liquidation.

R   is an interpreter who served the NHS and courts. He had a casual contract with his agency, but a new agency was appointed and interpreters were required to be self-employed to continue working through the new provider, which also does not pay travel time or expenses or insurance, as self-employed workers are obliged to cover those costs themselves. R is working in a group that is mounting a legal challenge to the decision to end their casual contracts, with union support.

S   was offered car mechanical work. He was driven a long way to the site to find they were breaking cars that had probably been stolen. He refused the work and was harassed for over a year by the contact. He didn't report it to the police.

You *are* familiar with British employment. Your ability to listen and take a strategic view is valuable. You can offer 'coaching' sessions or mediate when a refugee has difficulties at work. Having a neutral third party to help communication can reassure both refugee and employer, but be aware of the demand on your time and patience. Or you may move into an advocacy role, supporting the refugee to 'nudge' employers into remembering good practice, or 'poke' them with a potential or actual grievance (scrupulously following their procedures). If necessary, you might need to back the refugee to use 'slap' tactics, which could mean bringing in legal advice or even action from a trade union such as Unite, a community law centre or employment solicitors. In some very serious cases, the refugee might be well advised to involve the police.

Conclusion

Maybe one day your refugee member or client will retire on a handsome pension and look back over their career and remember you. Refuge is more than having permission to stay somewhere. It is about the people around you, having space and opportunities to build and create your own future. So that even if your old life is no longer possible, you still have a life you made yourself – just not the one you grew up expecting.

CHAPTER 11

Refugee Children and Young People – With and Without Families

Introduction

Even if your job doesn't centre around children, you may well find yourself supporting refugee children or young people at some point (Box 11.1). They may be with parents or members of their extended family or living with other adults. They might be on their own, as 'unaccompanied minors', in which case they are probably 'looked after children' in the care of the local authority.

If they arrived young or were born here, they might have no memory of life outside the UK, but their lives are fundamentally shaped by what their family has been through before and since arriving in the UK. Their experiences in the next few years could affect their whole lives.

Box 11.1	Being aware that children might be from refugee families, even if born here

Waiting in a primary school playground with the head teacher, watching the children say goodbye to parents at the start of a school day, I asked him how many refugee or asylum-seeking children there were in his school. 'We had one a couple of years ago,' he said. I was astonished. The playground was full of people from Afghanistan, Iraq, Sri Lanka, Somalia and other countries that people have been fleeing for years. I had expected him to say about a third of the school. He didn't see them as refugees.

Until someone reaches the end of their 17th year, up to their 18th birthday, they are still legally a child. Their rights and statutory entitlements in the UK are set by children's law which for statutory bodies is more important than immigration law or immigration status. Voluntary and community bodies and some health, mental health and youth services such as careers are more flexible around age, and young people's or youth services go up to 25 (Box 11.2).

This chapter looks at the issues you might meet if you find yourself working with refugee children (and sometimes their parent or parents). This chapter doesn't go into detail on 'mainstream' children's rights, services and good practice as that expertise is easily available elsewhere.

It looks at supporting children who have refugee status or other Leave to Remain, asylum-seeking children and those who have been refused asylum or have Unaccompanied Asylum-Seeking Child Leave (UASC-Leave) (revisit Box 3.11 and Glossary for a reminder of definitions).

Many of the definitions and issues were laid out in earlier chapters regarding definitions and entitlements (Chapter 3), daily necessities (Chapter 8), health/ mental health and disability (Chapter 9), and education (Chapter 10), and this chapter is best read in combination with those. Organisations and sources of expertise are listed in Appendix A.

Box 11.2 **The child was hungry**

A young man came into our office. An age ruling had found him to be over 18 and he was en route to dispersal accommodation. As he talked, he demolished a tin of biscuits, a whole bag of satsumas and 12 stale fairy cakes left over from a volunteers' meeting. I asked him if he'd had breakfast – yes, but no dinner last night or money for lunch today because the paperwork hadn't reached his temporary accommodation. I don't know how old he was, but he was still very young – fresh-faced and spotty. If an adult, then barely so. And he was hungry.

Persecution and experiences before reaching the UK

Some forms of persecution and abuse inflicted on children are different to those inflicted on adults. Children are conscripted into fighting forces and bullied and intimidated and brutalised into soldiers and 'camp followers'. Children are forced into marriage, sexually exploited, mutilated. They are exploited for their labour, and trafficked for labour and sexual exploitation. Abuse often takes different forms (and has different consequences) with children: not only physical violence, but emotional manipulation, neglect and denial. Everything is gendered.

It is difficult to keep up to date with all the news from around the world, but being aware of recent conflicts and persecution affecting children will heighten your sensitivity to what *might* have happened to the young refugee in front of you (Box 11.3). Maybe nothing too bad has happened – her mother or father got her to safety before anything serious happened to her, or maybe they didn't. And the children live every day thinking about people they have left behind.

	Countries from which children are fleeing to the UK because of persecution, conflict and harm
Box 11.3	

Country of origin	Forms of persecution and danger that children have fled from	Children with family or unaccompanied (UC) (UC mostly 10+)
Afghanistan	Violence, militias and forced conscription of boys and young men	Family and UC; UC mostly male; babies born here
Albania	Localised conflict appearing to target sons, trafficking of young men, economic migration	UC mostly male; most are refused
China	Targeting families of political and human rights activists, trafficking for labour, also impoverishment linked to ethnicity Arrivals increasing from 2017	Both
Eritrea	Forced conscription, slave labour and maltreatment of boys and girls, young women and men, ethnic persecution, female genital mutilation (FGM) practised on girls	Mostly UC male and female, mostly from early teens; earlier arrivals now settled
Iran	Persecution and murder of gay men, persecution of Christians, non-conformism, also conflict between religious groups, persecution of political activists affecting families	Family but increasing UC; UC mostly male
Iraq	Young men forced into militias, religious and ethnic persecution of families	Family and UC; UC mostly male
Nigeria	Religious persecution, forced marriage, persecution of gay and lesbian young people	UC mostly male; most are refused
Pakistan	Forced marriage, persecution of disabled people, persecution for political activity	UC forced marriage female; others mostly male
Somalia	Ethnic conflict over many decades, FGM practised on girls in a wide age range	Families, babies born here
Sri Lanka	Ethnic and political conflict and widespread violence, at height in 2009	Families of all ages; babies born since 2009
Sudan	South Sudan, persecution, violence and destruction, by ethnicity and religion in civil war. On and off for many decades, but increasing since 2017	15% of UC applicants in 2017*

cont.

Country of origin	Forms of persecution and danger that children have fled from	Children with family or unaccompanied (UC) (UC mostly 10+)
Syria	Widespread ethnic and religious violence in civil war, by government and non-government forces. Families and UC arriving in the EU/UK overland and across the Mediterranean. Also small number of families in the UNHCR resettlement scheme	Families and UC; UC includes families through the international resettlement schemes
Uganda	Persecution, murder and rape of young gay men and lesbians. Child soldiers	UC young people, female and male
Vietnam	Trafficked and escaping trafficking, increasing since 2017	12% of UC applicants in 2017*
Refugee children who do not reach the UK: children from Cameroon, Central African Republic, Chad, Democratic Republic of Congo, Myanmar, Niger, Northern Nigeria, Yemen	Huge numbers are displaced and in refuge outside their country of origin, but do not come to Europe/the UK	All ages including babies born in exile

* Refugee Council Quarterly Statistics, 2018

Refugee children, abuse, protection and safeguarding

After arriving in the UK, young people still need to be protected from further traumas, including sexual, financial and other forms of exploitation and abuse. Some people will target refugee children with racist and hate-filled actions (Box 11.4). Others might just seek to fool or manipulate. Traffickers can reconnect. Their own families might harm, neglect or exploit them. New peers, friends, girlfriends and boyfriends can wield a lot of power over a refugee child or young person, especially if the child or young person is relying on them for emotional support, social networks and peer identity. There is also the spectre of gangs and of radicalisation.

Box 11.4 Attacks on asylum-seeking youths

In 2017, in Croydon, three teenagers were found guilty of beating up an asylum seeker in a suspected hate-crime.

In 2017 a group that had been harassing a young asylum-seeking man for some days followed him when he got off a bus, and when he ran into a refugee charity's office block for help, they followed him into the reception area and beat him up.

In addition, we can't ignore the frightening possibility that people in professional or responsible positions, including staff, contractors, volunteers, members and participants *in your own organisation*, could end up in situations and relationships where they could abuse the young refugees you help.

There are some conditions that make refugee children particularly vulnerable to abuse. Any person who is isolated and can't communicate easily or anyone who doesn't know – or trust – the people who could protect them is vulnerable to abuse (see, for example, Box 11.5). Any child refugee (or any adult refugee, or any child anywhere) could be in this situation. Add to this the extraordinary experiences refugee children have gone through already, and growing up between conflicting cultural backgrounds, it is not unusual for young refugees to be unsure about what is and what is not OK for people to do. They are normal children in abnormal circumstances that make them unusually vulnerable.

Box 11.5 **Private fostering**

Private foster carers are adults who have privately arranged to care for someone else's child, under the age of 16, for more than 28 days. They should tell the local authority. Private foster carers are in a very powerful position, especially if no outside body or other person is aware the child is living with them. Although a lot of private fostering is perfectly fine, it can be a front for trafficking, and the potential harm these adults could do is almost without limit. You may remember the death of Victoria Climbié in 2000. She was an eight-year-old child from the Ivory Coast who was privately fostered with an aunt who tortured her and eventually killed her (vcf-uk.org). If you become aware that a child is privately fostered, you must tell the local authority, who will make contact with the carer and child and ensure that the child's care, education, safety and other needs are properly dealt with. See Coram Children's Legal Centre and the British Association of Adoption and Fostering.

Whatever your role is, it includes protecting children and young people from abuse. If you have any concerns, you must act. You might feel a child is acting strangely, has changed in some way, or they might say something that worries you. You cannot raise your concerns directly with the child, but you can create a safe space and a trusting relationship.

If a child – or parent, for that matter – does 'present' to you with their experiences and fears, stay calm. Remind them you will keep it confidential, but it is not a secret – make sure they know what 'confidential' means. Confirm and clarify what they have said to you without encouraging further detail. If there is an interpreter present, check that they understand safeguarding procedures too. As soon as you can, preferably within minutes of them leaving, write down everything the child said in the words they used, date and sign it, and contact your safeguarding officer as quickly as possible.

Safeguarding: Calm. Confidential. Confirm and Clarify. Record. Report.

There are no special safeguarding or protection procedures for refugee children – you just follow good safeguarding practice:

- You and your organisation's safeguarding knowledge should be sound.

- Policies and processes must be effective, clear and well known to all staff, volunteers and trustees, especially what an individual should do if they are concerned about a child.

- Make good use of the collected safeguarding resources on the NSPCC website (www.nspcc.org.uk), including checklists and free training.

- Sign up for local safeguarding networks or bulletins (if there are any) from the local Safeguarding Children Board so you know whom to contact if a concern arises, and so you can access advice and training which might include some free training.

- Safeguarding is more than protection from abuse; it is also about concerns to do with children's health and safety, their care and their development as they become young adults. If you feel there is a risk that a child will be harmed or be held back, it is a safeguarding matter. In addition, the ideas, actions, services and structures you create to give them positive support and experiences are also 'safeguarding'.

To avoid any doubt, the Home Office, National Asylum Support Service (NASS) and NASS landlords are also bound by obligations to safeguard and promote children's welfare.

Recovering and going forwards

Children and young people have a life ahead of them. Although refugee children are normal kids, they have been through extraordinary experiences and they have the potential to become extraordinary adults. The faster they can function and connect with others in their new context, making the best of their own strengths and opportunities, the sooner they will take control of their own futures.

Any list of the things young people might have to overcome must give us pause.

- Dealing with the consequences of some of the violence and persecution already mentioned above.

- Regaining health after poor nutrition or malnutrition, missed immunisations, illnesses and physical injuries, including living with impairments.

- Coping with loss, separation and bereavement.

- Their lives might not have had much relaxation, social interaction, happiness and play.

- They probably have a broken education and might have to start from scratch.

Within families, children still live with poverty and insecurity even if protected by a parent's tenacity, determination and long-term aspirations. But family structures can buckle under the pressure, break up or become less functional. Parents might become less able to nurture their children because of their own struggles. Parent-and-child relationships might not follow their expectations – or yours. You often find power and role reversals when even young children care for parents, act as interpreters and manage communication with formal organisations.

Now in day-to-day life there are new challenges:

- Identity is a big issue from teens onwards. Most avoid being identified as an asylum seeker or refugee (Box 11.10, CS/E), and some struggle to balance feelings of family and national identity with the fluidity and diversity of urban British identities.

- They have to form and re-form relationships, sorting out their relationships with ever-changing peers, including sexual relationships, and managing long-distance family relationships including expectations, but also where family might be lost or in danger.

- They depend on negotiating successfully with multiple staff in different support bodies simultaneously, and so often shop around a bit to find people and places they can trust, especially where they must relate to authority.

  - Many value trust and personal relationships over specialist knowledge.

  - Accessibility is very important, especially as young refugees' lives can be chaotic and – as for adults – lurch into crisis.

- At the same time they are sorting out a lot of practical realities – learning to manage money, making a room into a home, their changing physical life, health and emotions, exam pressures and life aspirations.

- Whenever someone is moved, they have to start all over again.

They are unlikely to see their situation the same way you do.

How do children end up alone in the UK?
In times of danger, families split up. Families get separated by detention and death. Children are sent ahead with relatives or friends. People get lost in the

chaos of flight or because of the demands of smugglers or traffickers' lies (see Box 11.6 on reuniting families). And there are also children who flee their own families for many reasons – including homophobia or to avoid being forced into marriage.

Box 11.6 **Reuniting families**

In 2017 the British Red Cross (redcross.org.uk) helped more than 2000 families reunite in the UK. Not all cases involved children under 18, but many did. Once someone has Convention refugee status, they have a right to family reunion – bringing their spouse or children under 18 to join them, although children cannot bring parents to join them. When a family member knows where other family members are, this is an arduous, expensive and even dangerous process. But when they don't, the Red Cross has a Family Tracing Service where a person appeals for their (free) help. They gather as much background detail as possible from that person, then connect with colleagues in the Red Cross and Red Crescent movement in the relevant countries to find out if there are camp or detention records or other ways to identify missing family members. There is no guarantee of success. The Red Cross needs volunteers to help this process.

Sometimes parents will make strategic choices and send their children away. It is traumatic for the child and often dangerous. But as with London's 1.5 million child evacuees in 1939 or the Kindertransport trains that brought 10,000 unaccompanied Jewish children to Britain from 1938 onwards, parents are trying to do the best thing. Get them away from the Taliban. Get them away from forced indefinite conscription into the Eritrean army.

Lack of hope also drives some parents' decision to send children alone across the world, and the children themselves are sometimes part of that decision. Families see that the national or local situation means their children will not get a decent education or a decent future and they look for somewhere they will stand a better chance.

Children seeking asylum in the UK and their care

How many children? Numbers rise and fall with crises around the world. For example, only six Iraqi children arrived alone in 2013, but 324 arrived alone in 2016.[1] Young Afghans and Eritreans (males and females) have been arriving on their own for more than 15 years, but their numbers also fall and rise in

---

[1]   The Refugee Council produces useful quarterly statistics from Home Office data on 'Children in the Asylum System' which are excellent for a quick picture for your own knowledge, very useful in training, policy-making and funding bids. These figures are from the report in November 2017.

close connection to events in their homelands. In the years leading up to 2015, up to (but usually fewer than) 2000 unaccompanied children claimed asylum in the UK each year. This rose to well over 3000 in both 2015 and 2016 with the crisis in Syria and Iraq, before falling back towards 2000 in 2017 and 2018. Unaccompanied children are predominantly males, and more than 60 per cent are 16 or older; fewer than 10 per cent are 13 or younger.

Although patterns in Home Office decision-making vary from year to year, generally a quarter to a third of unaccompanied children get Refugee Convention status or one of the other forms of Leave to Remain that will let them stay in the UK after they reach the age of 18. In 2017 more than half the children from Eritrea, Syria and Vietnam were given refugee status. Iranian and Iraqi children had many positive decisions, though under half. Only two of 228 children from Albania were given refugee status. Children's asylum processes are considered in more depth below.

About 4000 children arrived with families each year until the start of the Syrian and Middle East crisis when the number rose as high as 6000. The largest majority of those dependent children, about three-quarters, are under the age of ten. Families have babies born in the UK. If their parents are still in the asylum process, babies become asylum seekers at birth, but don't show up clearly in published statistics on asylum.

How likely are you to meet these children, with or without their families? It depends very much where you live and what you do. Wherever an unaccompanied child or young person comes to the notice of (or 'presents' to) authorities for the first time, they become the responsibility of the local authority for that area, regardless of immigration status. Highest numbers present to authorities that are responsible for the 'ports of entry':

- Kent (Port of Dover) registered 930 children in 2015 (although not all stayed in Kent).

- Hillingdon (Heathrow Airport) handles 800+ arrivals per year and looks after around 300.

- Croydon (where the Home Office's Lunar House processes up to 80 per cent of initial claims for asylum for much of the UK) looks after around 400.

- As context, about 60 unaccompanied asylum-seeking children present in Scotland in a whole year.

You might meet unaccompanied children if you work near one of these, or any busy airport such as Manchester or Edinburgh, if they are fostered by their authority in your area, or if they are one of the few transferred to the care of children's services in new areas to spread the load. Overall, the children are concentrated in the South, South East and London. Asylum-seeking families with NASS accommodation will be mostly in the main dispersal areas of the North West, West Midlands, Yorkshire and the Humber. Many families who do not have NASS housing and those who get Leave to Remain return to London or cities where they have existing contacts, despite the cost of housing.

Children and the asylum processes

This section is about being aware of the processes children go through in the asylum decision-making process (the care system is considered in the next sub-section). This section summarises the main processes for an overview, and is not intended for case work. When you work with a child who is still waiting for an asylum decision, don't forget that you cannot do immigration case work if you are not licensed to do so. It is important to be generally aware of asylum processes and more important to know who to talk to in a hurry, especially as a child approaches 18. The main specialists in this field are Coram Children's Legal Centre (known as Coram or CCLC) and the Refugee Council's Panel of Advisers, usually called the Children's Panel, which gives direct support and advice to individual children seeking asylum, and carers and professionals who work with them (also see Appendix A).

The Home Office might think someone is lying about their age in their screening interview. This happens in up to a quarter of older unaccompanied children's cases. If they believe the person's appearance 'very strongly suggests' that person is significantly over 18, that person will simply be treated as an adult thereafter.

If the Home Office doubts their age but cannot be sure, the benefit of the doubt must go to the young person. They will be referred to the local social services, which will take care of the young person until social workers have done a full age assessment. An age assessment must follow the 'Merton' principles: be done by qualified social workers, with the young person fully informed at each stage, and told the reasons behind the decision on their age – which they can respond to. The final decision and reasons will be shared in full with the Home Office (Box 11.7).

You can be asked to give an opinion on someone's age – school and college teachers, including ESOL teachers, even vicars sometimes get requests from social workers, but there is no obligation. If you don't have relevant training or expertise, you could give an opinion, making your level of contact with the child and background expertise or lack of it clear, but unless you are very confident your opinion is sound, you should probably refuse. There are many controversies and judicial reviews or even determinations in the High Court regarding age disputes.

Box 11.7 Age disputes

If the Home Office rejects someone's claim to be a child, they might be detained in adult removal centres. But sometimes a child looks physically aged by a harrowing journey, by sleeping rough and eating badly, and maybe substance misuse. The Refugee Council has a quick-response Age Dispute team which visits the person in detention and makes its own age assessment. If the team is convinced the person is under 18, they contact the local authority to take them into care.

Wrist and dental X-rays are not usually accepted as evidence of age, as they have a five-year margin of error (depending on nutrition, for example); some people also raise ethical questions about unnecessary medical interventions.

Children who arrive with or without family go through different processes for their asylum claim.

Children in families are usually included in the mother's or father's asylum claim. If a child is born to the parents after they arrive in the UK, that does *not* give either the child or their parents a right to residency or British nationality, and hasn't done so for more than 30 years.

Unaccompanied children (and some older children in families) submit a claim in their own name or it can be submitted on their behalf. Among other things, their social worker ensures the child has a solicitor who will handle the case on Legal Aid, and should make sure necessary steps in the process are followed properly, such as case reviews and filling in 'statement of evidence forms', and assisting the child to engage with the process.

Children aged 12 and over will have an initial screening, a welfare interview and a 'substantive' interview. Children under 12 can be interviewed if the child is willing and considered mature enough by his or her carers. Children can only be interviewed with a responsible adult present who is not connected with the Home Office – usually a parent, guardian or their social worker – in addition to their solicitor.

For the substantive interview, the unaccompanied child will need to provide evidence to support their asylum claim. A young gay man might be asked to give evidence of homosexual relationships or other activities such as attending a youth club for gay youth. A person claiming religious persecution will be expected to provide evidence that they are actively following their religion. The solicitor or child might also be looking for evidence to support their stated age. They might want evidence to strengthen their credibility, showing the young person is of good character, a good student, a good influence on their peers or playing an active role in the community. They might ask you for a letter that details their activities, or to confirm your opinion that they are gay or Christian or under 18, or a character reference. If you have any relevant expertise or experience in the matter in hand, or are a pillar of the community yourself, make this clear to strengthen the credibility of your statement (see Box 7.5).

If the family gets Leave to Remain, the whole family, including children under 18, are included in the parent's status, as is any child who turned 18 while they were waiting for the decision. If the family has a fixed-term Leave and the child is still under 18 when it is time for renewal, the child continues on the parent's claim. There is a substantial charge of around £1000 per head for extensions and more than £2000 for Indefinite Leave, so family applications can be very costly.

If a child is born in the UK and lives here continuously until their tenth birthday and is of 'good character', she or he can apply to register as British. If children do not register before they are 18, it becomes harder to apply. Many children, families, carers and even social workers are not aware that registration or nationality might be a problem when children reach 18, which is why there is an active campaign called Project for the Registration of Children as British Citizens.

If the family gets refused – if a parent is refused, sometimes the children might make their own claims, especially if approaching 18. If not, or their claim is refused, the family becomes subject to deportation. Since scandals in 2011 that shocked many, families with children are very rarely detained, but the father might be. Families are allowed to visit a relative detained in a 'removal centre' any day at set times, sometimes by appointment, as long as they can manage the travel. Any attempt to deport one member of a family – the father alone, for example – could be challenged on the basis of the right to family life enshrined in the Human Rights Act 1998.

If the unaccompanied child gets Leave to Remain when under 18 (except UASC-Leave), they will stay in the UK with the rights and entitlements of an adult with Leave to Remain, plus the continuing rights and support that any British 'care-leaver' has (see below).

If the unaccompanied child gets refused – about a fifth of unaccompanied children's asylum claims are refused outright – they can be deported, but only if the Home Office rules they can return to family support in their country of origin, or if there are 'suitable reception facilities' for children, which is not the case in most countries.

Those whom the Home Office rejects but accepts cannot be deported before they are 18 are given UASC-Leave. It lasts for 30 months, or up to the age of 17½ (often written 17.5), whichever is sooner. They might be detained 'in suitable facilities' from 17½ which usually means a separate section of an adult removal centre. On reaching 18, whether or not they have an appeal outstanding, they can be deported.

Asylum and refugee children in care and children's law

Children's law trumps immigration law and the Children's Act 1989 is fundamental. As someone is first and foremost a child until they turn 18, their rights and the support they receive are the same as a British child would get.

Practical details on accommodation, money, health and education will be covered in the following sections.

A **'child in need'** under **'Section 17'** of the 1989 Act (also called 's17') is any child – British or refugee, unaccompanied or with family – who is unlikely to be or stay healthy and develop well if they do not get support, and any disabled child. The local authority must safeguard and promote their welfare and should take the child's wishes and feelings into account.

The local authority assesses the child's needs and should make a 'child in need' plan. Needs of asylum-seeking children include ensuring they have solicitors accompanying them to Home Office interviews. It could also mean maintaining contact with the Children's Panel and providing other help such as starting to trace their families and applications for British nationality. The local authority might need to provide support including accommodation and cash and/or identify a range and level of other special support – anything from mental health, disability or education bodies to sports clubs and art projects. These needs might put the social work team in touch with you. You can make sure your local social services are aware of your activities and services. Remember, though, that they will need to be assured you have top-notch safeguarding in place.

A **'looked after child'** under **'Section 20'** ('s20') is accommodated by the local authority when the child would not be safe, or her or his welfare would suffer if she or he was not accommodated. There should be a care plan including immediate and longer-term health, education, emotional wellbeing, social relationships and self-care. Social services can apply for a court 'Care Order' ('Section 31') which gives the local authority as a body 'parental responsibility' for the child, formalising requirements that clarify duties such as the need to follow through on the asylum case and promote the child's longer-term welfare. Some argue this would be in the interests of refugee children. However, Care Orders are more often used for children of British families when adults may object to sharing care and decisions with the local authority.

Care-leavers. With actions starting from their 15th year, the looked after child (if she or he arrived more than three months before turning 18) will get 'leaving care' support for a smooth transition to adult rights and services, and to address their ongoing needs. For unaccompanied asylum/refugee children, this usually means financial support and accommodation up to their 21st birthday, plus advice and assistance with education, training and employment through a 'pathway plan'.[2] Support will be continued to their 25th birthday if they stay in full-time education or have a disability. Failed asylum seekers (including UASC-Leave) lose this support if they refuse to comply with 'removal directions' or deportation after they turn 18.

---

2   The Immigration Act 2016 includes scope to reduce the support for some migrant care-leavers.

Necessities for daily life – roof, food, money and essential resources for life

Regarding children's access to other necessities for survival – accommodation, food and money for daily life and necessities such as clothes – Chapter 8 has relevant background information.

Children with families

(A) A ROOF

Families in the asylum process make a single-family application to NASS. Families with disabled children who have care needs will usually be housed by NASS until a care assessment is done by the local authority where they are housed, if it is done at all. If you are aware of a disabled child, find out if they have had an assessment; if not, assist them to request one. As with disabled adults, if a disabled child needs a higher level of adjustment or special support than NASS can 'reasonably' provide, it becomes the local authority's responsibility to provide suitable support and possibly adapted accommodation.

If refused asylum with no claim or appeals outstanding, NRPF families usually get 21 days' notice to quit their NASS accommodation as NASS will no longer support them. If the local authority finds there is no reason the family cannot exit the country, they can also refuse 'child in need' support, even when a family is homeless, on the grounds that the family has a reasonable alternative – that is, to return to their country of origin. If a family is taking steps to return, they can reapply to NASS or the local authority. But it is all very complicated and often does not work smoothly or quickly. A family stuck like this needs specialist advice, and you do too – you can start with Coram Fact Sheets but you should help them access community law centres, Coram, ASAP or Shelter. The latter three have helplines; details are on their websites.

Families with Leave to Remain have the same entitlements to housing as families with British nationality. The 28-day period after first receiving Leave to Remain, where they have to access mainstream benefits including Housing Benefit or Universal Credit, may be even harder for a family as family accommodation is hard to obtain. A family without housing at this point can apply to the homeless team of the local authority where NASS had housed them, as that is their 'local connection'. The children might be considered 'in need', even if not destitute, so families may be considered 'priority need' for housing or get temporary support, such as a bed-and-breakfast room. The Refugee Council and local charities' hosting and deposit schemes mentioned in Chapter 8 are invaluable.

(B) Money for food and essential resources

For asylum seekers, the weekly NASS rate for children and babies is the same as for adults at under £38 per person, so a family of one adult and two children will receive 3 x £38 = £114 per week. For babies, there is an extra £5/week until they are one year old, then £3/week extra until they turn three to cover milk, nappies and so forth, and during pregnancy women can claim £3/week extra. Parents who receive the one-time-only maternity grant of £300 are expected to use that for expensive items such as prams (see Maternity Action, also their advice line). When a family is refused asylum, if there were children under 18 when the decision was made, they might continue receiving NASS support (see NRPF Network).

All children get free school meals and fruit in reception, Year 1 and Year 2 (and to Year 3 in Scotland). Some schools, including secondary schools, have free breakfast clubs. Parents and carers apply for free school lunches from Year 3, although a fact that surprises a lot of people is that asylum-seeking families who are not receiving NASS support might not get free lunches for their children. Many people feel this is at odds with safeguarding principles and policies. Some schools and local authorities choose to be flexible.

Families that have Leave to Remain follow the same processes and rules as British nationals to claim the full range of housing and financial support that British nationals can claim, including crisis loans, Child Benefit and means-tested benefits such as free school meals.

In addition to those services and resources already mentioned in Chapter 8, bodies that support children or struggling families with food, clothes and other daily essentials, include the following.

Daily essentials for babies and children under five:

- Health professionals – for example, health visitors, in addition to their health role, often find goods and services for mothers with few resources. GPs might prescribe baby milk, supplements, shampoos, and skin creams.

- Mostly run by local authorities, children's and family centres, family information services, Sure Start in Northern Ireland and Cymorth in Wales run health, educational, childcare, advice and other free activities such as toy libraries, and might receive donated goods. They often provide milk, fruit and snacks in play sessions.

- Food banks and homeless organisations or drop-ins might have nappies, milk powder, etc. in addition to food, plus advice workers. Children's charities/charity shops gather children's goods (Box 11.8, CS/A, CS/B), and have very cheap baby clothes (CS/C). There might be local charitable trusts and grants (see Box 11.8).

Daily essentials for school-age children, up to 18:

- Primary schools often have Family Support Workers who respond to practical needs. Secondary schools have welfare staff. Schools will often provide clothes, coats, shoes, uniform and other kit from lost property and might have uniform grants. You could contact schools on behalf of the family if they want to remain anonymous.

- Holiday play and lunch schemes in some areas, especially Scotland, provide food, activities and sometimes advice at times when access via schools isn't available.

- Some areas have free school travel, and even outside school hours, usually with conditions, although local bus companies usually require evidence or a pass with age or address. A letter from you might help.

| Box 11.8 | Channelling goods to families and children – Case Studies A–C |

A   collects donations of toiletries and treats specifically for refugee children, from a network of churches before Christmas, boxes and wraps them and gives them as gifts.

B   is contacted informally, when necessary, by local community health staff and will seek out donations such as baby buggies or cots and blankets on request – this is not limited to asylum seekers or refugees, but is for anyone facing homelessness.

C   is a regular drop-in for asylum seekers run by volunteers and relying on donations. It appeals specifically for donations of disposable nappies.

Unaccompanied children – roof, food, money and goods

In addition to the above, the support that is specific to looked after children and care-leavers includes:

- Foster carers in their own home.

- Children's homes – houses for two to eight children, staffed by paid workers. They mostly house older children or children with complex needs.

- From 16+ the local authority has to continue to provide or help the young person find housing. It provides money for food and essentials and to facilitate education (see below). Local authorities cannot refer asylum-seeking care-leavers into the NASS system.

- Supported living for any young care-leaver (refugee, asylum, refused or UK national), such as:

- 'staying put' with their existing foster care family

- assisted access to social housing

- lodging with an approved supportive carer for up to two years

- foyer schemes which provide independent accommodation with life skills and other training

- 'move on' and 'floating support' services to young people in private or social rented property

- in emergencies, Nightstop/Crashpad schemes for short- or medium-term accommodation with a 'supported accommodation' family – usually voluntary; also hostels, night shelters (see Homeless Link).

The local authority is responsible for care and maintenance for unaccompanied young women and men with Leave to Remain (except UASC-Leave), so the individual cannot access Housing Benefit, Income Support or Jobseeker's Allowance. They can access some mainstream benefits such as Child Benefit for a baby, or disability allowances. There are funds such as a 'home allowance' or 'leaving care grant' for essentials.

Health, mental and emotional health and disability

Regarding health, mental and emotional health and disability, there is relevant information in Chapter 9, although in mental health in particular there are specialist children's services.

Children get all health care and treatment free, whether primary, secondary or emergency care and prescriptions, including dentistry, speech and language, and mental health care and treatment. Safeguarding duties for any organisation must take into account children's health and physical safety, wellbeing and future health and development outcomes, including any long-term health conditions and disabilities.

Young refugees and physical health

Some of the risks to children's physical health have been touched on already, such as trauma from conflict, forms of persecution of children such as female genital mutilation, lacks and gaps in nutrition and immunisations or adult care. Where families don't engage with health services for any reason – ignorance, suspicion, beliefs or just not being able to read letters sent home from school – children still might not benefit from the screening, prevention and treatments available to them.

There are certain health services set up for or more likely to be useful to children – such as health visiting, child development, speech and language therapy, different paediatric specialisms, separate emergency streaming and processes. The GP, A&E, minor injuries/urgent treatment sections and 111 (which has interpreters) are still the initial contact and access point for almost everything. Babies, children and young people have routes into health care via children's centres, health visiting services, referral via schools and social services, and increasingly any body or professional such as you.

You can start by ringing 111 while the child or parent is there. The 111 service has interpreters, and you can hand over the phone. With this simple action, you can start off a chain of accurate advice, referral, even basic assessment and a direct appointment with the correct service for them, speeding up the whole referral process. Children should always be registered with a nearby GP; if you realise they aren't, help the family to register as covered in Chapter 9.

Young refugees and mental and emotional health

Young refugees are coping with huge changes and stresses. They may be coping with earlier traumas. Some children have difficulty forming trusting relationships or emotional bonds. They may feel disconnected and isolated even from immediate family, from peers and from support workers.

Certain mental health services focus on children (Box 11.9). All NHS areas have Child and Adolescent Mental Health Services (CAMHS, pronounced 'Cams') for children and young people, but waiting times even for a needs assessment can be terrible and many CAMHS services have no specialist trauma counsellors. In many places, secondary schools now have their own counselling services and can access bereavement counsellors, but school counsellors may not have training in trauma counselling.

Box 11.9 **Children's mental health – expertise and resources in the voluntary sector**

Freedom from Torture (Birmingham, Glasgow, London, Manchester and Newcastle) works with children and families, and therapeutic bodies such as the Baobab Centre in London and the Haven Project in Hull develop ideas, models, evidence and lessons from working with young refugees.

They pass this expertise on through training, conferences and publications found on their websites.

If you are not a trained counsellor, be cautious – don't encourage young refugees to open up to you. It is possible that you could speed up referral and waiting times by getting on the phone and writing letters arguing that their need is urgent. Remember, young people can also talk to their GP while they wait for counselling. If it is a crisis, get them to A&E – call 999 for the police and an ambulance if necessary.

Where young people need ongoing mental and emotional support, but are not at the level to need or get NHS interventions, or are waiting, other local organisations sometimes have young groups or activities (Box 11.10). Ask your local Mind/Support in Mind, Inspire (Northern Ireland), carers' organisations, disability groups and also youth bodies such as YMCA. Perhaps you can set up or find activities that include interaction and prevent isolation (Box 11.10, CS/D, CS/E) or could help build life skills (CS/F, CS/G) and a positive self-image through music, drama, exercise, relaxation or sports (CS/H). Remember, if someone wants to talk about how they are feeling, listen, witness and accept what they say, but you may need to alert someone in the safeguarding chain, so *don't* promise to keep what they say *secret*.

	Examples of projects for wellbeing and emotional
Box 11.10	**health for young people/refugees – Case Studies D–H**

D   Mosaic is a centre for young lesbian, gay, bisexual and transgender people where people from any background can socialise and also access other support.

E   Diversity was a partnership between two local youth organisations to expand refugee teenagers' social networks, building more links with young Britons. They named it 'Diversity' to avoid any link to 'refugee' or 'asylum' because of earlier experiences where young people avoided anything that might identify them as refugees or asylum seekers. The funding ended but the organisations still collaborate on other work.

F   Chrysalis is a life-skills course that helps young refugees up to age 25. It combines learning and other opportunities with social interaction, over two to three months.

G   STAR is Student Action for Refugees – more than 40 self-run groups of higher education students who campaign and volunteer with local refugee projects in their area, including schools, youth clubs, homework clubs and sports.

H   DOST was a small all-round refugee youth charity which had to close in 2017 due to lack of funding. They organised talks, walks, sports, tea, networking, safe space, gardening, sailing and campaigning. They never turned anyone away. They were hoping to reopen as an independent charity – search on the internet and see if they made it.

Young refugees and disability

Disabled children and their carers (including parents, other adults and siblings) have the same rights to support whether they are UK nationals or refugees or asylum seekers.

They are protected by laws on equality, disability, safeguarding, children in need and caring.

They are entitled to assessment and support by the local authority and an integrated approach involving other services which might include your own:

- The Early Help Assessment (EHA, replacing the Common Assessment Framework or CAF) which is a shared document which coordinates support for a child, to be overseen by a lead professional. Many different children's professionals can complete one. If there doesn't seem to be one for the disabled child you are supporting, and you aren't the right person to do it, ask the local children's centre, child's school or health professionals such as health visitors if they can help, or contact the local authority.

- The more detailed 'Children's Act assessment' by asking the local authority's disabled children's team directly. It should happen in less than 45 days although urgent care should start immediately, so if a refugee child with urgent care needs has just arrived in your area, they should be supported straight away, before the full assessment is completed and without waiting for medical diagnosis.

- Assessment by an educational psychologist, usually coordinated by the child's school, but parents/carers can request the school to arrange an assessment.

- Carer's needs assessment.

- Local authorities must also assess and plan for a smooth transition from child to adult services between 16 and 18 (Care Act 2014).

- Education, health and care plan up to age 25 for some children with special needs.

They should be able to access the normal resources that any disabled child should get:

- Information that the local authority must make available called the 'Local Offer' or 'SEND Local Offer' which should be in accessible forms including different languages. You search online using the local authority's name plus 'Local Offer' and you will usually get a directory or something similar.

- GP practices, nurseries, schools, children's services, etc.

- Local generalist disability services and rights groups or networks, some of which might be branches of national bodies (e.g. Carers UK, SCOPE) or national.

- Local or national condition-specific organisations (e.g. for blind children).

Learning English, education, training

Please read this section alongside Chapter 10, especially the education and training section. This section uses 'refugee children' as a general term, unless there is a reason to specify a child's immigration status.

All children in the UK must be in full-time education until at least 16. The local authority has a duty to provide places, regardless of the child's immigration status. In England, after 16 children can move into apprenticeships, traineeships or at least 20 hours a week working or volunteering, while in part-time education or training.

Education carries the promise of a good future. Refugee children can make remarkable progress, especially where their life experiences have given them skills and attitudes that support determination.

To start off with, refugee children might still have fresh memories of trouble and transit. It may also be a long time since they were last in school. Education in their original country may have been based on very different ideas about learning methods, content, examinations and goals. Or they may have moved schools several times during dispersal by NASS and after Leave to Remain.

Refugee children join at any stage in the school system, and often mid-year. They may have little or no English and their numeracy skills might be low, or just low in English. They might be behind or fall behind other children their age, but it is extraordinary how fast some children adapt and learn.

Refugee and migrant parents are sometimes surprised by the different relationships and responsibilities of child, teachers and parents – for example, by the use of play – or by poor behaviour in the classroom. They might not help their children to engage effectively in education. Unfortunately, some children develop behavioural problems, and suspensions and exclusions occur.

This section is not about educational methods or therapies to re-enable learning – that is for the specialists. It is focussed on how hands-on workers can help refugee children and families make the best use of education opportunities. Fortunately, the current ethos of formal education in Britain is to engage and nurture every child, and most schools are excellent at this.

Education for refugee children

Schools have much more than classes and exams. There is fun and interaction with other children and with kind and supportive though still authoritative adults. They are warm, safe, bright and friendly, positive places and spaces, with varied activities in secure routines (Monday to Friday, start time, play time, home time) and welfare such as food, drink, health checks and safeguarding included. These conditions are designed to engage children and make them feel enabled and confident, to nurture children and support their development.

At the same time schools give access to services that can provide urgent and longer-term specialist assessment, support and therapy for children with learning difficulties or trauma, for example, and some will support individual parents or families too.

The first thing you might help with is getting a school place. It can be disappointingly difficult.

- Children in initial accommodation cannot apply for a school and some wait months before NASS contractors house them.

- Parents need to choose a school but might not know it's useful to look at special educational needs (SEN) support, English as an Additional Language (EAL), 'inclusion' staff or welfare support. It is not only about exam results and Ofsted/Education Scotland/ETI NI/Estyn ratings.

- There might be confusion over multiple processes for different schools in the same area, and 'in-year' admissions.

- Poor spoken or written English and limited IT cause parents difficulties with phone calls, visits, brochures, forms.

- Parents can be asked for evidence such as council tax bills, utility bills, birth certificates that they might not have.

- If schools are full, children will be allocated a place at a school the parent/carer does not like or that is too far away, so hard-up parents and children have to make expensive bus journeys.

- Parents can appeal and apply to move the child. Moving school is often disruptive and difficult for children.

- There are many reports of older children waiting months for a place, even until the new school year, especially 15/16-years-olds at the top age for compulsory education.

Issues for refugee children, and opportunities, by age

(A) PRE-SCHOOL AND EARLY YEARS (0–5)

The pre-school and early years are increasingly seen as crucial to a child's development, and an important time to identify children who need 'early help', some of which is truly useful to refugee children. NHS health visitor home visits, clinics, weaning and parenting groups start from virtually the first week of birth and children's or family centres, commissioned or run by local authorities, mostly offer services for 0–5, from 'stay and play' baby and toddler groups or crèches open to all, to individual support and more specialist services by referral only. If the mother you are supporting is not making use of these already, strongly encourage her to do so. You can explain that they are free and safe, and help her read and understand the timetable of activities. It can be a great help if you go with her the first time she visits.

In some cases – for example, a parent sent on a training scheme by the Job Centre – child care will be paid for, but only if the childminder or nursery is Ofsted-approved. It is the parents' responsibility to choose and register for child care – difficult in an unfamiliar system and with poor English. You could form links with a couple of good local childminders you are happy to recommend, and help refugee parents get through the paper-heavy registration processes with them.

There are free nurseries attached to some primary schools that take children as young as two for a few hours per week, if the parents are on certain mainstream benefits – excluding asylum seekers and NRPF – although there might also be a postcode catchment area. There can be waiting lists and parents should apply early.

(b) Primary (4–11)

At five years old, full-time education becomes compulsory and children often start from four or four and a half. Schools have extra support for children who are behind, or need intensive help to learn English. There might be a deputy head responsible for inclusion, a SEN coordinator or 'SENCo' (England) or teacher who oversees English as an Additional Language (EAL). Throughout the UK there are school systems to plan extra support for individual pupils. This can be anything from an extra 15 minutes per week to referral for assessment by an educational psychiatrist.

Some schools may employ a family support worker giving extra help to parents and carers to understand and communicate with the school, and may help with practical necessities such as reading letters and filling forms, or accessing health or benefits advice. School lunches and uniform have been mentioned above. Refugee children will get support for extra activities like educational trips, based mostly on means testing. Some outside activities such as learning musical instruments must be paid for, although schools can often use discretion.

Collect a small fund to contribute to extra activities, build communication with inclusion and SEN staff, welfare or family support staff, write to governors. The individual who brings you into contact may be one of several refugee children at that school.

(c) Secondary (11–16)

Moving to secondary school is another big change for refugee children. Peer networks and identity are issues for all refugees, and children at this age are also hitting puberty, so identity and relationships outside the family are a big feature of secondary school life – adding new tensions inside the family unit. Many refugee children avoid any 'refugee' or 'asylum seeker' labels (Box 11.10, CS/E). Secondary schools can be huge, and children get less individual attention from teachers and must take more responsibility for their own progress. Help is available, but they may have to ask for it. There is a strong link between parents and carers being engaged and the effectiveness of extra support to help the child progress.

Unaccompanied children are more likely to arrive at secondary school age than primary. The school staff will be aware if they are looked after, though not necessarily that they are refugee children. Education is included in their care plan and they get guaranteed support such as priority for school places, coordination between school and social workers (involves foster parents too), and necessary funds for activities and trips.

The school puts children in the school year the child claims (or is ruled) to be and provides extra interventions to help children catch up. Schools with substantial numbers of migrant children often have specialist inclusion/EAL teams and quiet 'safe' spaces and support for children struggling with anxiety and mental/emotional health difficulties. There are activities within and outside the curriculum to prepare children for adult life, which can also help children from other nations and cultures learn about life in the UK: citizenship, life skills, physical, social, health education (PSHE), employability and career guidance.

Schools have activities and authoritative structures to tackle anti-social attitudes and behaviour where refugee children might be victims, but might also victimise – for example, bullying, harassment, discrimination such as racism, homophobia – and radicalisation. Schools provide easy access to certain health services, such as screening and immunisations. They safeguard and protect.

(D) FURTHER EDUCATION (17–19+) AND HIGHER EDUCATION (HE)
Chapter 10 discussed many formal English, education and training opportunities that are available to adults from 17 onwards, whether starting from scratch or moving from school.

Getting a place:

- Eligibility is based on qualifications to date, although interviews may give some young people the chance to impress admissions staff, who can waive normal requirements.

- As well as A Levels/Highers, if young people have the International Baccalaureate (also called 'IB'), this counts for HE/university admission.

- University access courses or schemes might enable a person without A Levels/Highers to get to university.

- The HE body will want assurance that the young person can stay in the UK for the full length of the course, as the institution is penalised when people drop out.

- Explore HE/university-level courses with modules or with distance learning elements, or work placements.

Fees are a problem. Looked after children/care-leavers will continue ESOL and other full-time education fee-free to 21 or longer, whether at school or college. But for children in families, if they are still in asylum when they reach 18, there could be fees, even for ESOL. The situation keeps changing, but fees can reach £7000 a year even at A Level and more in HE. An asylum seeker or person with discretionary leave, for example, might be assessed as due to pay overseas student fees up to £18,000/year for HE courses.

- There are schemes to continue free education and support for young people who are otherwise 'NEET' or 'not in employment, education or training' and young people can sometimes join schemes for refugees, ethnic minorities, etc., mentioned in Chapter 10.

- Student loans for fees and maintenance are available from government for approved Level 3 or HE/Level 4, 5 or 6 courses. Young refugees with Refugee Convention, Humanitarian or Indefinite Leave can apply if they will be over 19 when they start. Student loans for courses to access university might be written off when you finish your degree.

- 'Long residency' in the UK may mean people on limited leave can still pay home fees and access student loans if they have lived here for a 'substantial' part of their lives. See the 'Let Us Learn' campaign.

- Fees can be reduced through internal bursaries at the discretion of the establishment. Several HE bodies have asylum and refugee scholarship/ bursary schemes, but the student must almost always have a firm offer of a place on the course *before* applying. They must check the details or they will waste time and might miss a deadline on something more relevant. STAR (Box 11.10, CS/G) lists more than 50 HE bodies with refugee bursaries.

- Some trusts can fund studies. See Educational Trusts' Forum or contact Refugee Support Network for advice on refugee access to HE.

Living and eating while studying (looked after children – see above):

- There is the possibility of around £1000–£1200 per year for living costs for those with Leave to Remain and in a low-income household, as a '16–19 bursary' in England or the Education Maintenance Allowance (EMA) in the rest of the UK, as long as attendance and progress are good.

- Under certain conditions, young people with Leave to Remain can claim Jobseeker's Allowance while they study.

- Colleges continue to provide free meals up to age 19 (not if NRPF). Some cities give students free bus travel.

(E) Training and employment

In addition to material in Chapter 10 regarding trades and employability, it is worth looking at apprenticeships. Young people with Leave to Remain can do apprenticeships. It counts as paid work, so people in the asylum process, with UASC-Leave, refused or with NRPF cannot start apprenticeships. Those with Leave to Remain can start apprenticeships from 16 years, and can go as far as getting a degree-level qualification, without incurring any of the fees they might be charged for further or higher education. From age 16 to 18 the minimum apprenticeship wage is about half the adult 'living wage' for the UK, and from 19 years it is the UK minimum wage, but it increases as the person learns.

Those who can't do apprenticeships might still be able to get work experience during other studies (14+) or through volunteering, and there are many young persons' and youth volunteering schemes such as the Duke of Edinburgh's Award (14+; may be fees), National Citizenship Service/The Challenge (15+) and local schemes.

Putting on non-formal learning and education opportunities

Alongside formal education, there is always the non-formal. Chapters 5 and 10 are relevant. Talk to Children in Need for their advice, guidance and possible funding support, and check your insurance, safety and safeguarding.

You don't necessarily have to put something on yourselves, but can help young refugees make full use of the range of informal opportunities that others are already putting on for young people. What is there out there for young refugees?

- Libraries offering information and putting on activities directly, providing access to IT, books and materials, displays and exhibitions.

- Local authorities running or commissioning/funding organised activities in parks and public venues, plus sports and team games, sports and schemes at leisure centres and sports facilities.

- Children's, youth and specialist play associations, churches and other faith bodies run or host playgroups, youth clubs, Beavers, Cubs, Brownies, Guides and Scouts, plus alternatives like Woodcraft Folk, Girls' Brigade, Boys' Brigade, armed forces cadet groups (there may be 'subs', or subscriptions but these are usually low and might even be negotiable). Half an hour visiting and browsing noticeboards in a community centre or church hall normally gives better results than searching online.

- Some young people's bodies arrange camps and trips away which might be the only chance some children have for a holiday or time in the countryside, although parents might need reassuring.

- Private lessons and activities that adults or young people pay for: maths, English and homework 'cramming' schools; supplementary schools where children might learn their parents' language or religious teachings; dance lessons, sports teams, music and drama classes and choirs. Private or supplementary schools should be registered and inspected by Ofsted. If you suspect one isn't, you should contact Ofsted.

For older children:

- Consider if young people could visit or study your work or organisation. First Give is a scheme where young people research a charity and present what they learn to an audience; they might even win a prize for you.

- Offer work experience placements.

- Offer volunteering opportunities so young refugees can complete award schemes for citizenship or other skills, such as National Citizen Service/ The Challenge or the Duke of Edinburgh's Award.

- Run longer-term sports, music or homework activities, or offer sessions or training to other young people's organisations – a 'cook on a budget' night or 'fix a motorbike' day or 'make a film' course at a youth centre, children's home or if there is foyer accommodation for young people near you.

- Organise mentoring or coaching training for some of your staff/members who can then support a school or college's older students.

- And when you hear a child who you are supporting is in a play or getting an award, try to go.

For families – if you don't work directly with children or prefer not to, you could provide:

- Family activities: events, outings, advice sessions and case work, or concentrate on supporting just one family – for example, if there is a support scheme run by your local authority for families arriving through the Syrian Vulnerable Persons' Resettlement Scheme.

- Help for parents to engage effectively with schools – for example, in English classes you can include vocabulary and role plays to practise talking to teachers.

You might work with school, college or youth workers rather than directly with refugee children.

- You can provide information or promote events to raise awareness and help people develop their own resources to work with refugee children.

- You can offer to find volunteers, training, advisers, speakers (LGBT History Month? Human Rights Day? Holocaust Remembrance Day? Self-esteem for girls?) for them to draw on.

- Use your connections to fundraise or donate equipment they can use for children or pass on to families.

- Combine your networks, and exchange contacts as well as making sure you know what they offer, so you can refer refugee children and families to their services.

- Keep open good channels of communication in case you need to raise a concern. Bear in mind that you can contact senior staff, the local authority or regulators if you have a serious concern.

Conclusion

What I raised in Chapter 1 as the 'new role' for hands-on staff is strikingly clear when looking at support for child refugees. The many local specialist and referral services that once existed have largely gone. The expertise still remains but there is very limited capacity to provide services any more. Regular children's and young people's services and education have expanded their expertise and built strong networks for collaboration and coordination, so they can respond to refugee children's needs. To support refugee children effectively, you need to be part of those networks.

CHAPTER 12

In Need of Refuge

This chapter is dedicated to Judith Kramer, who brought people together.

Introduction

I set out to answer three questions, laid out in Chapter 1:

What matters most?

What do I need to know?

What can I do?

There is so much more than can be covered in one book. You can go much further, starting with sources in the Boxes and Appendices. Doing things is the best way to learn about them. Please share what you learn.

The book starts from the point that when you find yourself working with refugees, you are working with ordinary people. They couldn't carry on living where they lived because of how they were treated. They left, leaving their former lives behind.

Now you are meeting them in the UK. As you get to know them, they are still dealing with their past. They are managing with very little. As someone supporting refugees directly, any response you make to them must take their real, very diverse life experiences into account.

Refugees are usually impoverished and incapacitated to some extent by their experiences, but they are still doing what they can to rebuild their lives. They do so in a context shaped by dependency on many other parties, and their success, to some extent, relies on their ability to negotiate those relationships.

There are numerous formal organisations that control resources and 'the rules of engagement'.

There's you and your team, volunteers and activists like you. There are lots of other local and hands-on, practical staff and your peers and 'friends' within other organisations.

There's the social context: popular views and ignorance, other service users, your members or participants. There are people with doubts, and there are donors of food and clothes.

You provide a service to refugees. You arrange activities, interpret systems, advocate to other bodies. You create ideas and space. Maybe it's just doing your job and you are expanding your existing expertise to reflect these new relationships as you absorb the knowledge you need to support refugees properly. Just a normal part of professional development. Or maybe it's more than a job to you, and you are becoming a hybrid between professional and 'kind stranger'. But your focus might be growing wider.

You *and* the refugee have agency and can bring about change. It might be that you consciously try to change hearts, minds and paperwork. But simply by doing what you can to make things work, you also challenge other parties to be more aware, accurate and adaptable. And by making services work better for refugees, you make them work better for everyone – including me and my mum (thank you).

It's time to look back at a couple of fundamental issues about 'refuge' and 'refugees'. These queries have come from the discussions about giving practical support and go a bit beyond practice.

What is refuge?

What is 'refuge'? This question has emerged at several points in the book, wherever there has been a choice about the level of support for refugees, or the standards to aim for, which depend on what we are trying to achieve. What can we conclude?

Refuge is safety

Whether it is international refuge from persecution or a women's refuge in the next town, refuge starts from being safe now.

But refuge also means being safe tomorrow, and many asylum seekers, refugees with Leave and, of course, refused asylum seekers aren't safe, as they might still be sent back – if not tomorrow, perhaps in two or three or five years' time.

You aren't safe if you are scared to walk down the street because thugs are attacking asylum seekers in your area. You aren't safe if you can be identified and preyed on by traffickers or fraudsters, or if compatriots continue to persecute you in the UK. You aren't safe if you are vulnerable to discrimination or exploitation which others can inflict on you because you are so impoverished and dependent that you can't walk away. The state has a duty to protect refugees from such dangers, just as it must try to protect British nationals.

Someone who is giving good-quality, direct support to a refugee is also keeping them safe. If your organisation has proper safeguarding for anyone who might be vulnerable, you are quite literally keeping people safe. By being trustworthy, listening and treating what they say in confidence without letting it become a secret, you give people a safe connection to communicate fears, actual threats and harm. Then something can be done about it. When others might refer someone with a 'refugee' problem away, you take it on board and take action: you give refugees security.

Refuge is a decent life

Refuge must surely be more than survival. Living in the UK must be better than living in a temporary camp on the border between two countries at war.

A decent life means a certain standard of services and resources and practical goods and help. Practically, it means a decent roof over your head. It means being able to eat nutritious and even pleasant food. It means enough money, health care and a fair chance of getting a decent job.

It isn't only services, though. A decent life means leisure, social and peer connections. Not just a roof but a home. It isn't only about being able to see a doctor but about being healthy, both physically and mentally; it's about emotional wellbeing. Perhaps it also means being able to look in the mirror and know who you are.

In ordinary life all these practical things link together. If you have a home where you feel comfortable, you can invite friends over and cook them a good meal. Afterwards, you can clean everything up, bath the kids and still feel able to revise for half an hour before you go to bed.

Refugees have a lot to deal with before they can start building a decent life for themselves and their families. The UK's asylum system creates its own challenges, as people waiting for a decision and living on NASS rations know very well. Some difficulties, such as mental health problems or lack of capital, take time to overcome. So refuge isn't only about arriving and scraping together the means to live. It's longer term.

Refugees will often need support on and off over time and through a series of crises. Staff or activists who stay working in the same area might find themselves looking back on decade-long relationships. Building a new life is a long-term project for a refugee. I hope this book has shown how much a competent and willing practitioner can help along the road.

Refuge is respect and equality

In 2017 I had the privilege of asking a mix of over 100 refugees and supportive workers the question 'What is "refuge"?' The answers from the British and the professionals in the room had a strong theme of 'welcome'. So then I had to ask, 'What is "welcome"?'

There is warm welcome to a guest or a visitor, friendly, even enthusiastic and kind. Strangers making a special effort to help people get sorted out – creating a first impression that will never be forgotten.

There is also the kind of welcome given to a new member of staff. Equally enthusiastic and helpful, but with an eye to a longer-term relationship. You don't only help them out because they need help, but because they will have a role to play and you need them to play it well, as soon as possible. After orientation briefings and a 'honeymoon' period, everyone settles back into 'business as usual'. The no-longer-new employee becomes part of ordinary interaction between people getting things done with a degree of mutual interdependence.

The welcome to a refugee is not the welcome given to a guest, but to a new member of UK society. Refugees are ordinary people. Look them in the eye and connect, not as a friend (although friendly is nice and friendship might come), but as a fellow citizen worth arguing with. This is the origin of respect and equality.

Refuge is being able to take control of your future

Most of us expect to decide what kind of life we want to live. We don't expect it to be easy, and we will make mistakes, but they are ours to make. Refugees lost most of their power to make decisions about their lives when they had to leave their homes, or even before that.

Now in the UK, refugees are often disabled by attitudes and processes, whether it is 'We don't do refugees' from some organisations (see Chapter 2), constraints from the Home Office (Chapter 3), direct (Chapter 4) or indirect discrimination in access channels (Chapter 5), or the 28-day cliff edge after getting Leave to Remain (Chapter 8). They might be disabled by the side effect of cuts and scarce resources – for example, when free education only goes to the level that makes you employable in low-paid work. Unnecessary barriers make it harder for refugees to make decisions about their own lives. Sometimes it feels as if they are being set up to fail.

Where systems disable, to some extent you can re-enable. You help people obtain the means – English, for example – to tackle relationships for themselves. When you facilitate someone practically in their struggle for the daily necessities of life, and help them access services that will be useful to them, you free up their energy and resources to work on longer-term strategies.

When you build up your own contacts and networks, it makes you part of providing refuge because of your role as a safe connection. You provide refugees with a mesh of support from different people and organisations that they can navigate for a range of needs. You are also putting in place things they can grab hold of when they are at risk of falling.

Most of what you do is not about helping refugees (although a hand up now and then might be good) but about finding and creating more space for them to help themselves. They are active agents. If they are not held back, they'll get on with doing what they think is the best thing to do, even if it isn't what you think they should do. That is their choice.

Perhaps 'refuge' only exists when you can start to make your own decisions again, and take control of your future. If you are in a situation where you are prevented from doing that, perhaps the people who make it possible again are creating refuge.

Then you can get on with building a new life, beyond refuge.

Refuge is whatever a refugee thinks it is

What is refuge? It's only refuge if it feels like refuge to the person who needs it. In an English group I ran for interpreters, an older man told me he used to write poetry before he was an exile. Now that England was his home, he wanted to write poetry again, in English. Perhaps that is refuge, being able to do the thing that makes you feel like you, as a normal part of your new life.

Or perhaps you just need to go and talk to refugees and ask them yourself.

Who is a refugee?

We need to return to the question of defining 'refugee' one final time.

The definitions in Chapter 3 were chosen to let us distinguish between who is and who is not refugee for practical actions and therefore how we support people. This book has argued for defining a 'refugee' pragmatically by the experiences a person has had, as experience is the most important factor in working out how best to support them, and shapes how effective they are in engaging with us and the support we can offer.

Now I want to revisit the question of 'Who is a "refugee"?', still on the basis of experience, but putting aside the practical element for now. I want to unpick experiences until we get to an essential core of what 'refugee' means.

The refugees we have been talking about throughout this book are the people we find ourselves helping in the UK. The experiences related to being in a new country, or in the UK, are very significant for them. But a great deal of what they experience here is shared with other migrants. Besides, asylum could be very different in another country. Their experiences after arriving in the UK are often problematic, but they are not essential to what 'refugee' means.

They are people who have crossed an international border, leaving their country of origin behind. Is this crossing an essential element of being a refugee? Leaving your country of origin behind, where you have nationality, entitlements, rights, culture and language?

The rules change as you cross the border. People crossing no longer have certain access to services or a voice, which, as taxpayers and voters in their original country, they might have expected. Language, ethnicity and culture often change across borders too, and refugees are rendered inarticulate, maybe illiterate, by the new language. Their identities, arts and history are largely unknown to their new hosts.

People migrate across borders every day. Usually, they have fairly clear plans to return – but so do refugees, although it might not come to pass. What makes refugees essentially different?

To observers, refugees crossing an international border looks like a very big step. The government of the new territory they are in becomes aware of them for the first time, as their arrival has implications for rights and resources, and might create social and political unease. By crossing the border, the refugees become visible for the first time in the realm of international law.

But in terms of what refugees themselves are experiencing at the border, it might not feel like such a big deal. Refugees often lose their rights, culture and normal life a long time before they reach the border. State protection failed them well before they got there. Human rights to family life, freedom from degrading treatment and so forth have frequently been compromised, if not worse. Some may never have had a vote. And the culture and society they are leaving behind very possibly tolerated and even encouraged their persecution and tried to destroy their identity.

Ordinary life changed in substantial ways a while earlier, when people had to start being careful what they said in public, or the child first moved desk to stop the boy next to her kicking her. If there is a moment when you become a refugee, it is some time before that moment at the border. The border is one more set of changes in a long series of moves and changes.

It could be that moment of the first move that defines a refugee. Not the act of moving itself, but the reason for the move.

A move because if you don't move, you will be harmed – physically or in other ways. You have to move because you have to get out of danger and out of the reach of people abusing their power.

You have to move when there is nothing you can do to avoid the abuse, nothing you or a whole group of people like you can do to prevent or resist or stop them. They have the keys and the weapons, and people will let them get away with it. They have the power and they are in control, doing what they want to do. No one and nothing is going to protect you or can be trusted to stop the harm. The only power you have remaining is to walk away. You lose a lot by leaving, but you might lose more if you stay.

Therefore, the move is not just for safety. It is to regain at least some control in your life. Even though someone in search of refuge starts off with very limited control over what happens next.

But what if you are unable to walk away? They have too much power over you, or you would lose too much – your children perhaps, everything you know and have lived and worked for. Maybe you can't walk away because you have nowhere to go or the alternatives seem as bad as staying. Perhaps you are working on a plan, saving money, trying to contact friends, but are still stuck for now, powerless and without protection.

Which means the critical point is not when you leave, but when you *need* to leave.

That is when you become 'a refugee'.

Because you need refuge even if you haven't gone looking for it. You *need* to go somewhere else if you are to take back control of your life, from people who are abusing their power. You could be a refugee when you are still running your own business or cooking in your own kitchen.

Risk is a factor, too. Not just actual harm, but well-founded fear of harm from abuse. Any time there is nowhere to go. Any time protection is lacking. Maybe everything is fine for now, but getting worse. Or it could get worse and you wouldn't be able to stop it. If you could get away now, you would avoid the worst that might happen.

I don't think any of us can be completely sure this will never happen to us.

I don't want to be a refugee

I don't want to be a refugee. Ever.

I never want to be powerless, with no control over my life and my family's safety and wellbeing.

I live in a country where, for now, things are pretty much OK (for me) and I am in control of my life. If there was a problem, I would know where to turn. UK systems are far from perfect, and British society has some nasty streaks. On the other hand, there are strong movements of people who believe in inclusion and we have checks and balances on the powerful.

So I'm OK for now.

I am OK because I benefit from generations of people who have fought, sometimes literally, for the rights and protections I have. Over centuries, committed political and social activists and reformers have managed to build democratic and legal systems in the face of great opposition. These campaigners have pushed into place protections for the public, working people, women and men in all their diversity. The Human Rights Act 1998, the Equality Act 2010 and the fact that we are signatories to the Refugee Convention are because of them. And don't underestimate the achievement of laws protecting children, disabled people, people needing health and mental health care.

The great-great-grandchildren of their opponents are still part of UK society. We have constant reverses; exceptions are written into law that undermine equality, and other provisions have been downgraded. There are endless attempts to undermine human rights. Legal Aid has been stripped away. Ill-thought-through policies ignore diversity and cause injustice. Many people living in the UK would remove our rights to protection tomorrow.

At the local level, hands-on workers and activists inherit and develop knowledge, practice, structures and spaces that offer people security. It isn't only community law centres, housing associations or specialist refugee networks. Protection comes in the form of coffee mornings, work experience placements, an open door. Hands-on workers are not peripheral to a safe society: they are the protectors. We are an integral part of effective checks and balances on government in this country.

Interaction at the local level is where real life is lived and mass attitudes are formed. Organisations don't grow knowledge and change perceptions – you do. At present, inclusive social attitudes and informed debate in the UK are stronger than the nasty streaks. Diverse voices can just about be heard.

But it isn't only the malicious who are dangerous. Those people and organisations who 'don't do…' deny real needs and reject diversity. They close down space. They take away your power to choose and decide for yourself. This is also agency, but not for a safer society.

What we certainly don't have is some kind of magic force field that will just always be there, one that means it could never happen here. State-sanctioned persecution, civil wars, slavery and abuse of power have happened throughout Britain's history. Britain is a diverse nation and some people are stronger and better protected than others. Discrimination and inequality are part of daily life for many UK residents. And no one is 100 per cent safe.

We must always be afraid that abuse and persecution will happen again. We all have a part in preventing it, including the newest members of British society. Refugees must also use their voices and agency for a safe society, and be part of our democracy. We must learn from their experiences in a creative process that will make us all safer.

A little paranoia doesn't hurt.

Acronyms

Acronyms that are the names of organisations are in Appendix A.

Acronyms are not included if the full expression is used throughout the text, even if the acronym is given once for reference because it is likely the reader will come across it elsewhere in their working life.

A&E	Accident and Emergency Department (NHS)
ARC	Application Registration Card – given to asylum seekers as an identity card
CCG	Clinical Commissioning Group – local decision-making body contracting NHS services
EAL	English as an Additional Language (children)
ECM	Equality characteristic monitoring
EIA	Equality Impact Assessment
ESOL	English for Speakers of Other Languages (adults)
GCSE	General Certificate of Secondary Education – examination taken at age 16
GP	General practitioner – also known as a family doctor (NHS)
HE	Higher Education
NASS	National Asylum Support Service – see Appendix A
NHS	National Health Service
NRPF	No Recourse to Public Funds – also referred to as 'No Recourse'
PSED	Public Sector Equality Duty – in the Equality Act 2010
PTSD	Post-traumatic stress disorder
s17	Section 17 of the Children's Act 1989 – refers to care for children in need (Chapter 11)
s20	Section 20 of the Children's Act 1989 – refers to looked after children (Chapter 11)
s4	'Section 4', refers to NASS accommodation and subsistence support to some refused asylum seekers
UASC-Leave	Unaccompanied Asylum-Seeking Child Leave to Remain
UCSA	Unaccompanied child, seeking asylum
UK	United Kingdom of Great Britain and Northern Ireland

Glossary

This glossary includes words, terms and 'shorthands' that are used in more than one chapter and are not in widespread use outside refugee support work.

'Shorthands' are words or short expressions used in a specific way for this book. Although these expressions are used by some practitioners in direct discussions, they are not technical terms and might not be in widespread use. They should not be used in correspondence or formal exchanges.

This is not a legal book, and many terms are defined in pragmatic ways suitable for local, hands-on practitioners, activists and volunteers who are supporting refugees in welfare, social, health, wellbeing, learning and development. These definitions are not suitable for legal, immigration cases or detailed case work such as housing appeals. You must not give immigration advice if you are not licensed to do so (see Box 3.3).

If you want further explanation, you can find fuller discussions in the main text, using the Index.

Access	Routes and methods people have to follow to get or use resources and services, involving the notions of: pre-gate – before people know a service exists; gate – proving eligibility to be considered; queue – waiting and putting a case for the kind of resources and services needed; encounter – face-to-face or other direct interaction between the person seeking resources and the people who control them (Box 5.1).
Asylum seeker	Legal term, summarised as someone who has asked to stay in Britain on the grounds that if she or he goes 'home', she or he will be in danger, and who is still waiting for a final answer (Box 3.11).
Characteristics	Features of a person or their life, such as being right-handed. Nine characteristics that cannot be changed by the person (e.g. sexual orientation) and are known to be used as an excuse for discriminatory treatment (e.g. insults or refusing a service) are listed as 'protected characteristics' by the Equality Act 2010, making it illegal to discriminate against people because of any of these nine characteristics (Box 4.4).
Children's centre	A place where multiple services are provided in a pleasant and informal environment to babies and children under five and their families.

Convention refugee   Shorthand used in this book for a person who has status under the International Convention on the Rights of Refugees 1951 (Boxes 3.4, 3.11).

Country of origin   The country where a person was ordinarily living and where they had rights as a national, usually from birth, but left because of danger or persecution.

Detention   Held or detained in secure premises, for new arrivals, asylum seekers and refused asylum seekers, especially if they are due to be deported. It is officially not prison, so detainees are allowed phone calls, their own clothes, etc.

Direct discrimination   See *Discrimination*

Discretion   The ability to choose to do more or to do less.

Discretionary Leave to Remain   See *Refugee with Leave*

Discrimination   Treating people less favourably or in a way that disadvantages them, because of a characteristic they share with a group of other people (e.g. their ethnicity, sex or sexual orientation) where there is no objective or justifiable reason for doing so. Discrimination can be direct (roughly speaking, deliberate), indirect (incidental – e.g. a side effect of a decision); 'positive' (but illegal) aiming to boost a group that is seen as disadvantaged; or take other forms (Box 4.7).

Eligibility   Being legitimately entitled to a resource or service according to criteria and policies set by others – usually requires evidence.

Encounter   See *Access*

Equality   Having the same rights and being treated equally well, with equally good outcomes, regardless of a person or group/ population of people's different or shared characteristics.

Equality characteristic monitoring (ECM)   See *Public Sector Equality Duty*

Equality Duty   See *Public Sector Equality Duty*

Equality Evidence Review   See *Public Sector Equality Duty*

Equality Impact Assessment (EIA)   See *Public Sector Equality Duty*

Equality Objectives   See *Public Sector Equality Duty*

Failed asylum seeker   See *Refused asylum seeker*

Gate   See *Access*

Health visitor   Specialist nurse providing holistic support to individuals and families, including clinical and social work elements, usually 'in the community' and involving outreach and home visits.

Home country   See *Country of origin*

Home Office   Government department responsible for managing immigration into the UK.

Human rights	Individual protections for a safe and decent life, laid out in the Human Rights Act 1998, includes Article 2 Right to life, Article 3 Freedom from inhuman and degrading treatment/torture, Article 8 Right to family life
Humanitarian Protection Status	See *Refugee with Leave*
Immigration Bail	Conditions that asylum seekers must comply with or be detained, includes restrictions on activities, affects final and other support.
Indefinite Leave to Remain	See *Refugee with Leave*
Indirect discrimination	See *Discrimination*
Leave	Shorthand used in this book for Leave to Remain, a catch-all for several forms of permission to stay in the UK granted by the Home Office.
Local connection	Having attachments and investments in a local area that justifies having support from the local authority, using local taxpayers' money, usually based on residency, family, employment.
Migrant	Any person who has moved from one country to another; includes refugees, but also tourists, students, people with work permits, spousal visas, etc.
Mitigating action	See *Positive action*
National Asylum Support Service (NASS)	Service that handles accommodation and money for subsistence for asylum seekers and refused asylum seekers, part of the Home Office but working via prime and sub-contractors.
Naturalisation	Process of a person becoming a British national.
Negative decision	Refusal of a request for asylum. See *Refused asylum seeker*
No Recourse to Public Funds (NRPF)	Having NRPF means not being allowed to make use of resources or services that originate from tax money. A person with NRPF can still use several state-funded services if and only if it is specified that they can or if the services, such as parks, are open access and anyone can use them without evidence of being entitled.
'One plus One' principle	'Each time you refer a refugee to a refugee specialist, project or group, you also refer her or him to at least one other non-refugee specialist, project or group.'
Ordinarily resident	Someone who has lived in an area for a length of time, or who has just arrived but will be living there for the foreseeable future.
Overstayer	Migrant whose permission to be in the UK has run out but she or he is still here.

Positive action	Additional support, activities, resources or services for a group of people who are disadvantaged compared with the wider population, perhaps because of earlier discrimination, or other circumstances, justified from sound, objective evidence. *Mitigating action* is similar but taken to prevent disadvantages being caused in future by changes or decisions being made today.
Positive decision	A grant of Leave to Remain in the UK having requested asylum; may be permanent or fixed-term.
Positive discrimination	See *Discrimination*
Post-traumatic stress disorder (PTSD)	A condition of mental ill health, where someone who has suffered or witnessed trauma, such as injury, extreme fear, near death or witnessed death, is caused ongoing severe distress which may have a range of symptoms and affects their ability to function in everyday life.
Pre-gate	See *Access*
Protected characteristics	See *Characteristics*
Public authority	Broadly speaking, any state body that has powers given to it by law and/or operates with taxpayers' money – so councils, police, NHS, most schools, etc. are public authorities. Also agents of that body that work to deliver services and resources on its behalf, which includes contractors and charities with grants or commission to deliver services (see Box 4.12).
Public Sector Equality Duty (PSED)	All public authorities are bound by the duty, that they must pay 'due regard' to equality in all their work, and proactively work to eliminate discrimination, advance equality of opportunity, foster good relations. They have a number of procedures to follow and documents they must produce and make public, which they may call by different names but include: Equality Evidence Review, Equality Objectives, Equality Impact Assessments, Annual Report on the Equality Duty, Equality Characteristic Monitoring. See Chapters 4 and 7.
Queue	See *Access*
Reasonable adjustment	Obligation to take sensible and manageable steps to enable people to live, act and work equally with others.
Reflexivity	Change in behaviours and action, including how other bodies or people are seen and treated, simply through having a new experience that expands awareness.
Refugee	Shorthand, a subjective definition used throughout this book based on people's past and present experiences: 'Any person who feels she or he has sought refuge from persecution, in the UK' (Box 3.11).

Refugee with Leave	Shorthand used in this book especially in relation to entitlements; a person who has claimed asylum in the UK and been given some form of 'Leave to Remain', meaning permission to stay in the country that gives similar rights to resident British nationals (Box 3.11).
Refused asylum seeker	Legal term, summarised as 'people who have asked for asylum and received a negative decision'; broadly, the UK government will not give them refuge and expects them to leave the country.
Removal centre	See *Detention*
Slavery	See *Trafficking*
Smuggling	Also called people smuggling – moving people who want help to cross border; often secret, illegal, profit-making. But smugglers are also at times individuals helping people escape real danger, at serious risk to themselves.
Status	A person's immigration situation; how they are defined by the Home Office.
Sure Start centre	See *Children's centre*
Trafficking	Trafficking is a specific crime in international law (and different to smuggling). Traffickers control people; they buy and sell and own them. They move people within countries and also across borders to exploit them for labour, sex, benefits fraud, body parts or 'modern slavery'.
Unaccompanied	Here, used in relation to a child, meaning without any adult who is responsible for their welfare, safeguarding and development. Unaccompanied children are usually 'looked after' by the local authority (Chapter 11).
Unaccompanied Asylum-Seeking Child Leave (UASC-Leave)	Permission for a young person under 18 who has been refused asylum to remain in the UK until they are 18. It ends when they are 17.5 years old and they may be detained pending removal.
Undocumented	Someone who does not have papers that show they are legally entitled to remain in the UK. It doesn't mean they are necessarily illegally here.
Voluntary Assisted Return	Governmental scheme to remove people with their consent, providing them with a limited amount of support for the journey and reintegration to their country of origin only.

Appendix A

Organisations and Sources – By Theme

This list provides sources of expertise for support, knowledge and networking. It is not intended to be a complete list but to give you a starting point when you are looking for advice or projects. It includes large and smaller specialists and other relevant organisations, plus examples of the kinds of local organisations you would expect to find when you network in your region. Organisations supporting or serving children are grouped together at the end of the Appendix.

An online search will give you up-to-date contacts, projects and details of eligibility. Please remember how busy people are, and do your own research before you ring!

Local level organisations and networks
Statutory and democratic bodies
COUNCIL TEAMS AND SERVICES:

Social work departments rarely have a specialist asylum/refugee team but will probably have:

Vulnerable adults teams – disabled asylum seekers and refugees including those with mental health difficulties.

Looked after children (LAC)/LAC Transition teams – unaccompanied asylum-seeking children.

Domestic violence/violence against women and girls (VAWG) teams – including trafficking, forced marriage.

Housing and homelessness –may include Syrian Vulnerable Persons Resettlement support teams.

Public Health is usually responsible for the Joint Strategic Needs Analysis and has statistical data. They work on relevant issues such as TB and HIV, and often manage Health Visiting teams. Environmental Health will investigate housing and employment including asylum accommodation contracted by NASS.

Other council teams: Ask if you have a Stronger/ Safer/ Cohesive Communities, Integration team or carers' support teams. A few local authorities have in-house interpreting services where there can be a reservoir of expertise.

Council services across your area: Key points –libraries, children's, Sure Start, Cymorth Centres, primary schools.

DEMOCRATIC STRUCTURES:
The local Members of Parliament (MPs) (www.parliament.uk/mps-lords-and-offices/mps) and Assembly Members (AMs), nearby MPs/ AMs who have taken up refugee causes in the past; individual local councillors and Party groups (eg. Labour group, Liberal Democrat group, Conservative group); metropolitan authorities/Mayor's teams tackling integration/diversity, migration, equality and anti-hate-crime, health equality, homelessness, women and girls.

Voluntary, community and faith organisations

Refugees' (and other migrants') own community organisations (RCO or MRCO).

Local refugee support groups e.g. Refugee Support, Refugees Welcome (often set up where there is a Syrian Vulnerable Persons Resettlement scheme), City of Sanctuary/Places of Sanctuary, Student Action for Refugees (STAR). Thanks to REAP (West London) for supporting this book.

Citizens Advice/Citizens Advice Bureau (CAB), Community Law Centres and other community-based advice services, sometime hosted or run by the local authority.

Equality/identity-based bodies: women's centres, disability groups and Independent Living Centres, mental health e.g. local Mind/Support in Mind/ Inspire (NI).

Faith and inter-faith networks, local Age UK/Age Concern, carers support organisations, LGBT networks, a very few equality/race equality centres survive.

Council/Association/Alliances of Voluntary Services and/or Community Empowerment Networks or similar, where they still exist.

Activist bodies, e.g. Amnesty International, 38 Degrees, United Nations groups, groups focussed on a specific country for cultural reasons or to provide support, e.g. Syrian support groups. Local Union branches, e.g. Unison.

Local businesses that serve specific ethnic populations, e.g. food, clothing, cafés.

Churches, mosques, gurdhwaras, synagogues and other local faith bodies.

National organisations and networks
Refugee specialists
NATIONAL SPECIALISTS:
Refugee Council, Scottish Refugee Council, Welsh Refugee Council, Refugee Action. Others include Freedom from Torture (Manchester, Birmingham,

Newcastle, London, Glasgow), Right to Remain, STAR-Network, Refugee Support Network, Jewish Council for Racial Equality (JCORE). Also Home Office (NB Asylum Screening Unit, Lunar House, Croydon, and Further Submissions Unit, Liverpool).

SMALLER ORGANISATIONS WITH NATIONAL SIGNIFICANCE:
Bail for Immigration Detainees (BID), Yarl's Wood Befrienders, City of Sanctuary, Refugee Week, Migrant Help (including Trafficking – see also Anti-Slavery Commissioner), St Ethelburga's Centre for Reconciliation and Peace, UK Lesbian and Gay Immigration Group (UKLGIG), Holocaust Memorial Day Trust, Writers in Exile, British Museum, The Imperial War Museum and Jewish Museum.

SEEKING IMMIGRATION/ LEGAL ADVICE/ IMMIGRATION SOLICITORS:
Immigration Law Practitioners' Association (ILPA), Office of the Immigration Services Commissioner (OISC), Refugee Legal Fund, or the Law Society of England and Wales, Scotland or Northern Ireland.

REFUGEE-FOCUSSED 'THINK TANKS', POLICY AND ACADEMIC BODIES:
Queen Elizabeth House (known as QEH) Oxford. Many universities have small departments or teams specialising in refugee issues, e.g. London South Bank University, University of Sussex (Law) SOGICA and University of Aberdeen. Individual academics may have specialist research interests. See also All-Party Parliamentary Groups (APPGs).

Democratic engagement: Operation Black Vote and Parliamentary schemes.

ONLINE NETWORKS:
You usually need to contact the host or organisers (shown in brackets) to be invited to join more specialist networks.

ASAN (Asylum Seeker Appeals Network): Regarding case work around entitlements and support for asylum seekers (Asylum Support Appeals Project).

Disabled Refugees: Rights and Campaigns (HEAR Equality and Human Rights Network).

Frontline Network: Mostly homelessness but wider issues.

Homeless Link: Destitution, homelessness.

NRPF Network (No Recourse to Public Funds) mostly local authority but open to all.

Refugee Support: Projects (London-centric), (Refugee Council).

Women's Asylum Charter: Campaigning for gender-aware recognition of asylum-seeking women's realities (Asylum Aid).

Directly related organisations (not specific to refugees)

ADVICE AND LEGAL:

Citizens Advice, Law Centres Federation (LCF), Public Law Project, Charity Commission.

EQUALITY, ANTI-DISCRIMINATION AND IDENTIFY-BASED GROUPS:

Equality Policy: Equality and Human Rights Commission (EHRC), Equality and Diversity Forum, National Equality Partnership reports (NEP has ended). Also The Kings Fund, Runnymede Trust, Joseph Rowntree Foundation, British Future, Council of Midwives, brap (Birmingham), Race on the Agenda (RoTA), Women's Resource Centre, Age UK, Stonewall.

Regional and national inter-faith networks: Faith Forum, Council of Christians and Jews,

Unions, e.g. Unison and especially Union officials can be well connected in relevant fields.

OTHER RELATED SPECIALISTS:

(See further contacts by theme below.) British Institute of Human Rights (BIHR), Amnesty International.

Housing, homelessness, money, food and essential goods

Accommodation

NATIONAL SPECIALISTS:

Homeless and at risk of or already street sleeping:

Access to practical support: Homeless Link, Shelter Helpline, Combined Homelessness and Information Network (CHAIN), also Streetlink service.

Expertise: Frontline Network, NRPF Network, Housing Associations' Charitable Trust (HACT).

Housing entitlements, rights, advice and access for asylum seekers:Asylum Support Appeals Project (ASAP), Refugee Action plus CAB, LCF. National Asylum Support Service (NASS) – Home Office/ Government, accessed via Migrant Helpline.

Detention:

BID, Free Movement, also expertise from Association of Visitors to Immigration Detainees (AVID), Set Her Free Campaign (Women for Refugee Women).

Training for staff:

ASAP (also Factsheets), Shelter.

LOCAL HOUSING AND SUPPORT PROVIDERS:

Some advice and assistance from local authority homelessness teams but note there will be local variations in waiting lists, priorities, criteria, etc.

Housing Associations, e.g. ARHAG, YMCA, often regional or local, e.g. Birmingham HOPE. Night shelters: see Shelter. There may be very small specialist refugee housing agencies, e.g. Micro Rainbow (LGBT – two properties in London).

Local Home Office/NASS accommodation for asylum seekers is sub-contracted to agencies who often sub-contract further to private landlords. To find your local provider agency, ask directly at the accommodation or contact ASAP.

EXAMPLES OF OTHER VCS ORGANISATIONS AND PROJECTS:

Voluntary Hosting Schemes: Refugees at Home, Housing Justice, Rooms for Refugees (Refugee Council), Room for Refugees (Glasgow).

Rent Deposit/Bond Schemes e.g. Refugee Council, Wycombe Refugee Partnership, various Refugee Welcomes.

Holistic case-workers connected with specialist organisations: Freedom from Torture, Refugee Council's Therapeutic Case Work Team.

ADVOCACY:

Advice for Renters, CAB, Shelter, Crisis.

CAMPAIGNS:

28 Days Campaign (Refugee Council), Participation and Practice of Rights Project (Belfast). Also No Second Night Out.

Money and essentials

NATIONAL SPECIALISTS:

Advice on Entitlements and Rights: CAB, LCF, NASS/Migrant Helpline, Refugee Action, Refugee Council, ASAP, Frontline Network, NRPF Network, Joseph Rowntree Foundation, on poverty.

Money and debt: National Debtline (Citizens Advice), Money Advice Service. Also Credit Unions (see Association of British Credit Unions).

LOCAL SUBSISTENCE AND ESSENTIAL PROVISIONS
(OFTEN NOT REFUGEE SPECIALISTS):

Food: Foodbanks/free food, find via The Trussell Trust. Ask Gurdwaras, churches at Harvest Festival (late September) and Christmas, Mosques during Ramadan/Eid. Drop-ins, e.g. New North London Synagogue Asylum Drop In. Soup runs/soup kitchens by homeless and night shelter bodies and Gurdwaras, Salvation Army, some local YMCAs.

Clothing banks/charity shops, toy libraries, furniture-, bicycle-, IT-recycling projects. Municipal dump 'reuse' shops. Try British Heart Foundation, YMCA shops, Sue Ryder, local 'upcycling' projects.

Libraries, Children's Centres, Women's Centres.

CAMPAIGNS:
Still Human – Still Here, Asylum Matters (City of Sanctuary).

FUNDERS:
Vicars' Relief Fund, NCVO- 'Funding Central' for small organisations, 'GrantsforIndividuals' (both by subscription).

Physical, mental and emotional health and disability
Physical health
NATIONAL SPECIALISTS:
Health policy, rights and entitlements: NHS England, NHS Scotland, NHS Wales, NHS NI, Public Health England, Healthwatch England (access and patient rights and voice), National Institute for Health and Care Excellence (previously 'Clinical' Excellence; NICE), Kings Fund (social policy and health), Doctors of the World (access and rights), NRPF Network, ASAP, NHS Choices (online), NHS 111, Maternity Action, Royal College of Midwives, British Medical Association (BMA), Forward (Anti-FGM).

LOCAL HEALTH SERVICES AND PROVIDERS:
Available across the UK (www.nhs.uk): As above plus:

GP (General Practitioner)/Family Doctor Practices/Surgeries – anyone can register. It is very important to register. Community pharmacies, Health Visiting, community midwives; immunisation, safeguarding, TB teams. Primary care in clinics and delivered through schools. NHS dentists, Healthwatch in each local authority area.

NHS Minor Injuries Units, Urgent Treatment Centres, Accident and Emergency (A&E).

NHS Clinical Commissioning Groups (CCGs) – the body that commissions and oversees quality of health services delivered by hospitals, GPs and other providers. NHS England Customer Contact Centre.

Basic clinical assessment and referral is sometimes provided through (non-medical) drop-in sessions (see Food), street/homelessness outreach projects, also e.g. (medical) Doctors of the World/Project London walk-in clinic (see -also Praxis).

Examples of other VCS organisations and projects:
Advocacy:

Nudge: GP Practice Manager > Lead GP > the local Healthwatch. Poke: Patient Advice and Liaison Services (PALS) > local CCG > Doctors of the World. Slap: complaints processes > NHSEngland > Care Quality Commission > local MP.

Campaigns:

Project London (Doctors of the World), Docs not Cops, Maternity Alliance, BMA is also active.

Local CCG or 'providers' may commission or sub-contract activities and services through smaller, e.g. non-clinical, local charities and community groups running engagement or communication/self-care/health education activities/ active living sessions or projects.

Try contacting the Engagement and Equality team, Commissioners for Mental Health and/or Young People Safeguarding Nursing lead (also Sexual Exploitation, FGM).

Maternity Action, Age UK.

Mental health

National specialists:

As Physical Health, plus: information from NHS Choices, Mind online, NICE (offers clinical guidance on PTSD). Rethink, for anyone affected by mental ill health.

Survivors of violence, abuse, torture and sexual violence: Freedom from Torture, Helen Bamber Foundation. Expertise and training: Freedom from Torture; Bristol University.

Bereavement: Bereavement Trust, Cruse Bereavement Care, Mind.

Counselling, befriending, talking: British Association for Counselling and Psychotherapy and sister website itsgoodtotalk.org.uk for local practitioners. Samaritans, Refugee Council Therapeutic Services.

Available across the UK locally, mental health services and providers: NHS mental health care and treatment: GP practices, Community Mental Health Teams, A&E if actively life-threatening.

Examples of other VCS organisations and projects:

Refugee specialist: (Examples in South East) Room to Heal, Manor Gardens Centre, Refugee Resource Therapeutic Services Oxford. Also small self-help, self-run groups. Support services offered within housing associations or the women's refuge movement, e.g. Ashiana.

(National) Richmond Fellowship, Richmond Fellowship Scotland.

HEAR, Mental Health Foundation Scotland, Asylum Aid/ Women's Asylum Charter group.

Disabled refugees

NATIONAL SPECIALISTS:
Freedom from Torture: physical and mental health disabilities resulting from torture.

Rights and Entitlements: Terrence Higgins Trust (HIV/ AIDS), Scope, National Survivor User Network, Disability Law Service: Right to Community Care Assessments/ Care Act 2014 – Disability Law Service, CAB, HEAR and contact individual local authorities; Displaced People in Action (Wales). Also Department for Work and Pensions (DWP) support for disabled people in work/ employers through 'Access to Work'.

Information/ campaigns: Refugee Action, Asylum Aid, EHRC, earlier work by Joseph Rowntree Foundation.

Deaf refugees/ deafness/ Deaf rights: City Lit (London) – Centre for Deaf Education;Manchester University – Social Research with Deaf People team; Deaf Plus; British Deaf Association; Age UK for older people becoming deaf.

LOCAL SERVICES AND PROVIDERS:
Available across the UK: Refugees' own community organisations and deaf and disabled people's organisations in some cases; local independent living centres where they remain; carers' charities.

Learning, employability and employment

Non-formal learning

NATIONAL SPECIALISTS:
Non-formal English programmes and approaches: Faith Action/ Creative English, Speaking English with Confidence, Talk English Together, BBC Learning English team.

Online Resources: BBC online and many others – choose carefully.

LOCAL OPPORTUNITIES (THERE MAY BE ELIGIBILITY CONDITIONS):
Library activities: e.g. literacy activities, classes, writers groups, even children's story time for parents too. Online access – librarians will assist people to access courses and resources: provide local and authority-wide information about groups, classes, courses and activities.

Children's centres, including child development and health, e.g. weaning, parenting courses, English, health education, Job Clubs. Primary schools for parents, e.g. Stay and Play, school activities like events, parent information evenings, there might be 'community' activities for parents, even English groups.

Charities, faith bodies, equality and identity and refugee self-help groups, e.g. Tamil community groups; Women's Centre, e.g. self-esteem courses, arts and crafts, English. Community centres and church halls are a venue for many activities, though they don't necessarily run them directly – check the notice boards rather than online.

Outreach, e.g. Health Improvement; talks from health outreach staff, NHS Right Care Right Place, cancer screening, diabetes, etc.; Citizens Advice outreach trainings – usually delivered to existing groups (e.g. saving money, consumer rights); Volunteer bureaux might offer e.g. safeguarding, equality and diversity, book-keeping; housing associations often provide training and employability as part of their support packages, e.g. Crisis Skylight, Glasgow Housing Association.

Women's Institute, Women's Guild, University of the Third Age (U3A), Workers Educational Association, The Citizens Trust, Groundwork.

Teacher training centres and colleges often need opportunities for teachers to gain experience; they might provide free classes taught by trainees.

FUNDERS:
The People's Health Trust, Post Code Lottery, Awards for All (Big Lottery), local authority small grant schemes and councillors discretionary funds, Local Wellbeing structures. European Social Fund has been a significant funder of refugee employability up to 2019.

Formal learning including employability and employment (for children and young people see next section)

NATIONAL:
The Open University has free introductory to advance modules available online.

'Life in the UK' Government reference resources and commercial and some voluntary sector courses.

Professional Bodies' 'continuing professional development'; also may support requalifying, e.g. midwifery, engineering.

Evidence of qualifications and skills: UK National Recognition Information Centre (NARIC). Evidence of level of English: contact local colleges.

Supporting refugees into and in employment, including requalification: Refugee Council/Refugees into Jobs/Scottish Refugee Council, The Council for At-Risk Academics (CARA), General Medical Council (doctors), Transitions (engineering), The Entrepreneurial Refugee Network (TERN) (see also Chaigaram, StarBucks). Refugee Career Advisers Network (RCAN), contact via ELATT.org.uk, Refugee Advice and Guidance Unit RAGU at London Metropolitan University – London-based), Refugee Employment Network.

LOCAL OPPORTUNITIES (THERE MAY BE ELIGIBILITY CONDITIONS):
Education: Colleges of Further Education (FE); Colleges of Higher Education and education and employability programmes including placements and apprenticeships, student volunteering programmes. Increasing numbers of universities are offering scholarships (see STAR website for partial list).

Employment: Job Centre Plus including 'Job Coaches', NHSJobs.nhs.net, children's centres sometimes run job clubs. Apprenticeships can be accessed via colleges and some commercial brokers or directly through the potential employer if they are already committed to apprenticeships.

Volunteering: Volunteer Bureaux – ask libraries for contacts. Local authorities may run brokerage schemes. Schools can provide opportunities to parents and carers. Hospitals and CAB usually require a one- to two-year commitment. Ask at Food Banks directly.

ADVOCACY:
Education – poke: contact College Director. Slap: Ofsted, Education Scotland, ETI NI, Estyn Wales.

Employment and case work – CAB, Unions, LCF members may have employment specialists. Clarity on rights from Advisory, Conciliation and Arbitration Service (ACAS).

CAMPAIGNS:
Education – Action for ESOL, National Literacy Trust, Plain English Campaign. Right to Work – Refugee Council, Trades Union Congress, Movement of Asylum Seekers Ireland. Wage poverty – Living Wage Foundation, Joseph Rowntree Foundation.

Children and young people (CYP) asylum seekers and refugees (ASR)

In addition to services mentioned above:

NATIONAL:
Children's Panel Advisory Committee/Service, c/o Refugee Council; Scottish Guardianship Service; Refugee and Migrants' Children's Consortium (previously RCC) – a collaboration of several British charities and other organisations; Every Child Protected Against Trafficking (ECPAT).

CYP specialists supporting ASR: Children England, Barnado's, The Children's Society, Save the Children Fund, Aberlour Child Care Trust, Child Poverty Action Group (CPAG), Action for Children, Children in Need.

Legal support and lobbying for CYP: British Red Cross, International Organisation for Migration, Coram Children's Law Centre (CCLC), Just for Kidz Law.

Age Assessment: ADCS Association of Directors of Children's Services.

Family reunion: (International) Red Cross/ Red Crescent, Children and Families across Borders (CFAB), UNHCR.

Safeguarding: Safe Network, Children England, NSPCC, ChildLine, CASPAR (free weekly Safeguarding Bulletin). Also e.g. Victoria Climbie Foundation 'vcf.uk'.

Housing and accommodation: Foyers, Housing Associations, local authority responsibilities, e.g. P3, YMCA, Stonham, Centrepoint. See also Accommodation.

Fostering and Care: CoramBAAF (Adoption and Fostering Academy), Chrysalis (Sheffield). Local authorities' own connections.

Money for essentials: advice/case work ASAP/ASAN, CCLC, Educational Trusts' Forum (care-leavers).

Health, emotional and mental health (EMH) and disability: Baobab Centre for Young Survivors in Exile (London); Young Minds.

ADVOCACY:
Strategic Legal Fund (fund test cases), Local Safeguarding Children Board, Ofsted. Authors – Jill Rutter, Angelina Jalonen and Paul Cilia La Corte (JKP).

CAMPAIGNS:
Project for the Registration of Children as British Citizens; campaigns for family reunion (Refugee Action, UNICEF); Campaign for Equal Access (to university) (STAR/National Union of Students); Let Us Learn (c/o Just for Kidz Law).

Local opportunities (may have eligibility criteria):

As above, plus: Family Information Services, 'SEN offer' for your local authority.

Safeguarding: Local Safeguarding Children Board – local authority with NHS/CCG.

Housing, money and essentials: e.g. Haven (Hull).

Physical health, EMH, disability: children's centres, sports and youth clubs and centres.

Learning and Employability: children's centres/Sure Start centres, schools, colleges of FE and HE (especially ESOL departments), universities, apprenticeships.

CYP LGBT support groups: e.g. Mosaic.

Voluntary and community: sports, arts, National Citizen Service, Duke of Edinburgh, Princes Trust, Youth groups (e.g. Beavers, Cubs, Brownies, Scouts, Guides, Explorers, Woodcraft), other leagues including Armed forces cadets.

Examples of small organisations or projects: Young Roots, Salusbury World.

Funders:

Children in Need, Reaching Communities, Tudor Trust, Paul Hamlyn Foundation, Jack Petchey Foundation. Look into 'First Give'. There are often local schemes for children or youth welfare and activities, including looked after children and care-leavers: ask your council, library or council/association of voluntary organisations.

Appendix B

*Evidence and Documents Relevant
When Supporting Refugees*

You might find it useful to look up images online.

See the Index for explanations and discussion about use.

Remember:

- Only ask to see documents if you need to.

- Don't keep copies unless you have to and then only with permission; keep them safe and shred when no longer needed.

- It is better to make a written and signed note that you have seen the documents and note key numbers and dates, and then only if you must.

- If you are returning documents, check the safest way with the refugee.

Refugees find it helpful if you can make them copies, and might ask you to verify that the copy you give them is of a genuine original. You must be certain the original is genuine before you agree to do this, but for bank statements, course certificates, etc. there is a fairly low risk. If they need certified copies of birth certificates, identity papers, etc., refer them to a solicitor.

If you are satisfied, mark the copy with a company stamp, sign and date it, and state that in your opinion it is a true copy. Add your full name, job title and contact details on the copy itself.

Former national and earlier personal documents

National passport	With their status stamp in it.
Birth certificates	This confirms name, date of birth, etc. and states details such as whether they have Leave to Remain and what kind, whether work is permitted, No Recourse, etc. The spouse of a refugee counts as a refugee, but it might not say so in their passport.
Marriage certificate	For self and children.
Spouse's documents	Passport, immigration status.

Immigration-related documents

ARC	Application Registration Card (often called 'ARC card' by users): photographic ID with status.
Aspen card	Debit and/or cash card that is charged with money from NASS. Very difficult to replace. Do not lose them.
BAIL 201	Letter from the Home Office to an asylum seeker specifying conditions (e.g. no study, or regular reporting) that they must comply with to avoid being detained.
Decision letters	From the Home Office: give the person's actual status and date from which it comes into force, and sometimes detailed instructions on what they need to do next. They should read it carefully and keep it safe. They might want to make spare copies for safety.
Evidence of movements	Keep tickets and itineraries, especially for overseas travel, but any travel over a few days. They might be necessary for NASS and also in the long run for naturalisation as a UK national as the applicant must prove they have not travelled out of the country for too long a period or too often, and might need to give continuous proof of their location – for example, all addresses without gaps for several years if applying for certain jobs with security implications. Keep your own records of attendance for a decade or more.
Home Office number	Found on ARC and on letters from the Home Office.
NASS contract	Many people don't read the contract which is not in simple English, but it has important information in it such as what they should do if they need to be away from the accommodation for a period of time. If they break the contract, they will probably lose their financial support and accommodation.
NASS letters	NASS number, which is different to Home Office/asylum application numbers.
Refugee Travel Document	With their status stamp in it: an internationally recognised document they can use for international travel. It confirms name, date of birth, etc.

UK documentation

Bank account	See Chapter 8 on getting a bank account. Cards and statement can be used as ID for various uses. It is worth the trouble to get a bank account as soon as possible, as any bank account will probably prove useful in its own right or to help get credit ratings, etc. in future.
DBS certificate	Difficult to obtain for newer arrivals, but necessary if people volunteer or work with children or vulnerable adults. Refugees can get DBS checks from a couple of years after arriving in the UK, though they might not be accepted by the organisation/agency/employer if the checks are for a period under five years. DBS takes much longer if people have moved several times. They are free to do while someone is a volunteer. It is not good practice to keep copies of DBS papers, but you can note the name, date of birth, DBS number and dates if you need records to show your safeguarding is up to scratch or to complete a reference.

Disability	May be able to register with the local authority as disabled without examination or medical certification. Any medical letters or certificates from country of origin, Red Cross or UNHCR medics from transit, or from the UK might be useful for requesting care or reasonable adjustments. Some clinicians may charge for letters. A printed copy of a community care assessment is strong evidence.
NHS number/ GP registration/ HC2 cards	They do *not* need proof of address to register with a GP, but it helps. GP registration papers/letters and ARC/NASS together will be enough for them to get a HC1/HC2 certificate for free prescriptions.
NI number and card	Will only be issued when they receive Leave to Remain. If it does not arrive by post, chase via the Job Centre/Jobcentre Plus.

Other evidence and documentation

Evidence of address	If they don't have NASS accommodation, they might find it hard to get evidence of address as they don't have bills in their name, leases, mobiles are usually pay-as-you-go, etc. If their name is not on a lease, they can still ask landlords for a letter confirming they have the landlord's permission to stay there, but most landlords are reluctant.
	You can write and post a letter to the person on formal letterhead with your charity, company or other registration numbers so they have something. You can issue a membership card or volunteer identity card, and if yours is a charity, include the full name and Charity Commission registration number. Ideally, print with a photo, sign, laminate and provide with a lanyard with the organisation's name on. It might even help them get discounts, memberships, etc.
Library card	Gives access to free IT and numerous courses, and can be used as local ID and proof of living locally (e.g. at a sports centre). Usually needs proof of address. A letter from you to the library vouching that the person lives locally might be sufficient.
Ordinarily resident	They should try to get a local authority residents' card which brings many benefits; varies according to area.
Qualifications	National or British. As well as formal qualifications, refugees need and appreciate certificates of attendance at workshops and courses even if there was no qualification.
	Level of English will be required for some courses and jobs. As well as formal qualifications, informal evidence can sometimes be given by colleges or teachers through admissions procedures or for a small fee. A retired teacher might be willing to write a letter stating their assessment of a person's English.
Recognition/ references	Present a 'Notice of Special Effort', 'Recognition of Progress', 'Certificate of Volunteering', etc. to show appreciation and build up someone's portfolio to show course administrators or future employers. Write personal references and references describing participation and/or voluntary involvement in activities (see Box 10.9, Box 7.5).

References

Asylum Aid (2017) *Through Her Eyes: Enabling women's best evidence in UK asylum appeals.* Women's Asylum Appeals Project. Accessed on 05/07/2018 at www.asylumaid.org.uk/womens-project/throughhereyes

Asylum Aid (2018) *Women's Asylum Charter.* Accessed on 05/07/2018 at www.asylumaid.org.uk/womens-asylum-charter

EDF and REAP (2011) *Refugees, Migrants and the Equality Act 2010: A briefing for refugee and migrant community organisations.* Accessed on 05/07/2018 at www.edf.org.uk/wp-content/uploads/2011/06/EDF-Briefing_Community-Organisations_Web_draft-3.pdf

HEAR (2018) *A guide to the right to free and concessionary transport for disabled asylum seekers, refugees and reused applicants in the UK.* Accessed on 05/07/2018 at https://hearnetwork.files.wordpress.com/2016/10/rights-and-entitlements-of-disabled-asylum-seekers-refugees-and-refused-applicants.pdf

Joseph Rowntree Foundation (JRF) (2014) *Poverty and the cost of living.* Accessed on 05/07/2018 at www.jrf.org.uk/report/poverty-and-cost-living

REAP (2009) *We Don't Do Refugees – Refugees for Equalities Report.* Hard copy available from reap.org.uk

Refugee Council with Lisa Doyle (2014) *28 days later: Experiences of new refugees in the UK.* Accessed on 05/07/2018 at www.refugeecouncil.org.uk/assets/0003/1769/28_days_later.pdf

Refugee Council (2016) *The UKs role in the international refugee protection system.* Accessed on 05/07/2018 at www.refugeecouncil.org.uk/stats

Refugee Council (2017) *Children in the Asylum System – November 2017.* Accessed on 05/07/2018 at refugeecouncil.org.uk/stats

Refugee Council (2018) *Quarterly Asylum Statistics – May 2018.* Accessed on 22/07/2018 at www.refugeecouncil.org.uk/stats

Nayeri, D. (2017) 'The ungrateful refugee: "We have no debt to repay".' *The Guardian,* 4 April 2017. Accessed on 05/07/2018 at www.theguardian.com/world/2017/apr/04/dina-nayeri-ungrateful-refugee

WRC/REAP (2011) *One plus One: Supporting frontline organisations to work effectively with refugees.* Women's Resource Centre and National Equality Partnership; hard copies from reap.org.uk

Index